# SWING IT!

## AN ANNOTATED HISTORY OF JIVE

### BILL MILKOWSKI

BILLBOARD BOOKS

an imprint of Watson-Guptill Publications

New York

**Dedicated to the memory of Ric Weinman,**

**who personified the irrepressible spirit of Louis Jordan,**

**Austin Powell, Tiny Grimes, Slim Gaillard,**

**and Leo "Scat" Watson in every waking hour of his short,**

**but extremely hot, jive-laden life.**

———————●———————

Senior Acquisitions Editor: Bob Nirkind
Editor: Alison Hagge
Production Manager: Ellen Greene
Cover and interior design: Leah Lococo

First published in 2001 by Billboard Books, an imprint of Watson-Guptill Publications,
a division of BPI Communications, Inc., 770 Broadway, New York, NY 10003
www.watsonguptill.com

Library of Congress Cataloging-in-Publication Data
Milkowski, Bill
Swing it! : an annotated history of jive / Bill Milkowski.
p.   cm.
Includes bibliographical references (p. ), discographies, and index.
ISBN 0-8230-7671-7
1. Popular music—United States—History and criticism. I. Title.

ML3476.M55 2001
781.65'4—dc21
00-064233

The principal typefaces used in the composition of this book were Granjon and Bureau Eagle.
Manufactured in the United States of America
First printing, 2001
1 2 3 4 5 6 7 8 9 / 08 07 06 05 04 03 02 01

# ACKNOWLEDGMENTS

———————•———————

The author would like to thank the following institutions and individuals for their assistance, support, and continued inspiration throughout the course of this project: the New York Public Performing Arts Library; the Schomburg Center for Research in Black Culture; Dan Morgenstern at the Jazz Institute of Jazz Studies at Rutgers University (the mecca for all serious jazz scholars); Frank Driggs; Scott Yanow and Bill Dahl for their prolific contributions to the All Music Guides, invaluable reference books for all jazz and blues scribes; Peter Grendysa, whose liner notes and various writings under the auspices of Words on Music have been invaluable in putting this project together; Billy Vera, a true R&B hound who has chronicled the rich history of the music in his extensive, insightful liner notes for numerous Specialty and Capitol reissues; Bob Porter, whose syndicated "Portraits in Blue" radio broadcasts turned me on as a youth growing up in Milwaukee and whose detailed and thorough feedback was helpful in preserving the accuracy of several entries in this book; Toni Ballard from the Berklee School of Music in Boston for turning me on to the jivenator; Bob Nirkind, who finally picked up on what I was putting down back in 1985; and Alison Hagge for her expubidence and ebullience throughout the editing process.

Also, personal shout-outs to Natalie and Irv Weinman, Bert and Nancy Milkowski, Casey MacGill, and Sophie Milkowski. And a special thanks to Lauren Zarambo, whose mantra of "just keep working, honey" helped me to complete this book.

CONTENTS

"To swing is to communicate, is to convey the rhythms of one's own being to a lover, a friend, or an audience and—equally necessary—be able to feel the rhythms of their response. To swing with the rhythms of another is to enrich oneself—the conception of the learning process as dug by Hip is that one cannot really learn until one contains within oneself the implicit rhythm of the subject of the person. So to swing is to be able to learn, and by learning take a step toward making it, toward creating. To be with it is to have grace, is to be closer to the secrets of that inner unconscious life which will nourish you if you can hear it, for you are then nearer to that God which every hipster believes is located in the senses of his body, that trapped, mutilated, and nonetheless megalomaniacal God who is It, who is energy, life, sex, force, the Yoga's prana, the Reichian's orgone, Lawrence's "blood," Hemingway's "good," the Shavian life-forces; It; God; not the God of the churches but the unachievable whisper of mystery within the sex, the paradise of limitless energy and perception just beyond the next wave of the next orgasm."

— *Norman Mailer, "The White Negro"*

"It don't mean a thing if it ain't got that swing."       — *Duke Ellington*

# THE **411** ON **JIVE**

The funny thing about my relationship with hep talk, jive, scat, vout, and all of that "stuff" is that it began with the influence of someone who was, and still is, totally unhip to that very thing. And that person is my mother. Terry Hauser—who is still stompin' upon this sweet, swingin' sphere—used to sit me down in the kitchen back in Troy, New York, and teach me songs. Now, this would be in 1945 and 1946, and the songs had titles like "Chi-Baba-Chi-Baba-Chi-Baba," "Mairzy Doats," and of course, "Java Jive." These are the very first songs I learned, and unknowingly, it set me on a course that fifty-four years later still has me groovin'.

Mind you now, I never knew what jive was, and for that matter, never knew about jazz—that is, from a terminological, "scat"ological, or swingological point of view. I just heard the music, and loved it so. People like Louis Armstrong, Fats Waller, The Ink Spots, The Merry Macs, and The Mills Brothers were in my head since I was a little boy. Louis, with his handkerchief, trumpet, and smile of the century was one of my earliest favorite. And Fats Waller singing "Your feets too big . . . them's gigunda gunboat" and Deek Watson and the rest of The Ink Spots singing "I love coffee, I love tea/I love the Java Jive and it loves me." Imagine how I felt, when I moved Hollywood in 1975, and Ben Oakland, the writer of "Java Jive," and his wife Bea, invited me to live in their guest house in Beverly Hills. (I had to decline as my prodigious use of herb and rampant sense of promiscuity did not appear to have a Beverly Hillish complexion.) By the way, Ben also wrote "I Left Hat in Haiti," recorded by Billy "Mr. B" Eckstine. Too hip for the room.

My real jive initiation came in 1953, upon hearing Al "Jazzbo" Collins's recording of "The Three Little Pigs: A Grimm Fairy Tale for Hip Kids," (Brunswick 78RPM 86001 for all of you audiophile freaks). The flip side was Steve Allen's adaptation of *Little Red Riding Hood:* "Once upon a time in the land of Ooh Pah-pah Dow there lived three little pigs. One of them was very cool, another was on the more commercial side, and the third was definitely on the square." Man, that's just what I needed at the age of twelve. Jazzbo broadcasted on WNEW in New York and his popularity gave him presence in the newspapers, so we could see what he looked like. He was kind of stocky, sported a Dizzylike beret, and had this very hip goatee. I rapidly became aware that there was another world out there, and one that was only sixty miles from my house. I began to dream of being a beatnik in NYC.

Right on the heels of Jazzbo Collins came what I refer to as "Jock Jive." Yep, the Harlem Globetrotters would make their annual sojourn to Convention Hall in Asbury Park, and my dad was only too happy to bring me down to see those cats. Sporting those red, white, and blue uniforms, they would make their way on to the court to the tune of "Sweet Georgia Brown" whistled by Brother Bones. The incarnation of the Globetrotters that I experienced was the team that featured Goose Tatum. On that note, I need not say more. But every once in a while I take out my Brother Bones 78 (yep, I've got that one) and stick it in my Wurlitzer 1100, and remember Goose. That was Jock Jive at its best. Somehow something was piecing itself together in my head. I wasn't quite sure what it was, but there was definitely a dancing abstraction feeding my fantasy. But my real jive explosion came in the middle of 1955, when I discovered Harlem radio.

Growing up in a middle- to lower-middle-income environment has its benefits. The kids definitely have a more soulful veneer, and when I entered my first year at St. Rose High School, in Belmar, New Jersey, I got turned in the right direction. One day, in the yard, Nick Paduano, a thirteen-year-old pool shark, asked me if I had ever listened to Jocko. No, I hadn't. So Nick hipped me to WOV, 1280 on the AM dial. Thanks, Nick, you helped change my life forever. Douglas "Jocko" Henderson was one of a handful of radio jocks that broadcast in Harlem and Newark who spoke the poetry, music, and rhythm of jive, each for about two hours at a clip nonstop. There is absolutely nothing on the radio today that even comes close to what those cats delivered on a daily basis. In Harlem there were Dr. Jive (Tommy Smalls), Jocko, and Jack Walker The Pear Shaped Talker. In Newark there were Georgie Hudson,

Hal Jackson, and The Bruce (Say I Am the Bruce called Ramon). Here's an example of what I got to hear every morning, afternoon, and evening:

> **Mommyo, Daddyo, this is Jocko with the great big rocket ship show. You're ready for it ain't ya? Ya been ready for it. So fasten your seatbelts nice and tight, be prepared for the heavenly flight. Minus 6-5-4-3-2-1 blastoff big rocket ship. E to the D, it's WOV. Well o-root, bozar to boot, here's that big record-breaker, money-maker Miss Laverne Baker with one tagged Jim Dandy.**

And the music they played was nothing like I had ever heard. The hippest R&B music dished up with style and class. You know, I learned a lot about jivetalk listening to what they now call doo-wop. Those background vocals were rhythmic riffs sung with "scat"ological words. So, from Jazzbo to the Globetrotters to Jocko to the Moonglows, Clyde McPhatter, Ruth Brown, The Jesters, The Charts, and on and on, I got it. Hey man, did you ever hear "Rubber Biscuit" by the Chips? Or "Soup" by The Impacts? Sammy Strain was one of the writers of "Rubber Biscuit," and after the Chips he joined the Imperials, then spent seventeen years with the Ojays. He's now back with the Imperials. He once told me that the lyrics to "Rubber Biscuit" came from cadences that kids used to sing when they would get sent up to the "joint." And after their release, they'd bring it back to the streets of Harlem—"Cow Cow OOOh OOOh Cow Cow One-a-nebbuh duh. Chicken ona Jigajig golla-golla. Sow frow onea nebbuh dubbah dubbah. Ow frow hibben ana hibba-who."

You want jive talk? How deep you wanna go, baaaaaby?

Have you ever heard of Lord Buckley? At this point in time he's still too hip for the room, so I would like to say a few words about His Supreme Jiveness. My old pal Gene Pistilli called me up one day back in 1970 and asked me to come down to his apartment, as he wanted to play something for me that he considered very important. I walked in and he laid this huge joint on me. After putting me in outgear, he proceeded to play Lord Buckley's "The Nazz." I don't think I've ever been the same since that experience. When it comes to stand-up comics and jive, Lenny Bruce comes to mind, and most certainly George Carlin. I can also groove on early Redd Foxx and Moms Mabley. But let me tell you that if you ever ask George Carlin who's the king, he'll most certainly tell you His Lordship. Lord Buckley took great biblical stories, great historical characters—like Gandhi, Abe Lincoln, and the Marquis de Sade—and delivered them in the language of jive. But in doing so, he gave us a perspective on these cats that, at least for me, put their trips in a whole different light. "The Nazz" is one of the most brilliant jive experiences of all time. You must check out Lord Buckley. You must.

One more little story before I e-loose-a-date on Bill MacVoutski's neat piece of all reet that graces them sheets of papyrus moderne that mingle in your tingles. A great cosmic spirit that The Nazz, in all his or her unbounded love, decided to place in my path for a few moments that I might learn a thing or two. I speak of Baby Lawrence. Shortly after Manhattan Transfer got together, we began to try and figure out how to put our show together. I was still driving a cab, and one early morning, as I pulled in to the garage, another driver pulled in right behind me. He was an older cat, an alto player who lived in Newark. We went up to the diner on Ninth Avenue and Fifty-seventh Street and had breakfast, and talked about music. Eventually, the conversation moved to great hoofers. I spoke of Bill Robinson but he interrupted me and said, "No, not Bill Robinson. Baby Lawrence." I had vaguely heard of him, but lo, about two weeks later, while perusing the *Village Voice,* I saw a notice that the New York Jazz Museum was giving a Sunday afternoon program featuring the Harlem hoofers, and it was being led by Baby Lawrence. I don't believe in chance or coincidence. So in retrospect, I know this was one of those "guiding hand" scenes. I made my way down there, and couldn't believe what I saw. This wasn't tap dancing. That's on one level. This was in a totally other place.

The cats call it Jazz Tap Percussion. One by one they came out—Chuck Greene tapping out Lester Young, Bunny Briggs, Raymond Caylin. They were collectively known as The Copesetics. The performance ended with a display of cosmic tapetude with Baby Lawrence doing Charlie Parker solos with his feet. The effect it had on me was unworldly, so I found myself kind of levitating, and in that state, made my way to Mr. Lawrence. I explained to him that I was in this group that was doing four-part vocal harmony and was attempting to put lyrics to jazz solos and needed someone to help stage the show. He gave me his card and asked me to call him. I didn't call him. I think I was too intimidated. So, two weeks later, they did the same thing at the Jazz Museum, and there I was, again. But this time, Baby came over to me, and got in my face, and wanted to know why I didn't call him. Oh God, the student and the teacher. When the student is ready, the teacher appears. But why does he have to do it when I've got my thumb up my ass?

Well, we talked, and he said that he would check us out and would bring his girlfriend, Dorothy, with him. I can't begin to tell you the import of all of this. Dorothy Bradley was the wife of the late Buddy Bradley, who was the black Buzby Berkley. When Buddy passed away, he asked Baby to look after Dorothy. The two of them were not dancers. *They were dance.* I cannot put it any other way. I have performed on every stage in the world for the past twenty-eight years. I've been on television specials countless number of times, and for all my experiences I have never seen any dancer who even came close to these two heavenly souls. Baby Lawrence is now recognized as the greatest jazz hoofer and Dorothy Bradley, in my opinion, is unquestionably the greatest jazz dancer. Her every move is the absolute personification of jazz line. And it was all in the context of jive at its highest art form.

At the end of all our rehearsals, Baby and Dorothy would have us do the Shim Sham Shimmy to the tune of "Hit That Jive Jack." You know—"Put it in your pocket 'til I get back/Goin' downtown to see a man, and I ain't got time to shake your hand." They were like Siddhas bestowing the Kundalini energy on their disciples. And for the past twenty-eight years we have been putting asses on seats, moving and grooving to what they taught us. That's love. When Baby left the slow, vibrating material plane in 1973, his funeral service was attended by every hoofer in New York, led by Peg Leg Bates. And one by one, as they stood behind his gray coffin at the Emmanuel Lutheran Church, they walked down from the altar, and danced around him, gracefully touching the gray vessel that enclosed his heavenly body. A heightened celebration of love and respect on a level I don't believe I ever before experienced. That, too, was jive.

*Swing It! An Annotated History of Jive* by Bill Milkowski is a celebration of the love and respect that a whole lot of musicians and performers have bestowed upon us for the past eighty or so years. My experience with jive was a kind of haphazard wandering on a path God chose for a middle-class white boy who wanted to sing the blues. Not all of us have a course of that nature, but we all want to feel good. *You do want to feel good, don't you, baby?* Well, whether you know it or not, you are holding in your hand a lovely piece of literature that will open a door, which, upon entering will make you feel real good. And it will stay with you. The charm of *Swing It!* is that it's written by someone who genuinely loves the whole jive experience. And he has researched it thoroughly. *Swing It!* unfolds upon you as though someone was unrolling a beautiful Persian carpet. And what a ride—from Louis Armstrong right up to Big Bad Voodoo Daddy. All the cats and kitties are struttin' their stuff. But I must ask you to please be aware of one thing. Reading *Swing It!* is an eye thing. Yes, it will bring you some incredible images of another way of looking at life. But you must bring in your ear. And Bill is fully aware of this and has placed a most bozar discography for your lovely ears. Dig the stories and play the music of the cats and chicks to whom Bill's hipping you. Do this long enough and you will eventually "get it." And when you do, it will add to the beauty of your life. Now, ain't that a good idea?

*Tim Hauser*
*September 2000*

*Tim Hauser is the founder of Grammy Award–winning vocal group Manhattan Transfer. In his jiveiest fantasies, he is also L Dorado Kaddy, the sugar disco daddy. "I'm the boss with the sauce, the cat with the jive. I'll put gasoline on your Vaseline and give you a power glide."*

# TO JIVE OR NOT TO JIVE

I was driving home late one night in 1976 during my college years in Milwaukee when the lightning bolt struck. It traveled through my car radio, into my ear, and down to the very marrow of my bones. And it touched off a forest fire in my soul that hasn't let up to this day. What I heard that fateful Bicentennial summer night really blew my wig:

> *Greetings, gate. Am I late?*
> *Can I take the next eight?*
> *Solid, Pops, don't hesitate.*
> *That's on, Jack, that's on.*

Gate? Solid? Pops? Jack? *What was all this?* I thought while navigating my way bleary-eyed through the darkness back home. At once puzzled and fascinated by the secret code of it all, I was also swept up by the spirit of camaraderie and playfulness that the four jovial gentlemen exuded through the airwaves. After a few more verses of cadence and rhyme they launched into some acrobatic scat choruses that sent shivers up my spine. My ears burned, my foot patted involuntarily, I practically fell to the floor with my teeth chattering. It was my baptism in jive.

After that scintillating roller-coaster ride of scat and swing came to a jarring halt, the overnight disc jockey made the announcement: "That was The Cats & The Fiddle with 'That's On, Jack, That's On.' It's from a new RCA/Bluebird reissue entitled *I Miss You So*. And I'll be playing a lot more from this one in the coming hour 'cause I really dig what these cats are puttin' down."

I sat in that car for the next hour or so, parked inside my parents' garage, patiently awaiting the next barrage of jive from The Cats & The Fiddle. The payoff was a sizzling "Stomp Stomp," a swinging rendition of "Blue Skies," and the upbeat anthem "One Is Never Too Old to Swing."

I went hunting for that Bluebird record (remember vinyl?) the next day. The hilarious cover photo spoke volumes to me. (See pages 62–63.) Pictured were four Cats in matching herringbone suits, smiling and playing their instruments with acrobatic aplomb. One Cat was straddling the neck of his bass, riding it like a jockey and slapping the strings behind him like Angel Cordero applying the whip to a thoroughbred's rear down the homestretch. A second Cat straddled the body of the reclining bass like a backseat passenger on this horse, smiling as he chunked away on a four-string tenor guitar. Cat number three plucked his guitar under a raised leg while the tipple player strummed his ax behind his head, flashing a mischievous grin. I was floored by the sheer visceral appeal of that picture. It instantly conveyed an unashamedly ebullient spirit of showmanship along with a suggestion of some serious hotshot technique. These four Cats were to swing music what the Harlem Globetrotters were to basketball.

The contents of this compelling package delivered on that promise with insanely inspired scatting, humorous lyrics, and hepcat repartee (we took particular delight in the pot anthem "Killin' Jive") all underscored by that surging, irrepressible force of swing. The whole uplifting vibe of that carefree, good-time music was completely at odds with the caustic onslaught of punk music, which was taking hold across the States that Bicentennial summer. But I was hooked on these Cats. And their reissue twofer, my own personal Rosetta Stone of Jive, provided me and my best pal, Ric, with endless hours of syncopated bliss. We wore the grooves down on those precious platters, committing every scat chorus to memory, learning to "Swing the Scales" and chunk on our guitars in that loose-tight manner that makes for a real kinetic momentum. We were hopelessly lost in a jive time machine, eagerly picking up on what was being put down, circa 1939.

> Stomp stomp . . . start your hands a-clappin'
> Stomp stomp . . . start your feet a-pattin'
> Stomp stomp to the right, stomp stomp to the left
> Jack, you really come on

Sometime during that same summer of '76, I got ahold of an MCA greatest hits twofer on Louis Jordan, the Grand High Exalted Mystic Ruler of Jive. It was my introduction to Jordan's Tympany Five and such joyful, infectiously down-home jump blues numbers as "Caldonia," "Let the Good Times Roll," "Beans and Cornbread," "Choo Choo Ch'Boogie," and the protorap showcase "Saturday Night Fish Fry." Jordan blew his alto sax with blast-furnace intensity on those numbers (indeed, one of our personal heroes at the time, the powerhouse blues guitarist Freddie King, had mentioned in interviews that the sound he was going for on his guitar was inspired by the direct, piercing attack of Mr. Jordan's alto). But it was that same spirit of giddy fun and good times I had first picked up on with The Cats & The Fiddle—the very nature of Jordan's larger-than-life personality—that really grabbed me, making me a fan for life.

Previous to these two life-altering encounters, I had brief brushes with jive. I vividly recall my father coming home very late and slightly tipsy one night after a profitable day at the track and entertaining me into the wee hours with chorus after chorus of Fats Waller's "Hold Tight (I Want Some Seafood, Mama)." I also remember seeing Cab Calloway strutting and prancing manically in his zoot suit in *Stormy Weather*. I caught him again running down "Minnie the Moocher" in the Bing Crosby flick *The Big Broadcast of 1932* and "Reefer Man" in a scene from *International House,* a 1933 film starring a boyhood idol of mine, W. C. Fields. But for some reason, those expressions in jive didn't register as directly and deeply as did The Cats & The Fiddle and Louis Jordan (must've been the bold presence of guitar in those small-band settings—Tiny Grimes with The Cats, Carl Hogan and later Bill Jennings with Jordan's Tympany Five).

With that initial shot of The Cats & The Fiddle and a potent chaser of Louis Jordan and His Tympany Five, I was hooked on jive. And my insatiable habit would inevitably lead me to the harder stuff—Slim & Slam, Leo "Scat" Watson & The Spirits of Rhythm, Stuff Smith and His Onyx Club Boys, Harry "The Hipster" Gibson.

For a time, I believed that I was the only person on the planet, aside from my pal Ric, who even knew of the existence of this stuff. But, of course, I was not alone. I eventually ran into Paul Cebar, an equally enthusiastic jive scholar and musician who performed around Milwaukee, first as a solo act and later with his bands The R&B Cadets and The Milwaukeeans. Cebar was well versed (had his boots laced, in Calloway parlance) on all facets of jive and he spread the gospel around Mil-town back in the late '70s by including tunes by Jordan, The Cats & The Fiddle, and other jivesters in his act. Both he and I were slightly taken aback in 1981 when British pop star Joe Jackson came out with his Jordan tribute album, *Jumpin' Jive* (A&M), which we ultimately dismissed as well meaning but watered-down. We were too far into the real deal at that point to be fooled by imitations.

After moving to New York in 1980, I was elated to discover Tiny Grimes, the hot Charlie Christian–influenced guitarist with The Cats & The Fiddle, alive and well and playing a week-long engagement at Sweet Basil in Greenwich Village. I sought him out for an interview and guitar lessons, eventually establishing a friendship with him until his death in 1989. (Strangely, Tiny was the one to break the news to me about John Lennon's murder on the fateful night of December 8, 1980. As I recall, he interrupted his train of thought during an interview at Basil's to announce, "Hey, you know what? They done shot that Beatle tonight.")

Through the '80s and '90s, my passionate interest in all things jive had me ferreting out rare albums, articles, photos, and bits of memorabilia in record shops, libraries, thrift stores, and at collectors conventions. In 1994 I was heartened to witness the Broadway opening of *Five Guys Named Moe,* a tribute to the musical genius of Louis Jordan that had previously had a very successful run in London. In 1996 I was mildly amused to see jive make yet another comeback via the indie comedy movie *Swingers,* which launched the career of Big Bad Voodoo Daddy. Then in 1998 a TV commercial for The Gap (slickly choreographed to Louis Prima's anthemic "Jump, Jive 'n' Wail") brought jive to the masses, if only in one very effective sixty-second dose. That single, catchy ad served as a well-timed catalyst for a grassroots movement that had been slowly gaining momentum all through the '90s. Suddenly, in the wake of The Gap ad, retro swingers and hepcats began popping up in nightclubs all across the nation. And there were other key events that helped push this swing bandwagon into mainstream consciousness: Big Bad Voodoo Daddy's appearance at the 1999 Super Bowl half-time extravaganza and also on an episode of TV's *Alley McBeal* along with Brian Setzer's appearance on the popular sitcom *The Nanny.*

Although the nouveau jive thing seemed to have reached its real peak in the late '90s, interest in this retro phenomenon continues with the Broadway musical revue *Swing!* which premiered in January of 2000 and carries on the celebratory spirit of jumpin' jive through the hip musical contributions of Casey MacGill and The Gotham City Gates. MacGill—an ardent fan and jive scholar whose Los Angeles vocal group, Mood Indigo, was patterned after The Cats & The Fiddle and whose former band, The Spirits of Rhythm, takes its name from Leo "Scat" Watson's seminal jive group—was similarly transformed by his initial contact with these high-spirited, swinging sounds from the '30s.

"I'm totally into all that stuff . . . Leo Watson, The Cats & The Fiddle, Slim & Slam, Stuff Smith and His Onyx Club Boys," says MacGill. "I started out listening to The Rhythm Boys and also The Mills Brothers and then gradually worked my way back and got a little more esoteric. When I was eighteen or nineteen, I was turned on to older jazz music by a friend of mine who went on to play in a group called The Cheap Suit Serenaders with Robert Crumb, the cartoonist. These guys were all 78 record collectors but they also turned me on to a lot of LP reissues. In the late '60s, RCA had a thing called the Vintage Series. For $2.98 back then you could buy an album of reissues of 78s from RCA. They were really well collected. They had Fats Waller, chronological recordings from a particular year. They had the early Count Basie stuff with Bennie Moten. It was really a remarkable series and that kind of got me going. And I was well into it by the time they put out that Cats & The Fiddle [LP] on Bluebird. That was a whole new, wonderful discovery for me."

My own pilgrimage in jive culminates in the publication of this book.

First of all, let me state clearly: This is by no means a definitive document of the Swing Era or the deluge of big bands that thrived during the '20s, '30s, and '40s. Therefore, the reader is advised to look elsewhere for material on Artie Shaw, Benny Goodman, Ben Pollack, Jean Goldkette, Glenn Miller, Les Brown, The Dorsey Brothers, Charlie Barnet, Bob Crosby, The Casa Loma Orchestra, Woody Herman, Harry James, or Gene Krupa (like Richard Sudhalter's mammoth dissertation, *Lost Chords: White Musicians and Their Contributions to Jazz, 1915–1945*, which was published by Oxford University Press in 1999). And there are numerous jazz history books ripe with info on swing icons like Fletcher Henderson, Duke Ellington, Bennie Moten, Don Redman, Count Basie, McKinney's Cotton Pickers, Chick Webb, Andy Kirk, Luis Russell, or Jay McShann (like Stanley Dance's *The World of Swing*, which was published by Da Capo Press in 1979, and Gunther Schuller's *The Swing Era*, which was published by Oxford University Press in 1991). While those are all gifted musicians and great, swinging bands, my primary point of interest here is in those figures who have historically fallen through the cracks—the outrageous, outlandish entertainers over time who got their joyful message across with generous doses of swing. With the exception of Louis Armstrong, Cab Calloway, and Fats Waller, the rest have largely been dismissed by jazz scholars as mere novelty acts. Because of this unfortunate bias against musicians who are also entertainers, several significant jivesters have never gotten their due. They are part of a rather significant missing link, one that has never been discussed comprehensively in any one format.

As jazz critic Whitney Balliet wrote in a 1980 *New Yorker* profile on pianist-singer-jivestress Nellie Lutcher: "Somewhere she fell under the sway of a highly specialized group of musicians who were a compound of jazz and comedy, of improvisation and clowning. They were generally pianists, guitarists or bassists who sang novelty songs and used a variety of comic devices—Bronx cheers, growls, sighs, *basso profundo,* falsetto, roars. They sang scat style and they made up their own languages and sang them. They were expert, swinging musicians who had discovered early in their careers that their comic gifts outpaced their improvisational skills."

Too "jazzy" for rock scribes, too "silly" for jazz scribes, these jovial gentlemen of jumpin' jive are saluted in this Jive Companion. Their contributions—spreading joy, putting smiles on faces, and keeping feet a-pattin' with their infectious *joie de vivre*—should not be forgotten.

All reet!

*Bill Milkowski*
*August 2000*

# AN HISTORICAL PERSPECTIVE ON JIVE TALK

Originally a code word for those in the know, the term "jive"—loosely defined as "stuff and things worth taking note of," whether it be the latest dance craze, the hottest new sounds in jazz, or the latest hepcat expressions—has undergone several transformations in meaning over time. Louis Armstrong is said to have coined the phrase during the mid-1920s, around the time when he was revolutionizing the music in Chicago with his Hot Five and Hot Seven aggregations. Cab Calloway helped popularize the phrase in the '30s among the jitterbug set with hepster anthems like "Are You Hep to the Jive?" and "Jumpin' Jive." In the '40s it was used as slang for "marijuana" (as professed in the songs "All the Jive Is Gone" and "Killin' Jive") and by the '60s it had become a term of derision, as in "you jive turkey," the coarser "jive-ass motherfucker," and other sarcastic epithets hurled by the likes of comedians Redd Foxx and Flip Wilson or iconic jazz musician Miles Davis.

With the emergence in the '90s of several retro-swing bands, jive is suddenly back in mainstream consciousness, albeit in the form of affectation rather than as a rich, unique, and living language unto itself.

In his sociologically astute foreword to *Dan Burley's Original Handbook of Harlem Jive,* writer Earl Conrad explains how the origins of jive may go back to the very beginnings of the African experience in the United States—as early as 1619 when that first polyglot group of Africans was dumped on this continent (Jamestown, Virginia) to work the land—and were born out of a need to disguise meaning under adverse conditions:

"White America perpetrated a new and foreign language on the Africans it enslaved. Slowly, over generations, Negro America, living by and large in its own segregated world with its own thoughts, found its own way of expression, found its own way of handling English, as it had to find its own way in handling many other aspects of a white, hostile world. Jive is one of the end results."

Conrad speculates that jive talk may have originally been a kind of "pig Latin" that slaves talked with each other—a code used in the presence of whites. The word "ofay," for instance, may have been commonly understood within the African-American community to mean "a white person," though that same meaning eluded millions of white Americans. "Negroes needed to have a word like that in their language, needed to create it in self-defense," he writes. "The Negro has always had a way of passing on his thoughts, via jive, to his fellow blacks, when whites were around."

And whether the term itself morphs over time from "jive" to "soul" to "hip-hop," the codelike, fraternal aspect of black slang remains the same. Take, for example, the following excerpt from Burley's *Original Handbook of Harlem Jive.* Though originally written in November of 1944 and aimed at the jitter-bug set of that era, it could just as easily pertain to today's hip-hop culture: "Jive is a language in motion. It supplies the answer to the hunger for the unusual, the exotic, the picturesque in speech. It is a medium of escape, a safety valve of people pressed against the wall for centuries, deprived of the advantages of complete social, economic, moral and intellectual freedom."

In its most basic form, jive talk (or rap, for that matter) is simply a means of deriving pleasure from something the uninitiated cannot understand. In its highest form, slung by artful jivesters (or rappers), it is a vivid, vital, and dynamic language that can enthrall initiates while completely befuddling those who stand outside the inner circle of meaning. Jive, like cussing, is a language of emotion: a means of describing how one is affected by certain experiences or situations. Among those who contributed largely to the vocabulary of jive and helped build it up to its present-day fluency were many with little or no knowledge of formalized and classical English. The twisting of the language to suit the user has been one of the things that brought jive to its highest development. Burley addresses this kind of jive virtuosity in his handbook of jive:

"In a thousand and one places—poolrooms, nightclubs, dressing rooms, back stage, kitchens, ballrooms, theatre lobbies, gymnasiums, jail cells, cafes, bars and grills—on a thousand and one street corners, when the sun shines warmly and they have a half hour to kill, creators of the new Harlemese are busily adding words and expressions to their rapidly growing vocabulary of jive. No aerial gunner ever had more ammunition for emergency use than a jiver's repertoire when encountering his gang. Each new phrase, each rhyme is received with delight. Like copyreaders and editorial writers on newspapers, jive addicts take infinite care of their latest brain-child. They trim and polish, rearrange, revise, reshuffle and recast certain phrases until they have the best and most concise expression that can be devised. Reputations as "jivers" are eagerly sought and advanced apostles, real masters of the jargon, are looked up to with awe and admiration by their less accomplished disciples."

And so we get—courtesy of Burley and other jive-talkers from the '40s—such colorful, skillfully rendered expressions as "stashes her frame on a pig hide" (sits on a leather-covered stool), "digs the dipper for some brine" (asks the bartender for a beer), "got my rug beat" (got a haircut), "Are your boots laced?" (Do you understand?), "scoff ace deuce around the ticker" (three square meals daily), "playing the dozens with one's uncle's cousins" (doing everything wrong), and "layout across the drink" (the continent of Europe). If part of the function of jive (or any slang) is to alleviate the tedium of the mundane, this kind of playful use of the language goes a long way toward that end.

In his 150-page handbook, Burley not only sets out to "boot hepcats to the jive" with a comprehensive glossary of jive terms and phrases, he further entertains would-be hepcats by placing the lingo into a working context with cleverly worded jive interpretations of English lit classics. Everything from Shakespeare's *Hamlet* to "'Twas the Night before Christmas" is filtered through his unique jive perspective. Dig this hep tidbit from his jive version of Joyce Kilmer's poem "Trees": "I think that I shall never dig/A spiel as righteous as a twig./A twig, Jack, that may in heat time drape/A crib of feathers in its cape./Spiels are laid by lanes like me/But just the Knock can make a tree."

Burley's examples, concocted more than half a century ago, may be arcane by today's hip-hop standards. But these two modes of rhyming jargon—each a rich and wholly unique slanguage unto itself—both play a part in the continuum of the black experience in America. As Clarence Major rightly concludes in his introduction to *Juba to Jive: A Dictionary of African-American Slang,* "Black slang is a living, breathing form of expression that changes so quickly no researcher can keep up with it."

In his scholarly book *Black Talk,* author/musician Ben Sidran addresses the ever-changing nature of black slang over time and its inherent exclusivity. "When a facet or phrase of black, or hip, jargon gained too much currency within the white world, it was summarily dropped by blacks. This suggests that a 'secret' language functions differently within the black community than it does without, or, at least, that hip jargon is part of the Negro's drive for an 'ethnically singular' voice. At its most elementary, in-group language is simply a means of easy communication to integrate shared experience into its semantics and thereby exclude those who do not share a background. In the black community, as in the vernacular of other oppressed groups, it also serves as an emotional release, a means of softening the impact of oppression or of obscuring overt resistance to oppression. It served a double function: It rendered White America incommunicado."

Meanwhile, a savvy group of students at the University of Southern California has established a Web site (www.JiveOn.com) with the tongue-in-cheek mission of spreading the gospel of jive to all peoples of the world. As they state in their jive manifesto:

"Although jive was created and used exclusively by African-Americans, [we] would like to universalize this entertaining and expressive language form. Our goal is to have people of all racial, ethnic and religious backgrounds all over the world using jive in their daily conversations. In fact, we propose that jive be accepted as the official language of the world. Just think about it—a world of differences united by a common thread. Be a part of the dream by speaking jive today!"

Given the "aliveness" of jive lingo, the Web site is updated daily for the benefit of those who want to pick up on what is being put down, circa 2001. The terms may have changed from Dan Burley's and Cab Calloway's day, but the cause remains the same—uniting a group of like-minded individuals around a common mode of expression. So cop a squat, lace up your boots, and let me hep you to some of the killer dillers who kicked off this righteous jive continuum.

## CHAPTER 1

# THE **GODFATHERS** OF **JIVE**

**Louis Armstrong, Fats Waller, Cab Calloway**

The 1920s was an exceptionally fertile period in American history. It was the Roaring Twenties, the Jazz Age, a decade marked by a new vitality and spirit of experimentation in the wake of World War I and underscored by a prevailing air of good times in spite of the repressive era of Prohibition (1920–1933). It was also the time of the Harlem Renaissance, a period of unprecedented creative activity among African Americans in all fields of art.

From 1920 to 1930, great works were done by writers and poets like Langston Hughes, Countee Cullen, and Zora Neale Hurston, painters like William H. Johnson, Palmer Hayden, and Lois Mailou Jones, composer-bandleaders like Noble Sissle, Eubie Blake, Duke Ellington, and Fletcher Henderson, entertainment icons like Bill "Bojangles" Robinson, Paul Robeson, Ethel Waters, Josephine Baker, and Bert Williams. Two other geniuses who came up during this incredibly rich period in African American history and emerged full-fledged stars by the end of the decade were Thomas "Fats" Waller and Louis Armstrong. They were good friends and their paths crossed frequently, both socially and professionally, through-out the '20s.

Fats and Louis first met in 1923 while moonlighting with Fletcher Henderson's band at the Hoofer's Club in Harlem. They continued to work with Henderson through 1924, also appearing together on live radio broadcasts with Clarence Williams's Blue Five and at late-night jams at Connie's

Inn in Harlem. Early in 1925, before Armstrong moved to Chicago and made his revolutionary Hot Five sessions, they appeared together on a recording date for Vocalion by Perry Bradford's Jazz Phools. In 1927 the two kindred spirits crossed paths again in Chicago for a series of gigs at the Vendome Theatre with Erskine Tate's band. During his brief stay in the Windy City, Fats also sat in at several late-night jam sessions at the Sunset Cafe with Armstrong's own band, which included Earl Hines on piano.

In 1929 Louis and Fats were back together in New York working in the all-black musical revue *Hot Chocolates,* which opened at Connie's Inn in Harlem before moving to Broadway, where it enjoyed a lengthy run of 219 performances. Fats had written the music with Tin Pan Alley pitchman Andy Razaf (whose Macedonian given name was Andreamentena Razafinkeriefo), his most frequent collaborator. Armstrong's raspy rendition of the Waller-Razaf tune "Ain't Misbehavin'" helped make *Hot Chocolates* the hottest ticket in town. (The show would also help launch the career of Cab Calloway.)

Armstrong recorded "Ain't Misbehavin'" himself later that year with the Carroll Dickerson Orchestra and covered it on many occasions throughout his career, including on the 1955 tribute album to his pal, *Satch Plays Fats* (Columbia), which was recently remastered and reissued by the Columbia/Legacy label.

Though some in the post-bop jazz community had a strong distaste for the show-biz antics of Armstrong, Waller, and Calloway, their music was always spirited, joyful, and brilliantly entertaining. If jazz is the sound of surprise, jive is the sound of personality. And these three godfathers of jive personified that quality to the max. Together they set the tone for a strain of exuberant, swinging music and good-humored entertainment that has continued, in various mutations, up until the present day.

# LOUIS ARMSTRONG

BORN: August 4, 1901, in New Orleans, Louisiana
DIED: July 6, 1971, in Corona, New York

THE INVENTOR OF SCAT SINGING, the irrepressible spirit of jazz, and America's ambassador of goodwill around the world, Louis Armstrong was, in the words of writer Albert Murray, "a Promethean cultural hero," a joyous beacon who lit a path to the future of jazz. Quite simply, he was the most important and influential musician in jazz history as well as one of the most beloved entertainers of the twentieth century. As Scott Yanow points out in the *All Music Guide to Jazz*, "Louis Armstrong's accessible humor and sunny stage personality were major assets in popularizing jazz with larger audiences."

With his unprecedented, intuitive scat chorus on a 1926 recording of "Heebie Jeebies," Armstrong brought the tradition of jive into the realm of professional music. Jazz lore has it that he dropped the lyric sheet in the studio during a take and improvised nonsensical vocals on the spot. Whatever actually did occur in the studio on that day (February 26, 1926), the outcome forever altered the course of popular singing, greatly affecting everyone from Bing Crosby to Mildred Bailey, Billie Holiday, Frank Sinatra, Ella Fitzgerald, and every jazz singer who followed in Pops's wake. Anyone who has ever taken great liberties with melody and meter or otherwise exhibited any kind of rhythmic elasticity in their delivery—from scatmeisters like Jon Hendricks, Clark "Mumbles" Terry, and Eddie Jefferson to vocal expressionists like Tony Bennett, Betty Carter, Sarah Vaughan, and Mark Murphy, or current-day advocates of that same highly interpretive aesthetic such as Kurt Elling and Cassandra Wilson—owes a debt of gratitude to Armstrong's invention. And, of course, the whole lineage of jive musicians—from Cab Calloway, Stuff Smith, and Leo "Scat" Watson in the '30s, Slim Gaillard and Louis Jordan in the '40s, Louis Prima and Babs Gonzales in the '50s, on up to today's retro-swingers—flows directly from Armstrong's seminal, playful genius.

> **"If you have to ask, you'll never know."**
> — *Louis Armstrong*

One of jazz's first true virtuosos who played with the kind of operatic bravura that could raise goose bumps—peeling off flurries of impossibly high register notes as easily as breathing—Armstrong single-handedly shifted the emphasis of jazz from an ensemble art form to a soloist's art form while setting new standards for trumpeters worldwide. The sheer brilliance of his playing is perhaps best exemplified by his epochal masterworks from the mid-1920s like "Potato Head Blues," "West End Blues," "Hotter Than That," "Struttin' with Some Barbecue," "Cornet Chop Suey," and "Weather Bird," all marked by a passionate, robust attack, and dramatic, slashing

breaks that were wholly unprecedented for the time. As Murray writes in *Stomping the Blues,* "Everywhere Armstrong went in the 1920s, he created a revolution in musical sensibility. Which is not to say that he invented the form but that his assimilation, elaboration, extensions and refinement of its elements became in effect the touchstone for all who came after him."

Armstrong, nicknamed "Dippermouth" or "Satchelmouth" (shortened to Satchmo) for his extremely wide, toothy grin, cut his musical teeth in New Orleans playing in parades and on steamboat excursions with Fate Marable's band. In late 1918 he replaced Joe "King" Oliver in Kid Ory's band and honed his talents in that outfit for the next few years. Then in August of 1922 he left his hometown of New Orleans to join King Oliver's Creole Jazz Band in Chicago, where he caused an immediate stir. Louis remained with King Oliver's band through 1924 before moving to New York and joining Fletcher Henderson's big band. During this year, Armstrong enhanced his reputation by cutting several recordings with blues singers, including Ma Rainey, Sippie Wallace, and Bessie Smith. But his biggest impact would come as a leader in his own right.

After returning to Chicago in 1925—the same year that Josephine Baker introduced *le jazz hot* to Paris in *La Revue Nègre*—Armstrong undertook the first of his remarkable series of Hot Five and Hot Seven sessions for Okeh Records (cut from November 1925 through December 1928). Those historic recordings—the Rosetta Stone of Jazz—have recently been compiled, remastered, repackaged, and reissued by Columbia/Legacy. The brilliance of these recordings will, no doubt, continue to touch aspiring musicians for generations to come.

As Robert G. O'Meally writes in his astute appreciation of Armstrong's Hot Five and Hot Seven recordings accompanying that four-CD boxed set: "The recordings in this box showcase not Armstrong the old lion of middle-to-late years but the artist as a young man. Their importance to jazz history is so great that it cannot be overstated. Like Chaucer's poetry, which virtually begins the process of codifying the English language as a medium for sophisticated versification, Armstrong's Hot Fives and Hot Sevens provide a wide launching pad from which the history of jazz takes flight."

After making his revolutionary, exalted statements with these recordings, Armstrong began gradually focusing more blatantly on entertainment

**Louis Armstrong, circa 1944. Frank Driggs Collection**

at the expense of art. He had already hinted at this more lighthearted direction with his ribald, vaudevillian playfulness on the intro to "Tight like This" and in his frisky repartee with pianist Earl Hines to start off "A Monday Date," both from his Hot Seven recordings of 1928, or in his wild scat abandon in "Skid-Dat-De-Dat" from 1926 or "Hotter than That" from 1927. It was a direction that stern jazzophiles would come to view with increasing indignation over the years.

As Gary Giddins points out in *Satchmo,* "'Tight like This' manages to be cagey and direct, spare and effusive, vaulting and crude, high and low. In this three-minute spectacle, the entertainer and the artist are inseparable, and bound for trouble among the puritans. What manner of artist spices his performance with rude jokes about pleasures of the flesh? What sort of entertainer can so forthrightly convey the acute sadness of the human comedy? Setting up the final payoff, Armstrong interpolates an adolescent jingle ("Oh, the girls in France . . .") and then makes of that very phrase the stuff of great passion. Still, in 1928 Armstrong the entertainer was invariably at the disposal of Armstrong the artist. What would happen if the ebullience behind the artistry were to find shape in sheer personality, unleashed and unfettered?"

We begin to get a clue in 1929 as Armstrong wows audiences in the *Hot Chocolates* revue, which had its initial run at Connie's Inn in Harlem before moving to the Hudson Theatre on Broadway. It was in that show that Satchmo introduced "Ain't Misbehavin'," the Fats Waller tune that became his first big hit. Armstrong was featured with Leroy Smith's group during the run of the revue (at first performing from the pit and eventually taking his spot on stage, to the delight of audiences). His gravel-throated charisma helped make *Hot Chocolates* the hottest ticket in town.

In that same pivotal year of 1929 Armstrong would form his Savoy Ballroom Five and cut the pop song "I Can't Give You Anything but Love," charting a new course away from the cutting-edge Hot Fives and Hot Sevens and steering more toward the mainstream (though his version of that pop confection is indelibly etched with bold strokes of Armstrong's genius). As Giddins expounds:

"A new Louis Armstrong seemed to be taking over from the old. . . . Now he was looking the audience in the eye when he sang, dramatizing the song, making it come alive as a vehicle for the fun and games of his incomparable extemporizations. His utterly original way of putting over a song—of selling it, of keeping the audience enchanted with it—was as instinctive and ingenious as any other aspect of his achievement. He figured out how to make the music part of a larger presentation, the Louis Armstrong Show."

Clearly this was the model for entertaining that seminal jivesters like Cab Calloway, Stuff Smith, and Slim Gaillard would later draw on. And yet, Armstrong was attacked in some quarters for his "mugging" and "clowning" on stage. During his initial visit to England in 1932 he was described as "barbaric" by one intellectual, who admired his music but didn't think laypersons were ready for the shock of seeing him in the flesh. But as intellectuals and jazz snobs continued to stew, Armstrong began courting an entirely different audience with novelty numbers like "I'm a Ding Dong Daddy" and "I'll Be Glad When You're Dead, You Rascal You" (originally recorded in 1931 and reprised the following year in a *Betty Boop* cartoon in which Satchmo makes a cameo appearance), along with lightweight confections like "Sweethearts on Parade," which he nevertheless imbued with his transforming genius. Those ebullient numbers and a string of others like "Laughin' Louis," "Knockin' a Jug," "All of Me," and "Shine" inspired contagious fits of smiling all over the United States in the early 1930s, elevating the great jazz innovator to the new role of pop star.

A major turning point in Armstrong's career was striking up an association with manager Joe Glaser, a powerful music industry figure with mob connections who quickly steered Armstrong's career in a more commercial direction. As Giddins writes in *Satchmo,* "From the time they shook hands in 1935, Louis's star soared."

From the fall of 1935 up until the recording ban of 1942 Armstrong recorded exclusively for Jack Kapp's Decca Records. [At the height of World War II—July 31, 1942—The American Federation of Musicians, headed by James C. Petrillo, went on strike to seek royalties from the record companies to finance an unemployment fund to compensate musicians who lost work because of competition from recorded music. The strike dragged on for more than a year, drastically reducing the production of new commercial recordings.] After the ban was lifted in 1944, Armstrong recorded for Victor in 1946 and 1947, then with Decca from 1949 through 1958. During this second stint with Decca he was also "loaned out" to Columbia and Verve for one-off projects.

In 1936 Armstrong was featured in a major Paramount film, *Pennies from Heaven,* opposite Bing Crosby. In 1937 he appeared in two more movies and become the first black performer with a network radio show. In 1938 Satchmo recorded the first of his humorous mock sermons for Decca by the Elder

Eatmore, a jivetime persona he put on that blended Baptist preacher histrionics with his own innate comic timing. (Louis Jordan would later offer his own humorous spin on Armstrong's Elder Eatmore with equally emphatic mock sermons by Deacon Jones). That same year, Armstrong covered Slim & Slam's hit "Flat Foot Floogie" for Decca, backed by The Mills Brothers.

By the mid-1940s, at the height of jive's widespread popularity, Satchmo hit the road with a New Orleans ensemble, which included such great players as Jack Teagarden or Trummy Young on trombone, Barney Bigard or Edmund Hall on clarinet, Earl Hines or Billy Kyle on piano, Sid Catlett or Cozy Cole on drums, and Milt Hinton or Arvell Shaw on bass. Armstrong's traveling show at the time also featured risqué comedy routines with portly singer-dancer/comic foil Velma Middleton. This kind of lowbrow humor, of course, rankled the sensibilities of jazz stalwarts who rarely acknowledged any of Louis's work beyond the Hot Five and Hot Seven sessions.

The low point of this kind of unfortunate Satchmo bashing may have come in a September 1954 article penned by Wilfred Lowe for the British publication *Jazz Journal*. In his rather harsh indictment of Pops's tendency toward crowd-pleasing jive the irate scribe chides Louis for spurning jazz in favor of comedy, furthermore accusing him of selling his soul to the devil of Tin Pan Alley: "Armstrong, with his clowning, rolling eyes, suggestive growls and obscene asides, and his childish tantrums—his puerile utterances, drags his choice of music from the heights of art to the level of black face buffoonery. His concerts seldom rise above the plane of a coon carnival, complete with comedy, splits and other vulgarities."

He goes on to mock Louis as the "Clown Prince of Jazz" and questions how we can allow such buffoonery as "Two to Tango" to exist in the name of jazz. He further questions the title "King of Jazz," which was bestowed upon Armstrong decades earlier, suggesting that the appellation might be more fitting of someone like Roy Eldridge. In his summation, this pompous, sourpuss academe assesses the "damage" of Armstrong's contribution:

"The time has come for us to hand Louis Armstrong his cap and bells and to force his abdication before he can pull jazz music even further into the slime. Let us, by all means, treasure the memory of Louis when he was great. He has played his part. Now he must be allowed to either bow out gracefully or be forcibly ejected. We owe it to the pioneers as well as the future of jazz to ensure that Armstrong does no more harm. Place the crown on a head more worthy: clothe Louis in more fitting apparel—that of a jazz jester."

Satchmo the Jester may have been the source of embarrassment and con-fusion among some civil-rights spokesmen and black college students. But as Albert Murray so rightly states in *Stomping the Blues:* "He always counter-stated his clowning with his trumpet, which was never a laughing matter."

Writer-musician Ben Sidran eloquently defined that transcendent quali-ty that Pops possessed in *Black Talk:* "Louis Armstrong was most notable for the equipoise, the visceral balance between Western and Negro musical styles of his playing. Perhaps no one walked the fence between the two cultures bet-ter than he did. Like [Buddy] Bolden before him, Armstrong was an innova-tor whose influence seemed single-handedly to reform black music. The bal-ance of intellectual and emotional content in his playing impressed a vast and integrated audience. Armstrong combined the oral approach to rhythm and vocalization with an intuitive grasp of Western harmonic structure, creating a new synthesis acceptable to both blacks and whites."

And while he ruled the roost for thirty years, by 1957 there were rumblings of negativity regarding Satchmo's status. Two *Melody Maker* head-lines from October 12, 1957, represent a changing tide of sentiment toward the Great One: "Louis Doesn't Swing" and the defensive retort to a previous editorial, "Louis Is Not an Uncle Tom." And yet, Armstrong's widespread popularity continued to grow through the '50s and into the '60s on the strength of such pop hits as "Mack the Knife" (1956), "Hello Dolly" (1964), and the cloying "What a Wonderful World" (1968), along with worldwide exposure from whirlwind tours of Europe and Africa. He made his last recording, an animated reading of "'Twas the Night before Christmas," on February 26, 1971, at his home in Corona, Queens. He died on July 6, 1971, leaving behind an incredibly rich legacy with which over time musicians from all over the planet will be forced to deal.

# FATS WALLER

BORN: May 21, 1904, in New York, New York
DIED: December 15, 1943, in Kansas City, Missouri

A PRECOCIOUS CHILD whose pianistic talents emerged at an early age, Thomas Wright "Fats" Waller developed during the early 1920s under the tutelage of the great Harlem stride pianists James P. Johnson, his first mentor, and Willie "The Lion" Smith, a cigar-chomping sharpie who instilled the concept of sartorial splendor in the lad. The son of a Baptist preacher, Waller began playing organ in church and by the age of fifteen became something of a neighborhood sensation, performing as house organist at the Lincoln Theatre, where he entertained his schoolmates during the intermission between movie features.

**"Exuberance is the spontaneity of life."**

*— Fats Waller*

His prodigious, Johnson-derived stride work was first documented at the age of eighteen for Okeh Records. Two songs were recorded in late October of 1922—"Muscle Shoals Blues" and "Birmingham Blues." Shortly thereafter, Fats began collaborating on songwriting with another mentor figure: Clarence Williams, a great piano player, leader of the Blue Five and an astute businessman who would help guide Waller's career in the early years. That same year Waller also met Andy Razaf, a gifted lyricist who would become his most important writing partner. Together they would collaborate on Fats's most famous tunes—the winsome "Honeysuckle Rose," the melancholy "(What Did I Do to Be So) Black and Blue" and the oft-recorded "Ain't Misbehavin'," along with the music from such successful revues as *Load of Coal, Keep Shufflin',* and *Hot Chocolates.*

By 1924 Fats was a star on Harlem's rent-party circuit, well known for his piano rolls, radio broadcasts, and outsized comic personality. By November of 1926 he made his first recording as an organ soloist—a tango tempo rendition of W. C. Handy's "St. Louis Blues" and on the flip side his own "Lenox Avenue Blues," named for his old stomping grounds in Harlem.

In 1927 Fats joined his pal Louis Armstrong in Chicago for a series of gigs at the Vendome Theatre and also for several exuberant jam sessions at the Sunset Cafe, where Armstrong's band held forth. During his brief stay in Chicago, Waller also had a few encounters with the notorious Chicago gangster Al Capone. As Maurice Waller relates in his 1977 biography about his larger-than-life father:

"Suddenly, someone shoved a revolver into his paunchy stomach and ordered him into a car. He did what he was told. The gunman ordered the driver to take them to East Cicero, the home of Chicago's 'second mayor,' Al

---

**Fats Waller, 1939. Frank Driggs Collection**

"Fats" Waller

Capone, and Dad began to sweat it out. . . .

"It only took the shiny black limousine a little while to make it to its destination. The car pulled up in front of what appeared to be a hotel or fancy saloon. It was the headquarters of Al Capone. Dad's four escorts shoved him through the front door and then through a crowd of people, led him to a piano and told him to play. It was a surprise birthday party. Capone, who had heard Dad play at the hotel, was delighted when he saw the present the boys brought him sitting at the piano." Capone kept him there several days, shoving hundred-dollar bills into his pocket whenever he played a request and filling his glass with vintage champagne whenever Fats emptied it.

After his stay in Chicago had ended Waller returned to Harlem and to his old job as house organist at the Lafayette and Lincoln theaters. On December 1, 1927, he unveiled his inimitable vocal persona for the first time on record with "Red Hot Dan," which featured a red-hot scat chorus, and "The Digah's Stomp." As he gained confidence in his uniquely swinging approach to piano—an animated style that relied on a bouncing left hand in combination with an uncommonly graceful yet agile right hand (a style that influenced everyone from Count Basie and Teddy Wilson to Art Tatum and Dave Brubeck)—he gradually began allowing his inherent naturally buoyant personality and disarming sense of humor to come to the fore on stage. This penchant for crowd pleasing was described by Maurice Waller:

"Dad loved any kind of shtick and he used all kinds of costumes and gimmicks in his act. His favorite was the Hawaiian bit. As soon as the house lights dimmed, the band started playing a hula. Out slithered Fats from between the two giant folds of the house curtains. He would grab one end of the curtain and wrap it around his large, portly frame like an enormous hula skirt, roll his eyes suggestively and begin the funniest, lewdest dance ever seen. Then he would undulate those huge hips and sashay from side to side, finally making it over to the piano, where he would stare at the stool for a long moment. 'Hmmmm, how am I gonna put all of me on that little thing?' he'd ask, as he cautiously lowered himself onto the stool. Then he'd look down and shout, 'Hey, Fats, are you all there?' It was a little bit of hokum that always brought the house down."

Through the '20s and '30s, the jovial three-hundred-pound Fats continued to rock audiences with his dazzling piano playing ("A Handful of Keys," "Smashing Thirds," and "Jitterbug Waltz"), funny ad-libs, mugging, and risqué patter, frequently punctuating vocal choruses with his jivey trademark phrase, "Yass, yass, yass!"

His 1937 recording of "The Joint Is Jumpin'" is a classic example of Waller's extroverted, off-the-cuff style. The track opens with rollicking partying sounds by male and female friends. As the partying increases, Fats intones: "No baby . . . not now, I can't come over right now. Don't you hit that chick, dat's my broad. Put this cat outta here before I knock him through his knees." Later in the tune, with a siren wailing in the distance, Fats reassures the group: "If we go to jail, I got the bail." And with the cops knocking at the door, he adds, coyly, "Remember, don't nobody give his real name."

Examples abound of Waller's good-humored, jivey approach to delivering a lyric. His recordings of Tin Pan Alley fare like "There's Honey on the Moon Tonight," "On the Bumpy Road to Love," and "The Sheik of Araby" are imbued with uncanny rhythmic invention and a sense of irony that could deflate a particularly sappy song. He also regularly injected a healthy dose of ad-libbing and hip running commentary into his recordings. On "Serenade for a Wealthy Widow," Fats comments, "Woman, they tell me you're flooded with currency." On "Mandy," as he begins a very fast-paced solo, he giggles, "This tickling is so terrific. Oh, stop it baby." On "Somebody Stole My Gal" there's a monologue never intended by the lyricist: "Sherlock Holmes, go find that woman. . . . She's gonna come back in June? Well, go get her. . . . Oh, Sherlock, bring her right back." No one, save Louis Armstrong, ever took such great liberties with a song.

In 1939, an astoundingly prolific year in the studio, Fats released a bevy of recordings imbued with broad strokes of comedic panache, including such popular melodies as "Two Sleepy People," "Good for Nothing but Love," "I Can't Give You Anything but Love" (a duet with a teenaged Una Mae Carlisle), "You Meet the Nicest People in Your Dreams," "Honeysuckle Rose," "Ain't Misbehavin'," "Tea for Two," "Squeeze Me," "Handful of Keys," two particularly jive-laden offerings in "It's You Who Taught It to Me" and "Your Feet's Too Big," which includes the cryptic and oft-quoted tag line "one never knows, do one." Another wildly popular number from that same year, "Hold Tight (I Want Some Seafood Mama)," contains the nonsensical scat syllables "brrrrrrr-yaka-zakee," which would become a kind of jive mantra picked up on by several jivesters of the day, including Leo "Scat" Watson, who referred to it on his signature number of that year, "It's the Tune That Counts," and The Cats & The Fiddle, who nimbly inserted the Fats line into their 1939 anthem, "We Cats Will Swing for You."

While humor was always the watchword with Waller, the music beneath the frolicking was always stellar. As pianist Butch Thompson points out in his liner notes to *A Good Man Is Hard to Find* (RCA/Bluebird, 1938–1940): "Fats' sustained high level of musicianship throughout this huge body of work is nothing short of astonishing, and the constant (and often brilliant) barrage of 'jive' just insures that things don't get too precious."

By 1940 Fats was a superstar, his name and voice known to millions in America and Europe. That year he played to 120,000 fans at a concert at Soldier Field in Chicago. His longtime record company, Victor, now billed him as its outstanding comic performer. And with the release in 1943 of the Hollywood movie *Stormy Weather,* co-starring Bill "Bojangles" Robinson and Lena Horne, he was a bona fide household name.

Sadly, his years of late-night carousing, overeating, and heavy drinking finally caught up with him near the end of 1943. He died on December 15, 1943, of bronchial pneumonia on a train pulling into Union Station in Kansas City, Missouri. On December 20, Fats was given a royal send-off in Harlem. At the church service, the Reverend Adam Clayton Powell Jr. summed up Fats's contribution succinctly and eloquently: "Fats Waller always played to a packed house. We are gathered here this morning to mourn the passing of a simple soul, a soul touched with the genius of music which brought relief from our cares and woes. Because God gave him genius and skill, he in turn gave the world laughter and joy for its difficult and lonely hours. Thomas Waller and his songs shall live again. His sweetest songs are yet to be heard . . . in glory."

Fats Waller's sly, good-timey jive has generated steady record sales over the years for RCA Victor. His recordings and sheet music continue to do a phenomenal business in Europe. And there has been renewed interest in Waller's legacy since the Broadway musical *Ain't Misbehavin',* which opened as a limited-run cabaret act at the Manhattan Theatre Club on February 8, 1978, but was so well received that it soon moved to the Longacre Theatre on Broadway. (The show featured the music of Fats Waller and reproduced the atmosphere of a Harlem nightclub in the 1930s. It ran for 1,604 performances and enjoyed a brief revival in 1988.)

Fats's music—that irrepressible attitude in sound born out of a larger-than-life personality—continues to reach out and grab people over time, assuring him a place in the pantheon of jive for the ages.

# CAB CALLOWAY

BORN: December 25, 1907, in Rochester, New York
DIED: November 18, 1994, in Hockessin, Delaware

A CHARISMATIC ENTERTAINER whose frantic stage moves and wild showmanship laid the groundwork for everyone from Louis Jordan and Louis Prima to Little Richard and Jerry Lee Lewis to Michael Jackson and Prince, Cab Calloway took the seeds of jive planted by Louis Armstrong and Fats Waller in the 1920s and reaped a righteous harvest in the 1930s. A household name by 1932 (on the strength of his breakthrough hit from the previous year, "Minnie the Moocher"), the handsome, dapper man helped to bring jive into mainstream consciousness through such jive anthems as "Are You Hep to the Jive?" "Are You All Reet?" "We the Cats Shall Hep Ya," and "Jumpin' Jive" as well as appearances on radio, in movies (*Big Broadcast, International House, Song of the Island, Stormy Weather*) and cartoons of the day *(Betty Boop, Jack Frost)*. The publication in 1936 of *Cab Calloway's Hepster's Dictionary* (which was updated and reprinted in 1944) helped to spread the gospel of jive talk and fanned the flames of this popular fad.

At the height of the Depression, Calloway was making $50,000 a year and living in a manner to which he had become accustomed— wearing the finest clothes, driving a big green Lincoln convertible around town, flashing a smoldering sensuality, and attracting throngs of admiring females wherever he went. As Al Quaglieri writes in the liner notes to the 1994 compilation *Are You Hep to the Jive?* for Columbia/Legacy: "That toothy, worldwise grin . . . that thin moustache . . . those lascivious eyes . . . that tangle of shiny black hair dangling carelessly over his forehead. Since time began, whenever parents warned their daughters about dangerous men, this was the very guy they meant."

"Hi-De-Hi-De-Hi-De-Ho."
— *Cab Calloway*

The Dean of Jive, Cabell Calloway was born on Christmas Day in Rochester, New York, and raised in a middle-class section of Baltimore. A star basketball player in high school, young Cab had aspirations of becoming a pro but eventually decided on singing as a new kind of hustle. While still in high school he began sitting in at the Gaiety, a little speakeasy next to a bur-lesque house. With Chick Webb as a main inspiration, he turned to drums and played briefly in the ten-piece Johnny Jones Arabian Tent Orchestra, a Baltimore version of a New Orleans Dixieland band. After graduating from high school in 1927, he joined an all-male quartet that was featured in a tour-ing production of a black revue called *Plantation Days*. The show eventually traveled to Chicago in September of that year.

In Chicago, Cab lived with his older sister Blanche, a successful actress and vivacious woman who was not only also appearing in *Plantation Days* but was responsible for getting Cab his audition for the gig. In January of 1928, he got a side gig singing at the Dreamland Cafe, right across the street from the Sunset Cafe, where Louis Armstrong was turning heads with Carroll Dickerson's band. In the spring of '28, Calloway would become house singer and emcee at the Sunset, where he and Armstrong worked together for about six months. Two years later, Armstrong would be responsible for getting Cab his first major gig in New York, in the cast of *Hot Chocolates*.

"I suppose that Louis was one of the main influences in my career," says Cab in his autobiography, *Of Minnie the Moocher and Me*. "Later on, I began to scat sing in The Cotton Club with all of that hi-de-hoing. Louis first got me freed up from straight lyrics to try scatting."

When Armstrong and Carroll Dickerson left Chicago in the spring of 1929 to take up residency at Connie's Inn in Harlem, their spot as house band at the Sunset was filled by Marion Hardy's group, The Alabamians. Cab quickly took over the helm of that eleven-piece band and molded it into a crack outfit. As he writes in his autobiography: "We developed a style of nov-elty arrangement in which the band members all had megaphones, and I would sing a line and they would hold up their megaphones and respond. The crowds loved our jumpin', jiving style, and the dance floor at the Sunset was always hopping."

Cab took The Alabamians on the road for three months and finally landed in New York for a gig at the Savoy Ballroom in November of 1929, a month after the stock market crashed. While The Alabamians returned to Chicago after their engagement at the Savoy, Calloway stayed in New York and Armstrong helped him land a spot as juvenile lead in the *Hot Chocolates* revue. Cab toured with the show before returning to New York in the spring of 1930 to take over leadership of The Missourians, a hot Kansas City outfit that had been heavily influenced by Bennie Moten's band. Their first engagement was at the Savoy and later they began to make some noise at The Plantation Club on 126th and Lenox Avenue. It wasn't long before gangsters stepped in and persuaded them to move to The Cotton Club. As Cab writes: "The Cotton Club mob bought out my contract and The Missourians' contract the easy way—pure muscle."

Cab and The Missourians were hired during the summer of 1930 to sub for Duke Ellington while he and his band were in Hollywood shooting the Amos 'n' Andy film, *Check and Doublecheck*. Their revue that summer, "Brown Sugar—Sweet but Unrefined," was a combination of vaudeville, burlesque, and great music and dancing with music and lyrics by the team of Ted Koehler and Harold Arlen. Cab and the group would return for another extended engagement in the fall of 1930. By the end of the year, Cab was the king of The Cotton Club, where he wowed the wealthy white patrons with his dazzling showmanship, slick brand of jive, and a voice that has been described as exuding "a joy and festive spirit which moves one to instant gaiety."

"Sometime during 1931," Calloway writes, "when it became clear that I was a hit and that Duke would be on the road most of the time, we changed the name of the band from The Missourians to Cab Calloway's Cotton Club Orchestra. Suddenly I was one of those celebrities that I had been watching from a distance. Everywhere I went people knew Cab Calloway. And, Jesus, what money I was making—more than I'd ever expected in my life."

Calloway's big breakthrough was partly due to the overwhelming response of his big hit record of 1931, *Minnie the Moocher*, which involved audiences in a raucous call-and-response chorus of "Hi-De-Hi-De-Hi-De-Ho." A composite of two other popular titles of the day—"Minnie the Mermaid" and "Willie the Weeper"—it quickly became Cab's theme song and spawned a string of spin-off tunes, including "Minnie the Moocher's Wedding Day" and "You Gotta Hi-De-Ho" in 1932, "Keep That Hi-De-Ho in Your Soul" in 1935, "The Hi-De-Ho Miracle Man" in 1936, "Hi-De-Ho Romeo" in 1937, "Mr. Paganini, Swing for Minnie" in 1938, and "Hi-De-Ho Serenade" in 1939. (Jimmie Lunceford finally put the Minnie fad to rest in 1940 with his recording of "Minnie the Moocher Is Dead.") But Calloway would be forever associated with "Minnie the Moocher," which he continued to perform for thrilled audiences through the '80s and into the '90s.

Drawing on the lessons of phrasing he had picked up from Armstrong before him (and, to a degree, from his older sister Blanche), Calloway took great liberties with rhythm and melody in his colorful, pyrotechnic approach to delivering a lyric. While his flashy suits, physical gyrations, and flying lock of hair set the tone of his frantic stage presence, Calloway always kept first-rate musicians in his band, often hiring them away from other bands. He got tenor sax great Chu Berry in 1937 from Fletcher Henderson's band, hired trombonist Tyree Glenn away from Benny Carter in 1940, and lured trombonist Quentin Jackson from Don Redman's group that same year. At other times, Calloway's outfits included such stellar instrumentalists as tenor saxophonists Ben Webster and Walter "Foots" Thomas, clarinetist Eddie Barefield, guitarist Danny Barker, trumpeters Lammar Wright, Doc Cheatham, and Jonah Jones, bassist Milt Hinton, drummers Panama Francis and Cozy Cole. And in 1939 he shook up the band by hiring an impetuous twenty-two-year-old trumpeter named Dizzy Gillespie, who gave Cab headaches about sticking to the charts before he went off on his own to forge a new path in music with fellow bebop pioneer Charlie Parker.

Calloway first hit the silver screen in 1932 with an appearance in *The Big Broadcast,* in which he performed "Minnie the Moocher" and "Hot Toddy." He followed that up with an outrageous cameo in *International House,* a 1933 comedy vehicle for W. C. Fields in which Cab performs the risqué pot anthem "Reefer Man" and the equally taboo paean to cocaine, "Kicking the Gong Around." That same year he also made cameo appearances in three *Betty Boop* cartoons, singing "The Old Man of the Mountain," "You Gotta Hi-De-Ho," and "St. James Infirmary."

When The Cotton Club finally closed in 1940, Cab took the band on the road for an extended tour. He eventually returned to New York for a steady engagement downtown at the Coconut Grove in the Park Central Hotel and later at the midtown Cafe Zanzibar, where he served up a classier version of his swinging, extroverted jazz. That same year, he asked the musical question, "Are You Hep to the Jive?" Judging by his overwhelming popularity, the answer all across America was a resounding "All reet!"

His 1942 recording of "Blues in the Night" (a year after Jimmie Lunceford's version) became a big hit and his appearance the following year in the all-star Hollywood movie *Stormy Weather* brought his star up a notch. With the big-band era fading, Calloway had to reluctantly break up his orchestra. As he writes: "The big-band era came to an end for me in 1947, and the years after that are not easy to talk about. I went from being a guy

**Cab Calloway, 1936. Frank Driggs Collection**

whose gross was $200,000 a year to someone who couldn't get a booking. No work at all, and no money coming in. Jesus, that was demoralizing."

He scaled down to a septet he called the Cab Jivers (Danny Barker on guitar, Tyree Glenn on vibraphone, Milt Hinton on bass, Al Gibson on clarinet, Jonah Jones on trumpet, Ike Quebec on tenor saxophone) and in 1947 tried reviving some of his past glory by cutting "The Hi-De-Ho Man (That's Me)." That same year he shifted his attention to an emerging sound of the day by recording "The Calloway Boogie," an early example of rock 'n' roll that predated Jackie Brenston's "Rocket 88" and Bill Haley's "Rock Around the Clock" by several years.

In 1950 Cab opened on Broadway as Sportin' Life opposite Leontyne Price in a revival of Gershwin's *Porgy and Bess*. That musical ran for three and a half years, including one year in London. Then in 1967, at the age of sixty, he began a three-year run as Horace Vandergelder opposite Pearl Bailey in an all-black production of the hit musical *Hello Dolly*. He also worked with the Harlem Globetrotters in the 1960s, performing at half-time shows. As he writes: "The whole auditorium, 15,000 to 20,000 people most of the time, would be hushed and listening to see what I was going to put down, and by the end of halftime I would have the whole damned place echoing with 'Minnie.' I could feel the mood of the crowd even in a huge auditorium. And it was a ball, me just swinging and swaying with my hair flopping down on my forehead and my arms stretched out, singing my heart out. There's no feeling like that for me in the world."

Through the '70s, Calloway made special appearances at the Catskills and Florida resorts for fans who never tired of hearing him sing "Minnie the Moocher." His cameo appearance in the popular 1980 film *The Blues Brothers* helped spark renewed interest in this celebrated jive pioneer.

---

## Jivenotes:

Another group that was hugely influential in the 1920s was **The Mills Brothers.** Their impeccable vocal harmonies, acrobatic scatting, and manner of simulating instruments (trumpet, tuba, saxophone) with the human voice paved the way for a bevy of popular vocal harmony groups that followed in their wake, from The Ink Spots, The Spirits of Rhythm, The Cats & The Fiddle of the late '30s and early '40s to the doo-wop groups of the '50s, right up to contemporary times with Take 6. Hailing from Piqua, Ohio, the four Mills brothers (Donald, Herbert, John, and Harry) first sang as a group in 1925. Beginning in 1927 they appeared regularly on radio station WLW, where they were billed as The Steamboat Four and The Tasty Yeast Jesters. After a number of local appearances around the Cincinnati area, they finally came to New York in mid-1931 for a broadcast on the CBS radio network, sparking interest in their fresh new sound. Their first recording session for the Brunswick label on October 9 of 1931 produced a tongue-twisting scat rendition of "Tiger Rag" and the ballad "Nobody's Sweetheart Now." A month later they shared the bill with Bing Crosby in the crooner's debut at the New York Paramount and culminated that breakthrough year with another recording session, backing Crosby on a sizzling scat rendition of "Tiger Rag."

In 1932 the Mills Brothers, billed as "Four Boys and a Guitar," had a cameo appearance in *The Big Broadcast,* which starred Crosby and also featured Cab Calloway and The Boswell Sisters. And in 1938 they collaborated with Louis Armstrong on a rousing version of Slim Gaillard's jive anthem "Flat Foot Floogie."

By 1943, with the success of their smash hit "Paper Doll," the group smoothed off the rough edges and became a mainstream pop act, scoring thirty-two chart hits from 1943 to 1968. Their flawless harmonies, instrumental imitations, and rhythmic bass lines had an immense impact on black music, providing a foundation for jive, R&B, and doo-wop vocal styles.

## *Recommended Listening*

*NOTE: The resurgence in the popularity of swing music has created a ripple effect in the industry. A lot of older recordings have recently been rediscovered and reissued. The recommended listening section, which appears at the end of each chapter, lists CDs that are currently available. The dates listed—either in parentheses following the label info or in the title of the CD—note when the music was originally recorded (and not when it was re-released). Under the heading of each artist, the CDs are listed roughly chronologically.*

**FATS WALLER**

*Giants of Jazz,* Time-Life (1922–1943)

*Classic Jazz from Rare Piano Rolls,* Music Masters (1923–1929)

*Fats Waller and His Buddies,* Bluebird (1927–1929)

*Turn on the Heat: The Fats Waller Piano Solos,* Bluebird (1927–1941)

*The Joint Is Jumpin',* Bluebird (1929–1943)

*Swingin' the Organ,* Bluebird (1955 release of mid-1930s performances)

*Fats Waller and His Rhythm: The Middle Years, Volume 1,* Bluebird (1936–1938)

*A Handful of Keys,* Buddha (1999 release of a live 1938 radio broadcast)

*A Good Man Is Hard to Find: The Middle Years, Volume 2,* Bluebird (1938–1940)

*Fine Arabian Stuff,* High Note (1939)

## LOUIS ARMSTRONG

*Portrait of the Artist as a Young Man,*
Columbia (1923–1934)

*The Complete Hot Five & Hot Seven*
*Recordings,* Columbia/Legacy
(1925–1929)

*Rhythm Saved the World,*
GRP (1935–1936)

*You're Driving Me Crazy,*
Columbia (1939)

*Satchmo at Symphony Hall, Decca (1947)*

*The California Concerts,*
GRP (1951–1955)

*Satch Plays Fats,* Columbia/Legacy (1955)

*Porgy & Bess,* Verve (1957)

*Bing and Satchmo,* MGM (1960)

*Louis Armstrong and Duke Ellington,*
Roulette (1961)

## CAB CALLOWAY

*Cab Calloway and The Missourians,*
JSP (1929–1930)

*Cab Calloway 1930–1931,* Classics

*Cab Calloway, 1931–1932,* Classics

*Cab Calloway and Company,*
RCA (1931–1949)

*Keep That Hi-De-Hi in Your Soul,*
Jazzterdays (1933–1937)

*King of Hi-De-Ho,* Giants of Jazz
(1934–1947)

*The Hi-De-Ho Man,* RCA (1935–1947)

*Jiveformation Please,* Jazzterdays
(1938–1941)

*Cab Calloway,* Epic (1939)

*Are You Hep to the Jive?* Sony/Legacy
(1939–1947)

## THE MILLS BROTHERS

*Four Boys and a Guitar,*
Sunbeam (1931)

*The Anthology: 1931–1968,*
Decca/MCA

*Louis Armstrong and the Mills Brothers,*
Decca (1954)

*Singin' and Swingin',* Decca (1956)

**CHAPTER 2**

# THE GOLDEN ERA OF JIVE

**Louis Jordan, Slim Gaillard,**

**The Cats & The Fiddle, Leo "Scat" Watson, Stuff Smith,**

**Jimmie Lunceford, Lucky Millinder**

With the end of Prohibition in 1933, speakeasies (which had been thriving, albeit illegally, all over the country) became legitimate nightclubs overnight. In New York a new slew of clubs opened up on Fifty-second Street to accommodate the partying needs of the public. And a number of entertainers emerged on the scene to provide that good-time service with their spirited brand of jive.

As pianist Dick Katz reminisces in his liner notes to *52nd Street Swing: New York in the '30s:* "In this era of the celebrity jazz superstar, who performs in concert halls and festivals around the world, it is hard to believe that between 1934 and about 1949 there was an area, only a city block and a half long, where world-class jazz of all styles and types could be heard nightly. You didn't have to reserve $35 tickets in advance, or wait in line to pay a $40 admission (plus minimum, tax, and tip) to hear one set in a club."

Known as "The Street" or "Swing Street," Fifty-second Street stretched from Fifth Avenue to Seventh Avenue in Manhattan. It was a musical and cultural mosaic, a phenomenon that nurtured and developed some of the greatest jazz music and soloists the world has ever known. "Spawned by Prohibition, the cluster of brownstones on that street were well-attended speakeasies until alcoholic beverages became legal again in 1933," writes

Katz. "At that point, many of these watering holes evolved into showcases for state-of-the-art jazz. Musical novelty groups also flourished there. From 1935 on, The Street was really jumping."

They were jumping at the Three Deuces and right next door at the Club Downbeat, across the street at the Onyx Club, and over at the Famous Door, The Spotlite, Tondelayo's, Club Carousel, Club Samosa, The Yacht Club, Kelly's Stable, Jimmy Ryan's, and The Hickory House. And as Katz points out, "The close proximity of the clubs created an ideal climate for sitting in by musicians of all styles. This was a near-essential activity that launched many a budding career—most leaders didn't care who you were, if you could play. The jam sessions were a big draw and most of the clubs featured them regularly, until increasingly strict union rules against playing for free eventually killed the practice."

In the late 1930s one could catch a bevy of jazz stars on Swing Street, including Fats Waller, Billie Holiday, Art Tatum, Coleman Hawkins, Roy Eldridge, and the Count Basie Orchestra. The early 1940s offered the likes of Erroll Garner, Ben Webster, George Shearing, and Slam Stewart. And the boppers—Charlie Parker, Dizzy Gillespie, Bud Powell—would come along by 1945. On the West Coast a similarly vital scene was happening in Los Angeles at places like The Club Alabam, the Down Beat, Jack's Basket, Lovejoy's, the Last Word, and the Turban Lounge on Central Avenue; at Billy Berg's on Vine Street; at Streets of Paris on Hollywood Boulevard; or at the Swanee Inn on LaBrea Avenue.

This golden period on both coasts (roughly from 1934 to 1946) produced an avalanche of jivesters who gained popularity not only through club appearances, but from radio broadcasts and record sales as well. Among them were drummer-trombonist-scatman extraordinaire Leo "Scat" Watson, who appeared frequently on Fifty-second Street with The Spirits of Rhythm; violinist Stuff Smith, who premiered at the Onyx Club on Fifty-second Street in 1934; pianist-guitarist and resident madman at Billy Berg's, Slim Gaillard; and Louis Jordan, who by the mid-1940s would become the biggest star in jive. A personal favorite to come out of this Golden Era of Jive was The Cats & The Fiddle, an irrepressibly swinging four-piece vocal harmony group in the mold of The Spirits of Rhythm that formed in the late 1930s and made frequent appearances on R&B touring packages through the late 1940s.

On the big-band tip the Jimmie Lunceford's orchestra got into the jive act in the mid-1930s with jovial offerings like "For Dancers Only," "Rhythm

Is Our Business," and "Tain't What You Do, It's the Way That Cha Do It" along with flashy bits of showmanship. And Lucky Millinder, fronting the Mills Blue Rhythm Band, contributed good vibes and a vigorous conducting style through the '30s and '40s.

All these jumpin' jivesters were consummate entertainers as well as accomplished musicians. They succeeded in putting smiles on faces, eliciting polite yuks and genuine guffaws while simultaneously swinging their asses off.

## LOUIS JORDAN

BORN: July 8, 1908, in Brinkley, Arkansas
DIED: February 4, 1975, in Los Angeles, California

THE GRAND HIGH EXALTED MYSTIC RULER of jive was known as "King of the Jukeboxes" at the height of his popularity in the 1940s. Early on in his career he billed himself as "Louis Jordan, His Silver Saxophone and His Golden Voice." Later on he became known simply as "Mr. Personality." A consummate, effervescent entertainer who strung colloquial rhyming couplets together as nimbly as the "baddest" rappers out there today, Louis Jordan was one of the chief architects and prime progenitors of R&B and early rock 'n' roll.

From 1942 to 1951 "Mr. Personality" scored an astonishing fifty-seven R&B chart hits (all on Decca), beginning with the humorous blues "I'm Gonna Leave You on the Outskirts of Town" and finishing with "Weak Minded Blues." He was particularly popular during World War II and recorded prolifically for the Armed Forces Radio Service and the V-Disc program. Jordan's massive appeal also translated onto the silver screen. A series of short films for "Caldonia," "Reet, Petite & Gone," "Look out Sister," and "Beware"—essentially the first music videos—give us an enlightening peek at just what made him such a beloved entertainer.

"Hey everybody! Let's have some fun! You only live but once and when you're daid, you're done."
—*Louis Jordan*

"He was a complete original," says Ray Charles. "He was such a great showman, with a sense of humor and an unforgettable tongue-in-cheek style that, after hearing him once, I couldn't forget him, and I became a great fan."

So was Sammy Davis Jr., who once said, "Louis Jordan was the first recording artist to project life and situations of the black community on records with humor and dignity." (This is exemplified by Jordan classics like "Saturday Night Fish Fry," "Blue Light Boogie," and "Buzz Me Blues.")

"Louis Jordan was a great musician and in my opinion was way ahead of his time," writes B. B. King in the liner notes to 1999's *Let the Good Times Roll* (MCA), his personal love letter to his idol. "As people get to know more about him, they will realize what a great contribution he left to the music of today." Or as writer Nick Tosches put it in *Unsung Heroes of Rock 'n' Roll: The Birth of Rock in the Wild Years before Elvis* (Da Capo, 1999): "Jordan did more to define hep and to prepare white folks for the coming of rock 'n' roll than any other artist of that era."

Another Jordan fan, Casey MacGill of the Broadway musical *Swing!* also reflected on Jordan's immense contribution. "The way he economized the whole sound of big bands and distilled it into a smaller combo and took a lot of the excess filigree and stuff off of it was brilliant. He broke it down to its essential swing elements and then reintroduced a healthy dose of the blues. Also, the way he would mix blues and entertainment, I think, was really a very big contribution. He became the touchstone that a whole generation of guys picked up on that made the next step towards rock 'n' roll."

A powerfully direct alto saxophonist and an appealing singer with a comedic gift—his onstage mugging and cavorting were inspired by black vaudevillians like Bert Williams and Mantan Moreland—Jordan was a graduate of Chick Webb's Savoy Ballroom Orchestra of the 1930s, and he went on to form his own band in 1938, the year Slim Gaillard hit big with "Flat Foot Floogie."

Through the '40s Louis Jordan and His Tympany Five set the tone for jump blues—which is characterized by surging twelve-bar shuffles with an infectious swing feel—with a constant run of hits, including "Caldonia," "Choo Choo Ch'Boogie," "I'm Gonna Leave You on the Outskirts of Town," "Five Guys Named Moe," "What's the Use of Gettin' Sober," "Ain't Nobody Here but Us Chickens," "Ration Blues," "G.I. Jive," "Is You Is or Is You Ain't (My Baby)," "Beans & Cornbread," and "Saturday Night Fish Fry," his last monster jukebox hit from 1949. These lively, up-tempo, novelty-tinged shuffles not only made a huge impact on rock 'n' roll pioneers Chuck Berry and Bill Haley, bluesmen like B. B. and Freddie King and Clarence "Gatemouth"

**Louis Jordan, 1946. Bill Milkowski Collection**

Brown, and soul star Ray Charles, they also helped Jordan make significant inroads with mainstream audiences. Black and white audiences coast to coast were breathlessly jitterbugging to Jordan's jumping jive.

As Charlie Gillett wrote in *The Sound of the City:* "The pattern for jump combos was set by Louis Jordan's Tympany Five. Jordan presented a style that appealed equally to black and white audiences. Nobody satisfied both tastes so effectively until the rock 'n' rollers Fats Domino, Chuck Berry and Little Richard."

The son of a musician, Jordan was fluent on all the reed instruments as a youth but focused primarily on the alto sax. At the age of twelve he ran away from home and for two consecutive summers played with Ma and Pa Rainey's Rabbit Foot Minstrels traveling show while also supporting classic blues singers Ida Cox and Bessie Smith. Later on he majored in music at Arkansas Baptist College and in 1932 he moved with his family to Philadelphia, where he joined the Charlie Gaines Orchestra. In December of that year, the band accompanied Louis Armstrong on a recording session (a medley of Armstrong's previous hits). In 1934 Jordan made his vocal recording debut on the risqué "I Can't Dance, I Got Ants in My Pants" with Clarence Williams and His Washboard Band. He came to New York in the autumn of 1935 to play a show at the Apollo Theatre in Harlem and applied for a New York City Musicians Union card. During the mandatory six-month waiting period for residency status, he commuted back and forth between Philadelphia and the Big Apple, working in Philly with the Gaines Orchestra and in New York with a band led by former Fletcher Henderson drummer Kaiser Marshall.

A major turning point in Jordan's career came in the spring of 1936 when he was hired by drummer Chick Webb, whose orchestra was a mainstay at Harlem's Savoy Ballroom, a popular haven for jitterbugs. A few months later, Ella Fitzgerald would join the band and by 1938 would become the band's star vocalist on the strength of her breakthrough hit, "A-Tisket, A-Tasket."

Jordan played alto sax and sang with the Webb orchestra while introducing some of the numbers from the bandstand, all of which helped to shape his appealing stage manner. He made his solo vocal debut with Webb in January of 1937 on "Gee, but You're Swell" and a bright, engaging "Rusty Hinge," which offered a hint of things to come.

After honing his stage presence and vocal skills in Webb's orchestra—and feeling the need to branch out as a performer and instrumentalist—Jordan decided to strike out on his own in the summer of 1938. He made his first recording for Decca on December 20, 1938 ("Honey in the Bee Ball"), and christened his nine-piece group the Elks Rendezvous Band, named after the small club in Harlem where he had secured a residency. Eventually he cut the lineup down to six players, then added a guitar to make it seven. They traveled to Chicago to play intermissions between the Mills Brothers's sets, proving to be a big hit with the mostly white audiences at the Capitol Lounge.

From 1939 Jordan fronted the Tympany Five, a hard-driving jump blues outfit that actually had six members and no timpani whatsoever. Some well-known musicians passed through the ranks of the Tympany Five, including pianists Wild Bill Davis and Bill Doggett, guitarists Carl Hogan and Bill Jennings, bassist Dallas Bartley, drummer Chris Columbus, and in later years saxophonists Paul Quinichette, Charlie Rouse, and Sonny Stitt. It was with this solidly swinging unit that Jordan would set the world on fire with his infectious jumpin' jive.

Jordan's invigorating new sound was marked by the combination of his own blistering alto sax work (a model for the likes of Hank Crawford) and the Charlie Christian–inspired guitar playing of Carl Hogan (a model for young Chuck Berry). The rhythms really jumped and Jordan galvanized the proceedings with his own slick delivery and inimitable stage presence. He was quick with a rhyme and a well-turned phrase, a protorapper fully in command of his verbal chops. Dig these rapid-fire rhymes from "Beware, Brother, Beware":

> If she's used to caviar and fine silk
> and when she goes out with you
> she wants a hot dog and a malted milk.
> If she's been used to goin' to Carnegie Hall
> and when you take her out nightclubbin'
> she wants to hear one meatball . . . (that's all).

Coming down the homestretch of that up-tempo swinger, he puts it into high gear and lets loose with this verbal onslaught:

> If you get home about two
> and you don't know what to do
> and you pull back the curtain

*and the whole family's looking at you.*
*Get your business straight*
*and set the date, and don't be late, gate.*

Jordan's first big hit came in 1941 with "I'm Gonna Move to the Out-skirts of Town," a tune that was quickly covered by Jimmie Lunceford, Big Bill Broonzy, and Jimmy Rushing, and which Ray Charles would cover twenty years later. During the recording ban of 1942 to 1944 he stockpiled material and came back strong in the summer of '44 with "Is You Is or Is You Ain't (My Baby)" and a version of Johnny Mercer's "G.I. Jive." That same year he also had a cameo appearance in the big-budget Hollywood wartime musical *Follow the Boys,* and also went into the studio on July 26 to cut two sides with Bing Crosby ("Yip Yip De Hootie, My Baby Said Yes," and "Your Socks Don't Match").

At his absolute peak, in 1946, Jordan held the top four spots on the race charts for the year. In descending order they were: "Choo Choo Ch'Boogie," "Ain't That Just Like a Woman," "Stone Cold Dead in the Market," and "That Chick's Too Young to Fry." That same year—which also produced "Let the Good Times Roll," "Ain't Nobody Here but Us Chickens," and "Jack, You're Dead!"—Jordan's record sales were second only to Bing Crosby. In short, Jordan was a major crossover success years before the term had even been coined. America had fallen in love with his unique brand of jive.

His first duets with Ella Fitzgerald ("Stone Cold Dead in the Market" and "Petootie Pie") were recorded in October of 1945. In April of 1949 he was back in the studio with Ella, dueting on "Baby, It's Cold Outside" and "Don't Cry, Cry Baby." Their teaming came as no surprise, since they had already developed an onstage chemistry in Chick Webb's band, so they went at it again on August 15, 1950, recording "Ain't Nobody's Business if I Do" and "I'll Never Be Free." Eight days later, Jordan dueted with Louis Armstrong on "Life Is So Peculiar" and "You Rascal You."

A brief attempt at fronting a big band in 1951 proved an ill-fated venture, but it didn't diminish his vitality. In 1952, tongue firmly planted in cheek, he offered himself as a candidate for the highest office in the land on the amusing Decca outing "Jordan for President," a tune that would later be covered by B. B. King.

In 1953, a year before he left Decca, Jordan recorded in Los Angeles with

Nelson Riddle's Orchestra. Riddle's lush arrangements of "I Didn't Know What Time It Was" and "Only Yesterday" predated his work with Sinatra for Capitol.

By 1954, after an incredible run of a decade and a half, Jordan experienced a slackening off of his sales. He had switched to Aladdin and released tunes like "Dad Gum Ya Hide, Boy," "Gal, You Need a Whippin'," "Whiskey Do Your Stuff," "Messy Bessy," and "If I Had Any Sense I'd Go Back Home," which were performed with the same irrepressible spirit yet lacked the sheer firepower and visceral appeal of former hits like "Choo Choo Ch'Boogie" and "Caldonia." In 1955 he switched to RCA's short-lived "X" imprint and tried to gain a foothold in the growing musical trend of the day by issuing *Rock 'n' Roll Call,* the title track of which is a blatant nod to Bill Haley's "Rock around the Clock."

Jordan vindicated himself the following year with *Somebody up There Digs Me* (reissued on Bear Family as *Rockin' and Jivin'*). This 1956 recording for Mercury deftly updated Jordan classics for the rock 'n' roll crowd and featured Quincy Jones and Ernie Wilkins's arrangements of "Ain't Nobody Here but Us Chickens," "Let the Good Times Roll," "Salt Pork, West Virginia," "Run Joe," "Early in the Morning," "Caldonia," "Let the Good Times Roll," "Knock Me a Kiss," "Choo Choo Ch'Boogie," and "Beware." Protorock guitarist Mickey Baker and tenor sax star Sam "The Man" Taylor added muscle to this overlooked Jordan gem. With their publicity launch of the album, Mercury decided to bill Jordan as "The Original Rock and Roller."

A 1957 album for Mercury called *Man, We're Wailin'* was also a sizzling indication of what a fine saxist Jordan still was at that point in his career.

In the early 1960s Ray Charles signed his onetime idol to his own Tangerine label. The soul genius himself participated in the 1962 sessions for *Hallelujah, Louis Jordan Is Back,* which included a remake of Jordan's "Saturday Night Fish Fry," a cover of Charles's signature piece "What'd I Say" and a cover of Roy Milton's "Hop, Skip and Jump." But in spite of Ray's good intentions (and the strong material), that record got poor distribution and quickly disappeared from the shelves without making a dent in the public consciousness.

Late in 1962 Jordan cut tracks in England with British trombonist Chris Barber and his band, then in 1968 he recorded for bandleader Paul Gayten's West Coast label, Pzazz. That session featured the great tenor saxophonist Teddy Edwards and New Orleans drumming legend Earl Palmer (who had played on all of Fats Dominos's biggest hits from the '50s). But that album, too, faded quickly without making any noise, a source of great disappointment to Jordan.

A 1973 album for the French Black & Blue label found the sixty-five-year-old Jordan covering Mac Davis's loungey "I Believe in Music" while also reviving his past glory with new renditions of "I'm Gonna Move to the Outskirts of Town," "Caldonia," "Is You Is or Is You Ain't (My Baby)," and yet another take on "Saturday Night Fish Fry." Also in 1973 he recorded for Johnny Otis's Blue Spectrum label. Jordan's last recordings came in August of 1974 with New Orleans trumpeter Wallace Davenport on *Sweet Georgia Brown,* a purely instrumental session for Davenport's My Jazz label.

Jordan continued to perform right up until October of 1974, when he suffered a heart attack during a gig at the Golden Nugget Casino in Sparks, Nevada. He had a short stay at St. Mary's Hospital in Reno, Nevada, and then returned home to Los Angeles to recuperate. On February 4, 1975, he went shopping with his wife. Shortly after he returned home, he suffered a fatal heart attack. He was flown to St. Louis for burial in the Mount Olive Cemetery.

In 1990 a musical by Clarke Peters entitled *Five Guys Named Moe,* which featured music written or originally performed by Louis Jordan, opened in London. Four years later it overtook *Irma La Douce* to become the longest-running musical ever at the Lyric Theatre. After initially lukewarm reviews, another production enjoyed a decent run on Broadway in 1992.

A source of joy for generations of entertainers, players, and listeners alike, Jordan's towering influence continues to this day through such nouveau jivesters as Brian Setzer and his orchestra, Big Bad Voodoo Daddy, and Royal Crown Revue, among dozens and dozens of other regional jump blues and jive ensembles around the world.

"My whole theory, my whole life has been: When you come out to hear me, I want to make you happy," Jordan explained in Arnold Shaw's *Honkers and Shouters.* "Now I hardly ever do any sad tunes or any tunes that would suggest that you cry. I wanted to make you smile or laugh."

While Cab Calloway once surmised that jazzmen "play mostly for themselves," Jordan declared, "I want to play for the people." And he did so with unrelenting panache and a good sense of humor for four decades, spreading the gospel of jive in every recording and concert appearance of his fabulous career.

# SLIM GAILLARD

BORN: January 4, 1916, in Detroit, Michigan
DIED: February 26, 1991, in London, England

WITHOUT A DOUBT, Slim Bulee Gaillard was the most inspired madcap humorist and natural-born showman in the history of jive. At once subversive and hilarious, he concocted his own jive patois, called "vout," which was a combination of foreign words and phrases with the nonsense suffixes "orooney" and "oreeney" added to just about every other word and bits of Cab Calloway's jitterbug jive phraseology like "all reet," "all root," "solid," "gate," "got my boots on," and "killer diller" thrown in as well. Through the '40s, Slim amassed a wacky repertoire that included such Slim signatures as "Boip! Boip!" "Yep Roc Heresi" (which featured lyrics that were adapted from items from a Syrian restaurant menu), and "Chicken Rhythm." He often wrote about food ("Potato Chips," "Matzoh Balls," "Dunkin' Bagel," "Avocado Seed Soup Symphony") and machinery ("Cement Mixer," "Poppity Pop"), frequently dabbled in unadulterated silliness ("Ya Ha Ha," "Laughin' in Rhythm," "Splogham," "Serenade to a Poodle," his Yma Sumac parody, "Soony Roony," "Chicken Rhythm," "Mishugana Mambo," "Sighing Boogie") and occasionally indulged in social satire ("Federation Blues," "Make It Do"). But this comedic sense of the absurd often overshadowed his considerable musical skills. As Bob Porter stated in his liner notes to *Black California, Volume 2: Anthology*, "So much attention was given to Slim's high jinks that his splendid guitar work is rarely recognized."

> **"Laguna oreeney laguna orooney, laguna oreeney. Lyin' in the sun and havin' fun."**
> — *Slim Gaillard*

He played guitar like a disciple of Charlie Christian, could beat out a mean boogie-woogie on the piano (including backhanded, with his knuckles), and he sang like a tan canary on dramatic ballads (sometimes in Spanish, Greek, Japanese, Chinese, Yiddish, or Voutian). A cult figure in the mid-1940s, Gaillard inspired a generation of followers, including radio and TV host Steve Allen along with hepcat disc jockey Al "Jazzbo" Collins, to start speaking in "vout." I even have childhood memories of my father at the dinner table asking to pass the "spaghett-oreeney and meatballs-orooney."

Dig this classic Gaillard intro from a 1945 radio broadcast:

**Well, we have a little specialty. . . . We'd like to beat out
a very groovy-rooney special. It's a little number titled shred-
ded vout-orooney.**

Gaillard's own personal history has a kind of absurdist bent to it. Born in Detroit (though he sometimes claimed Cuba as his birthplace), young Bulee shipped out the summer of 1928 (at the age of twelve) with his father, a steward on the luxury liner S. S. Republic. Somehow, goes the Gaillard myth, he accidentally got left behind on the island of Crete, where he remained for six months. During his time in exile, he learned functional Greek, which he would later incorporate into his comedy routines. Legend has it that he traveled the eastern Mediterranean countries, picking up bits of Turkish and Arabic along the way before somehow returning to Detroit, where he drove a delivery van for bootleggers and had a solo act playing guitar while tap dancing. In 1936 Gaillard turned up in New York and soon found bassist Leroy "Slam" Stewart, who had worked out a neat gimmick of bowing solos while simultaneously humming along an octave above. They teamed up as Slim & Slam and the rest is history-orooney.

Slim & Slam scored some early success on the popular "Major Bowes Amateur Hour" radio program, which led to a long-standing series on radio station WNEW as a featured act on disc jockey Martin Block's highly rated "Make Believe Ballroom." Their hilarious jive patter and good-time comic ditties caused a sensation, and they were soon booked at Kelly's Stable, one of Fifty-second Street's most popular clubs. Their very first recording, 1938's "Flat Foot Floogie" became their biggest hit ever and was quickly covered by everyone from Benny Goodman to Louis Armstrong and The Mills Brothers. (Although the popular tune was initially titled "Flat Feet Floogee," the title and spelling were later altered.)

Slim's work during this early period with his Flat Foot Floogie Boys was heavily influenced by the antic jive of Fats Waller. Indeed, tunes like "Matzoh Balls" and "Chitlin' Switch Blues" from 1939 bear a strong resemblance to jovial Waller confections like "Hold Tight (I Want Some Seafood Mama)" and "Your Feet's Too Big." One of his most hilarious pieces from this period, 1941's "African Jive," features a twenty-year-old Forrest "Chico" Hamilton on drums and interpolates jive banter like "watchu know, Jack?" and "I don't know nothin', gate" into the fabric of hypnotic chants.

Slim & Slam's popularity grew on the strength of joyful ditties like "A Tip on the Numbers," "Palm Springs Jump," and "Chicken Rhythm," along with cameo appearances in the zany 1941 film *Hellzapoppin!* and two films from 1942, *Almost Married* and *Star Spangled Rhythm*. They continued working as a team until 1943, when Slim was drafted into the Army, ultimately serving in the South Pacific as a bomber pilot. Slam went on to join the Art Tatum Trio during the war years and had subsequent high-profile spots in bands led by Benny Goodman, Erroll Garner, and other top names.

Discharged from the Army in 1944, Gaillard relocated to Los Angeles and began working with his new partner, rotund bassist Tiny "Bam" Brown, whose frantic, way-out vocals matched well with Slim's cool, if nonsensical, vocal approach. Their exuberant chemistry on vout-laden numbers like "Tutti Frutti," "Cement Mixer (Put-ti Put-ti)," and "Poppity Pop (Goes the Motor-sickle)" caught on with the public and Slim soon found himself enjoying high-profile gigs on Central Avenue, Los Angeles's answer to New York's

**Movie still from *Sweetheart of Sigma Chi*, 1946 (from left to right): Slim Gaillard, piano; Leo "Scat" Watson, drums; Bam Brown, bass. Frank Driggs Collection**

Fifty-second Street. That same year, Slim became San Diego's first black disc jockey, spinning jazz records for several months from a used car lot.

On December 29 of 1945, Gaillard led an unusual date for Beltone Records with Bam Brown on bass, Dodo Marmarosa on piano, Zutty Singleton on drums, and Jack McVea on tenor sax with special guests Charlie Parker and Dizzy Gillespie. On this now-legendary session, entitled simply "Slim's Jam," Gaillard acts as a kind of mellow emcee, introducing each of the participants as he shows up for the session. Slim, caught in the middle of placing a double order of "reetie vooties with a little hot sauce on it," sounds surprised as Parker enters. And the following jive repartee ensues:

> "Oh, here's . . . Well lookit! Charlie Yarbird-orooney."
> "Hey there, Slim. How's it goin', Jim?"
> "Oh, everything is mellow, man. Lookit, this cat's got his horn with him there. Blow some?"
> "Yeah, I got my horn with me, man. I wanna blow some, too, but I'm having a little reed trouble."
> "Haven't got a reed?"
> "Yeah."
> "Well, McVouty's got a reed. He can trim it down a little. That's great?"
> "Yeah, that's great."
> "Well, that's solid then. Well, let's get together 'n' blow. We're in A flat. Take the next one. You got it."
> "I got it."
> "All reet."

After a scorching alto sax solo by Bird, Slim is about to order an orange soda when Gillespie strolls in. Again, he is caught off guard:

> "Well, lookey . . . Here's Daz McSkivven Vouts-orooney with his trumpet there . . . Take the next chorus before you cut out. That's killer. All reet."

Throughout the 1940s in Los Angeles, Gaillard had a strong following, using such sidemen as Zutty Singleton and Dodo Marmarosa. He continued to make appearances on both coasts through the early 1950s, including a lengthy residency in 1951 at Birdland on Fifty-second Street in New York. He recorded a reunion album with Slam Stewart in 1958 but during the

1960s he was largely outside of music, running a motel in San Diego. In 1970 there was a Slim & Slam reunion in Monterey but little else was heard from Gaillard until his cameo role in the blockbuster TV series *Roots: The Next Generation* brought him back into national notice.

By the late 1970s, Gaillard was back joking and jiving on a part-time basis, still singing "Flat Foot Floogie" and making audiences howl with his zany vout talk. In 1982 he moved to London and made appearances at various European jazz festivals, occasionally flying over the pond for a rare stateside gig. On November 15, 1983, he appeared at the Village West, his first New York showcase in twenty-five years. In a *Village Voice* review of the show, writer Stanley Crouch called Slim "a masterful entertainer whose strong suit was nonsensical routines composed of invented words as well as homemade prefixes and suffices." Crouch also wrote: "On opening night, he was one of the funniest men I have ever seen. His bizarre verbal interpolations were of a piece with his uncanny associative leaps. At one point, he stood up and talked with the maitre d' in fluent Greek; at another he struck up a conversation in Spanish with one of the waiters, which moved him to a hilarious salsa parody. His piano playing made satirical mincemeat of overdone styles and his perpetual banter always caught the audience, the musicians and the lyrics off guard."

Gaillard had a cameo spot in the 1985 film *Absolute Beginners,* a vehicle for enigmatic British rock star David Bowie. That appearance gained him widespread popularity around London, where he continued to live and perform up until his death in 1991.

As a performer for more than fifty years, the puckish, six-foot-five-inch Bulee Slim McVouty Gaillard may have best summed up his philosophy in a quote he gave *Down Beat* in 1949: "I'm an entertainer, not a musician. I've been an entertainer ever since I got out of the army. I have my fun and enjoy myself. I get a big bang when I see the people out there and can make them happy and laugh."

## THE CATS & THE FIDDLE

FORMED: 1937 in Chicago, Illinois

ALTHOUGH GENERALLY lumped in with R&B vocal groups because of their tight, four-part vocal harmonies that influenced such groups as the Four

Clefs, the Charioteers, the Orioles, the Robins, The Clovers, The Coasters, the Moonglows, and Little Anthony & The Imperials, The Cats & The Fiddle were truly unique for their time. A self-contained vocal/instrumental group, patterned somewhat after The Spirits of Rhythm, they swung relentlessly and outrageously on upbeat, original material that was fresh and different for its day. Their playful sense of abandon in scatting—particularly by front man

**"Come with me and you see, we cats will swing for you."**

— *Cats*

Austin Powell (which was no doubt influenced by the inspired vocal lunacy of Leo "Scat" Watson)—combined with their formidable instrumental prowess to give them a jazzier edge than any other vocal harmony groups that were following in the wake of The Mills Brothers's success.

Formed in 1937 by Chicagoan Austin Powell, who had previously fronted a high school vocal group called the Harlem Harmony Hounds, this novel four-part harmony group chose as its name a nursery rhyme that implied two things: "fiddle" represented the stand-up bass and they were all "hepcats." Joining Powell, who sang lead and played a four-string tenor guitar, were Chuck Barksdale on bass vocals and bass fiddle, Jimmie Henderson on first-tenor vocals and tipple (a ten-stringed instrument that looks like a ukulele and sounds more like a Puerto Rican *charango*), and Ernie Price on second-tenor vocals and tipple.

The Cats & The Fiddle performed early on at weddings, proms, and graduations around Chicago. It was at one of those functions that an RCA Victor agent, Lester Melrose, offered to record them for his Bluebird subsidiary label. The group's twenty-one discs for the label would appear on Bluebird's 8000 "race" series (although the distributors' catalogs at the time listed The Cats & The Fiddle releases under the inappropriate heading of "Hillbilly Music").

With Austin Powell's silky smooth crooning and sly, syncopated phrasing, reflecting the jive-oriented influence of Cab Calloway, Fats Waller, and Slim Gaillard, The Cats & The Fiddle caught on with hipsters in the late '30s, though widespread public acceptance came slowly.

As Lawrence Cohn readily admits in his liner notes to The Cats's Bluebird/RCA reissue twofer *I Miss You So* from 1976: "Their music does not stand heavy analysis, nor was it intended to be regarded by the heavy thinkers in the jazz world. Even the serious need occasional relaxation from their weighty deliberations and the Cats & The Fiddle provide their share of happy, free-and-easy swinging music."

The Cats's first recording session for Bluebird came on June 27, 1939. They cut ten songs that day, including the jivey "Gang Busters" and its companion piece "We Cats Will Swing for You," the frentic up-tempo "Nuts to You," the pot smoker's anthem "Killin' Jive," and "Killer Diller Man from the South," which features a slickly spoken call-and-response rhyming couplets vocal intro that predates today's rappers by sixty-one years. Their second session for Bluebird, on December 7, 1940, produced another eight sides, including "Mister Rhythm Man" (which bears a reference to Slim Gaillard's 1936 hit, "Flat Foot Floogie"), two jive numbers from Powell in "That's on, Jack, That's On" and "Public Jitterbug No. 1," a highly syncopated take on Oscar Hammerstein's "When I Grow Too Old to Dream" and Powell's melancholy "Just a Roamer." By far the most successful track from this session was Jimmie Henderson's ballad "I Miss You So," which ended up as the group's signature song (and title track of a Bluebird two-LP reissue set of 1976). That tune was just beginning to break in mid-1940 when Henderson contracted meningitis. He passed away by the end of the year and was replaced in the lineup by Herbie Miles, who appeared on The Cats's July 31, 1940, session that produced another eight tunes, including such infectious jumpin' jive as "Hep Cat's Holiday," "Swing the Scales," and "Pig's Idea."

Lloyd "Tiny" Grimes, a pianist and dancer who had taught himself to play guitar, came aboard in the fall of 1940, replacing Miles in The Cats's lineup. Along with his hard-driving Charlie Christian–influenced lines on a four-string tenor guitar, the native of Newport News, Virginia (born on July 7, 1917) also contributed several affecting originals to the band's repertoire. The first Cats session with Grimes, held on January 20, 1941, produced eight tunes, including Tiny's melodious offering "I'm Singing (So Help Me)," "I'll Always Love You Just the Same," and his anthemic "One Is Never Too Old to Swing," which features an outstanding Christian-styled electric guitar solo by Grimes on top of a hard-driving groove. His bold guitaristic presence is also felt on Powell's ballad "Until I Met You."

Grimes contributed two memorable pieces to his second session with The

Cats & The Fiddle, held in October of 1941—the rockin' "Stomp Stomp" and the surging "Sighing and Crying," which features Tiny's two-fisted boogie-woogie piano work. His forceful guitar signature is also apparent on a hepcat remake of Irving Berlin's "Blue Skies" and on "Lawdy-Clawdy," in which he shares vocal jive bantering up front with Austin Powell.

Grimes left the band in 1942 and moved to the West Coast where he joined Slam Stewart in 1943 when the bass player's duo partner, Slim Gaillard, was drafted into the Army. Tiny and Slam began jamming informally with the legendary jazz pianist Art Tatum, eventually formalizing the arrangement and moving back East, where their volatile improvisations took New York by storm. Because of the American Federation of Musicians recording ban from 1942 to 1943, Tiny did not venture into the studio again until 1944, when he cut with the Art Tatum Trio for Brunswick.

Grimes's spot in The Cats & The Fiddle was filled by Mifflin "Pee Wee" Branford. When Austin Powell was drafted into the Army in 1943, his front-man role was taken over by Hank Haslett, who in turn was replaced in 1945 by Herbie Miles. In 1946 the new Cats lineup cut sessions for the Manor label, including a remake of "I Miss You So" with Ernie Price handling lead vocals. The other tunes included "Life's Too Short," a remake of Tiny Grimes's "Romance without Finance is a Nuisance" and "My Sugar's Sweet to Me." Powell was discharged from the Army in April of 1946 and rejoined the group shortly thereafter, fronting an edition of The Cats & The Fiddle that included violinist Claude "Fiddler" Williams and the first female cat, Shirley Moore. They made more recordings for Manor and Decca, but the group eventually fell apart in 1950 and mutated into the Austin Powell Quintet, which did some recording for Decca. Powell led his own groups in Brooklyn in the '50s and '60s, with a brief stint in 1957 with Louis Jordan and His Tympany Five.

Meanwhile, Tiny Grimes had relocated to New York, where he began working in late 1944 with his own quintet featuring alto sax great Charlie "Yardbird" Parker. Their time together was documented on some notable recordings for Savoy, including Tiny's jive-oriented "Romance without Finance Is a Nuisance" (September 15, 1944, session). During the mid-1940s he recorded with The Ike Quebec Quintet and his own Swingtet for Blue Note, with Hot Lips Page for Savoy, Cozy Cole for Continental, Coleman Hawkins for Regis, and Billie Holiday for Aladdin and Decca. He also recorded with J. C. Higginbottom before forming The Rockin' Highlanders in 1948 (see chapter three).

# LEO "SCAT" WATSON

———◆———

BORN: February 27, 1898, in Kansas City, Missouri
DIED: May 2, 1950, in Los Angeles, California

A MULTI-INSTRUMENTALIST (trombone, drums, tipple) and eccentric vocalist, Watson had a wild, stream-of-consciousness scatting style that made a huge impact on hepcats and jivesters in the 1940s. The influence of his inspired zaniness can be felt in the liberated scat abandon of jazz singers over time, including Loumell Morgan, Ella Fitzgerald, Eddie Jefferson, Joe Carroll, Betty Carter, Mel Torme, Bobby McFerrin, and Casey MacGill.

Early in his career, Watson sang on the black vaudeville circuit. After moving to New York in 1929, he joined Virgil Scroggins, Buddy Burton, and Wilbur and Douglas Daniels in a musical novelty act called Ben Bernie's Nephews. By 1932 great guitarist Teddy Bunn replaced Burton in the group and they changed their name to The Spirits of Rhythm. This lineup, which consisted of three tipples, a guitar, and a drummer playing brooms on a suitcase with incredible aplomb, first recorded in 1933 for the Brunswick label ("Nobody's Sweetheart" and "I Got Rhythm").

> **"Make it sweet or make it bounce, tiddly-hoy-hoy-hoy it's the tune that counts."**
> — *Leo "Scat" Watson*

The Spirits initially worked at Chick Groman's Stables in New York and in February of 1934 began what turned out to be a long residency at the Onyx Club, which had recently transformed from a speakeasy to a legitimate club on Fifty-second Street, the fabled jazz strip that (in the words of writer Arnold Shaw) "brought Harlem downtown."

Watson's uninhibited scat vocals with The Spirits of Rhythm caused a sensation in the '30s. Only Watson—who was once dubbed "The James Joyce of Jazz"—could come up with a line like "I love a parade, love a beret, love a lemonade, love a gray day in the shade now." No one else (except for the equally zany Slim Gaillard or Bam Brown) could organically incorporate references to NBC, Bing Crosby, and Model-T Fords along with snippets of "Darling I Am Growing Older," "Swanee River," "Jingle Bells," and "Take Me out to the Ballgame" into the fabric of a scat chorus. Everyone after 1938, the year that Slim Gaillard hit big with "Flat Foot Floogie," was slinging

around the popular phrase of the day, "floy floy." But no one else incorporated rhyming phrases like "ship ahoy" and "piddly-hoy-hoy-hoy" into his lexicon of jive. Watson's rhythmic assuredness allowed him to take great liberties with both time and melody while his associative powers had him freely improvising surreal lyrics and spinning whirlwind choruses of zany vocalese with mind-boggling ease and agility. On a wild scat version of "Honeysuckle Rose," his stream-of-consciousness cup runneth over:

> *Oh honey, sock me on the nose*
> *yama yama yama yama root de voot de voot*
> *Oh honey, so sock sock sock sock sock cymbal sock cymbal*
> *rymbal dymbal a nimble nimble nimble . . .*
> *So sock me on the nose . . . ose gose*
> *goose goose goose goose moose gavoose*
> *bablow your nose . . . hello rose how's your toes*
> *put some papowder on your nose*
> *ah rosettah are you feeling bettah . . .*
> *ah rose nose nose me lamble damble damble*
> *roozy voot mop mop broom broom sweep sweep . . .*
> *So honey, sock my nose.*

When he sang he would move his right arm up and down as though he were manipulating a trombone slide. Spurred on by Watson's over-the-top exuberance, The Spirits were teeming with drive, pep, and an unadulterated sense of *joie de vivre,* helping them to gain a huge following on Fifty-second Street.

Leo "Scat" Watson made some guest appearances on recordings with the Washboard Rhythm Kings and in 1937, after The Spirits of Rhythm disintegrated, he worked on Fifty-second Street with John Kirby at the Onyx Club. He had a brief stint in the fall of 1937 with Artie Shaw's second band. His inspired scat and breezy vocal delivery are prominently featured on the clarinetist's recordings of "Shoot the Likker to Me, John," "I've Got a Strange New Rhythm in My Heart," and a swinging rendition of the Walt Disney ditty from *Snow White,* "Whistle while You Work." By the summer of 1938 he joined Gene Krupa's orchestra and was a featured vocalist on the band's burning rendition of "Nagasaki," Slim Gaillard's hit song "Tutti Frutti,"

**Leo "Scat" Watson, 1940. Frank Driggs Collection**

"Jeepers Creepers," and "Do You Wanna Jump Children?"

After an ugly altercation with a Pullman porter on a train, Watson left the Krupa band. He then put in some time with Jimmy Mundy's big band before forming his own group in 1939 and recording four sides for Decca—"The Man with the Mandolin," "Utt Da Zay (The Tailor Song)," a wacky vocalese rendition of "Ja Da," and his jivey signature number "It's the Tune That Counts."

In the summer of 1940 Watson appeared with a reunited The Spirits of Rhythm at the New York World's Fair. He moved to the West Coast in 1942 and began working there with jive icon Slim Gaillard, appearing on such classic bits of McVoutereenia as "Palm Springs Jump," "Groove Juice Special," and Slim's magnum jive opus, "Avocado Seed Soup Symphony." When Gaillard was drafted into the Army in 1943, Watson joined guitarist Teddy Bunn in a re-formed edition of The Spirits of Rhythm. A January 1945 session with the group featured bassist Red Callendar, second guitarist Ulysses Livingstone, drummer George Vann, and jazz critic Leonard Feather on piano. In December of that year he reunited with Gaillard for a hilarious rendition of "Avocado Seed Soup Symphony," a comic highlight of the Armed Forces Radio Service "Jubilee" broadcast from Billy Berg's nightclub in L.A.

In 1946 Watson cut four sides for Bob Thiele's Signature label, backed by trombonist Vic Dickinson's swinging quintet. Among those sides is a jumped-up version of Cole Porter's "Night and Day," coyly retitled "Tight and Gay." Watson worked with pianist Charley Raye in 1948 before illness disrupted his career. He was hospitalized in early 1949 and succumbed to pneumonia on May 2, 1950.

# STUFF SMITH

BORN: August 14, 1909, in Portsmouth, Ohio
DIED: September 25, 1967, in Munich, Germany

VIOLINIST HEZEKIAH LEROY GORDON "STUFF" SMITH began delighting audiences in the clubs on New York's Fifty-second Street in the mid-1930s with His Onyx Club Boys, a lively, jivey outfit, which also featured trumpeter-vocalist Jonah Jones and drummer Cozy Cole. Smith swung manically while playfully ignoring the rules of technically correct violin play-ing. As Count Basie's great drummer Jo Jones once said in summing up Stuff's talents: "He's the cat that took the apron strings off the fiddle."

Smith's loosey-goosey singing style was heavily indebted to Louis Armstrong (as can be clearly heard on his Pops-like takes on "I Hope Gabriel Likes My Music," "I'm Puttin' All My Eggs in One Basket," "T'ain't No Use," and "After You've Gone" from 1936 sessions for Vocalion with His Onyx Club Boys).

The son of a barber and amateur musician, Stuff began playing in his father's band, the twelve-piece Calument Entertainers, at the age of nine. A few years later, he won a music scholar-ship to Johnson C. Smith University in Charlotte, North Carolina, and in 1925 was in a traveling musi-cal troupe called Aunt Jemina's Revue. Beginning in 1926

**"I'se a muggin',**
**boom, da-**
**dee-yah-da."**
— *Stuff Smith*

he worked with Alphonso Trent's territory band. Trent's band was considered one of the best in the country and is said to have been the inspi-ration for Jimmie Lunceford's style. In addition to playing violin in the group, Smith was prominently featured as a vocalist and comic during their fourteen-month stand at the Adolphus Hotel in Dallas.

In 1927 he moved to New York to play with Jelly Roll Morton but soon returned to the Trent band, where he became a featured player on hot and sweet numbers as well as the comedic front man. Smith recorded with the Trent outfit in 1928 and 1930, before marrying and settling in Buffalo, where he met and teamed up with trumpeter Jonah Jones.

In 1934 Smith led a big band for a brief engagement in New York and then returned in early 1936 with a sextet to begin a long residency at the Onyx Club on Fifty-second Street. The group recorded "I'se a Muggin'" for Vocalion on February 11, 1936, and soon became a big attraction on fabled Swing Street on the strength of that minor hit, which was quickly covered by Andy Kirk, Mezz Mezzrow, and Jack Teagarden. Smith's "You'se a Viper" and "Here Comes the Man with the Jive," recorded in March and August of 1936, respectively, were among the many songs of that era (along with Cab Calloway's "Reefer Man" and The Cats & The Fiddle's "Killin' Jive") to address the hepcat's fondness for the medicinal benefits of marijuana.

The absurdist humor that the Onyx Club Boys exhibited on a lighthearted

1936 recording of "Knock, Knock, Who's There?" was no doubt a big influence on the wild and zany jive of Slim Gaillard, who hit big in 1938 with "Flat Foot Floogie," also for Vocalion. Here's a sample of that syncopated hokum:

**Knock, knock . . . Who's there?**
**Onyx . . . Onyx who?**
**It's an onyx-pected pleasure.**
**Knock, knock . . . Who's there?**
**Tangerine . . . Tangerine who?**
**Tangerine the bell before you come in?**
**Knock, knock . . . Who's there?**
**Gorilla . . . Gorilla who?**
**Gorilla my dreams, I love you.**

Stuff spent most of 1938 in Hollywood, where he appeared in the film *Swing Street* while also holding down a residency at the Famous Door. In early 1939, his band had a four-month stint at the Blue Fountain Room of the LaSalle Hotel in Chicago and by the summer he was back in New York, cutting tracks for Varsity with a new outfit while holding down a residency at the Edison Hotel.

Smith fronted various groups in New York and Chicago over the next few years (including a stint in 1943 where he briefly took over leadership of Fats Waller's band after the pianist's death), then returned to the Onyx Club for a six-month engagement in the winter of 1944 with a sensational trio of Jimmy Jones and John Levy, which recorded for the Asch label. Jones's replacements on piano were first Erroll Garner, then Billy Taylor. When Taylor quit, Smith disbanded the group and moved to Chicago, where he opened a restaurant while continuing to play regularly with his own small bands.

In the early 1950s he relocated to California. Norman Granz used him on an Ella Fitzgerald record date and then on several albums of his own, including one with Dizzy Gillespie. In 1957 Granz booked the violinist on a European tour with Jazz at the Philharmonic. Smith was felled by a liver ailment in Brussels and underwent an operation from which his recovery was deemed near-miraculous. After a year's engagement at the Royal Tahitian Room in Ontario from 1963 to 1964 and a record date with Herb Ellis, Smith followed up with club, festival, and TV appearances along with a stint with

**Stuff Smith on Fifty-second Street, 1936. Frank Driggs Collection**

pianist Joe Bushkin at New York's Embers.

In 1965 Smith returned to Europe, touring concert halls, clubs, and festivals. Again, he was hospitalized, this time in Oslo, but soon resumed touring until he collapsed in Paris and underwent a dangerous double operation to cure his ulcers as well as a liver condition. Doctors described Smith as a "medical museum" and doubted that he would ever play again. But three days after the operation, Smith was entertaining other patients with his music, and soon had to be discharged.

With his home base now in Copenhagen, Denmark, he continued to tour the continent, appearing at festivals and in clubs and making several recordings. His last recordings, as unrestrained and swinging as ever, came from 1967, the year he died in Munich, Germany. He was buried in Copenhagen.

Said the wholly unique musician: "I try to give the public a combination of entertainment, comedy, novelty, and swing. Variety is the keynote."

# JIMMIE LUNCEFORD

BORN: June 6, 1902, in Fulton, Mississippi
DIED: July 12, 1947, in Seaside, Oregon

BANDLEADER/CONDUCTOR JIMMIE LUNCEFORD got into the jive act from 1934 to 1942 with a string of jovial, swinging offerings like "White Heat," "Rhythm Is Our Business," "My Blue Heaven," "Organ Grinder's Swing," "For Dancers Only," "Margie," and "Tain't What You Do, It's the Way That Cha Do It."

"Rhythm is our business, rhythm is what we want."
— Jimmie Lunceford

Other novelty numbers in the band's book included "I'm Nuts about Screwy Music," "Slumming on Park Avenue," "Rhythm in My Nursery Rhymes," "I'm Laughin' up My Sleeve," "What's Your Story, Morning Glory?" "Whatcha Know Joe," and "Wham (Re-Bop-Boom-Bam)."

With gifted arrangers like Eddie Wilcox and Sy Oliver aboard, the orchestra presented highly polished and sophisticated music while also indulging in flashy bits of showmanship—saxophones swaying, trombones rotating in circles, trumpeters pointing skyward, throwing their horns at the ceiling, and catching them in regimented unison.

Although he was trained on several instruments, Lunceford primarily wielded a baton on the bandstand, conducting his orchestra in the formal manner of Cab Calloway and Paul Whiteman before him. Lunceford grew up in Denver, where he studied music with Wilberforce Whiteman (Paul's father). He played alto sax with George Morrison's orchestra in 1922 and later earned a bachelor of music degree at Fisk University, where he met fellow students (and future colleagues) Willie Smith, Ed Wilcox, and Henry Wells. From 1926 to 1929 he taught music at Manassa High School in Memphis. There he organized a student band called The Chickasaw Syncopators, which made four recordings before turning professional and hitting the road (known by then as the Jimmie Lunceford Orchestra) in 1930. The band had engagements in Cleveland and Buffalo before relocating to New York City in 1933.

Starting in January of 1934 Lunceford's group had a six-month stay at the celebrated Cotton Club in Harlem, where they had replaced Cal Calloway's orchestra as the house band. Nightly radio broadcasts from The Cotton Club enhanced the band's reputation and helped Lunceford land a recording contract with Decca. By 1936 he was dubbed "The New King of Syncopation" and had achieved notoriety comparable to that achieved by Duke Ellington and Count Basie.

The Lunceford Orchestra later appeared in the 1941 film *Blues in the Night* and scored a hit record that year on Decca with the title cut. A few years later, in 1947, he collapsed and died while signing autographs at a music shop in Seaside, Oregon. The band continued performing and recording under his name after his death, eventually breaking up in 1949.

# LUCKY MILLINDER

BORN: August 8, 1900, in Anniston, Alabama
DIED: September 28, 1966, in New York, New York

ESSENTIALLY A NONPLAYING FRONT MAN, Lucky Millinder was an occasional singer who conducted several impressive big bands through the 1930s and 1940s. Born Lucius Venable Millinder in Anniston, Alabama, he grew up in Chicago, worked as a tap dancer, and became a bandleader in 1931. His dancing background contributed to his acrobatic showmanship and vigorous conducting style, no doubt influenced by Cab Calloway. After leading an orchestra in France, he relocated to New York in 1934 to take over the reins of the Mills Blue Rhythm Band. (Prior to Millinder's arrival, the Mills Blue Rhythm Band had covered Satchmo's "Heebie Jeebies" and Cab's "Minnie the Moocher" in 1931, then "Reefer Man" and "Minnie the Moocher's Wedding Day" in 1932.) The group remained intact through 1938, often subbing for the Duke Ellington and Cab Calloway orchestras at The Cotton Club.

**"Who threw the whiskey in the well?"**
— *Lucky Millinder*

In 1940 Millinder formed his own, self-titled orchestra, which worked at the Savoy Ballroom. Most notable among his sidemen were pianist Bill Doggett, singer-guitarist Sister Rosetta Tharpe (who turned in rousing renditions of "Shout, Sister, Shout," "Trouble in Mind," and "I Want a Tall Skinny Papa"), and, for a brief time in 1942, trumpeter Dizzy Gillespie (whose solo on "Little Johnny Special" was a precursor to the bop anthem "Salt Peanuts"). In 1944 with Wynonie Harris aboard as singer, the Lucky Millinder Orchestra scored hits for Decca with "Hurry Hurry" and "Who Threw the Whiskey in the Well." Millinder broke up his band in 1952. He spent his later years as a liquor salesman and a disc jockey.

———————————●———————————

## *Jivenotes:*

Clarinetist-alto saxophonist-bandleader **Skeets Tolbert** deserves mention here for penning the Louis Jordan vehicle "You're My Meat" and the anthemic "Hit That Jive, Jack," which was promptly covered by Slim Gaillard and **Nat "King" Cole.** A gifted pianist who would gain mainstream stardom in the 1950s as a superb pop ballad singer, Cole flirted heavily with jive in the early years of his celebrated trio (Oscar Moore on guitar, Wesley Prince on bass) by cutting such hipster novelty numbers as "Straighten up and Fly Right," "Gone with the Draft," "Scotchin' with the Soda," "Stop! The Red Light's On," "I Like to Riff," "Call the Police," "Are You Fer It?" and the aforementioned "Hit That Jive, Jack," all of which sound greatly influenced by vocal jive groups like The Spirits of Rhythm and The Cats & The Fiddle.

Bandleader **Andy Kirk** also contributed to the jive canon with 1936 recordings of "All the Jive Is Gone" and "I'se a Muggin,'" featuring Pha Terrell on vocals, and a 1941 offering called "47th Street Jive." Other entertainers of note who emerged during the Golden Era of Jive include **The Four Blues,** a Cats & The Fiddle–styled band from the mid-1940s that hailed from Louisiana; **The Four Blazes,** a Chicago-based vocal jive group that kept that Cats & The Fiddle tradition alive through the 1940s and into the early 1950s; **The Three Peppers,** a vocal trio from the late 1930s that dabbled in giddy jive fare like "The Duck's Yas Yas Yas," "Fuzzy Wuzzy," and "Swing out Uncle Wilson"; **Loumell Morgan,** an ebullient Fats Waller–styled stand-up pianist from the mid-1940s with a zany Leo "Scat" Watson vocal streak; **Artie Simms,** a Nat "King" Cole disciple from the mid-1940s who recorded Cole's catchy jive number "Call the Police" in 1946; **Putney Dandridge,** another Fats Waller–styled pianist and singer who recorded several jivey sides for Vocalion between 1935 and 1937, including "Nagasaki" and "When I Grow Too Old to Dream"; trombonist **Leo "Snub" Mosley,** who hailed from Little Rock, Arkansas, where he got his start with Alphonso Trent's territory band and who also played with the orchestras of Claude Hopkins, Louis Armstrong, and Fats Waller in a career that spanned more than fifty years. Mosley's claim to fame was the slide saxophone, his own unique invention that was a kind of cross between a trombone and saxophone. Beginning in 1938 Mosley billed himself as "The Man with the Funny Little Horn" and he entertained audiences with extroverted vocals on exuberant jivey fare like "Pretty Eyed Baby," "Snub's Blues," and his signature number, "The Man with the Funny Little Horn."

And lastly, a nod to two great jazz trumpeters—**Hot Lips Page** and **Jonah Jones.** Page, a potent soloist with the Bennie Moten and Count Basie Kansas City bands of the early '30s, revealed his jive side on a number of lighthearted recordings he made as a leader in the mid-1940s, including "Sheik of Araby," "They Raided the Joint," "Open the Door, Richard," and "Uncle Sam's Blues." He was also in particularly exuberant form singing "When My Sugar Walks down the Street" and "St. Louis Blues" in recordings from 1952, just two years before he died. Jones first gained wide attention for his playing with Stuff Smith's Onyx Club Boys from 1936 to 1940. He became a star soloist with Cab Calloway from 1941 to 1952, staying with the singer even after his big band became a combo. He began leading his own quartet in 1955 at the Embers on Fifty-second Street. He scored huge hits in 1957 with shuffle-swing versions of pop tunes like "On the Street Where You Live" and "Baubles, Bangles and Beads." He garnered a Grammy in 1959 for his *I Dig Chicks* album and ten years later did a one-off album for Motown. Jones continued to lead bands in his jivey, good-natured swinging style through the '70s, '80s, and into the '90s. His final performance came in November of 1999 during a Jazz Foundation of America benefit concert at the Blue Note club in New York. He died at the age of 91 on April 30, 2000.

# Recommended Listening

**LOUIS JORDAN**

*Let the Good Times Roll,* Decca/MCA
(1938–1953)

*At the Swing Cat's Ball,* MCA (1938–1954)

*Look Out! It's Louis Jordan,* Charly
(1939–1953)

*The Best of Louis Jordan,* MCA (1942–1947)

*Five Guys Named More,* Decca/MCA
(1942–1952)

*The Best of Louis Jordan:*
*The Millennium Collection,*
Decca/MCA (1942–1953)

*Just Say Moe! Mo' of the Best of Louis*
*Jordan,* Rhino (1943–1973)

*Louis Jordan & Friends,* MCA
(1944–1950)

*One Guy Named Louis,* Blue Note (1954)

*Rock 'n Roll Call,* RCA/Bluebird (1955)

*No Moe! Greatest Hits,* Verve (1956)

*Man, We're Wailing!* Mercury (1957)

*I Believe in Music,* Evidence (1973)

**SLIM GAILLARD**

*The Groove Juice Special,*
Columbia/Legacy (1938–1942)

*Slim Gaillard, 1939–1940,* Classics

*Slim Gaillard, 1940–1942,* Classics

*The Legendary McVouty,* HEP
(1941–1946)

*Slim Gaillard, 1945,* Classics

*Laughin' in Rhythm,* Verve (1946–1953)

*Slim Gaillard and His Friends at Birdland*
*1951,* HEP

**THE CATS & THE FIDDLE**

*Killin' Jive: 1939–1940,* Dee-Jay

*Hep Cats Swing: 1941–1946,* Dee-Jay

**LEO "SCAT" WATSON**

*The Original Scat Man,* Indigo (1933–1946)

**STUFF SMITH**

*Stuff Smith and His Onyx Club Boys,*
Classics (1936–1939)

**JIMMIE LUNCEFORD**

*Jimmie Lunceford and His Orchestra,*
*1930–1934,* Classics

*Jimmie Lunceford and His Orchestra,*
*1934–1935,* Classics

*Stomp It Off,* Decca (1934–1935)

*For Dancers Only,* Decca (1935–1937)

*Jimmie Lunceford and His Orchestra,*
*1935–1937,* Classics

*Margie,* Savoy (1946–1947)

**LUCKY MILLINDER**

*Let It Roll,* MCA (1939–1943)

*Ram Bunk Shush,* Charly (1941–1946)

*Mills Blue Rhythm Band (1934–1936),*
Classics

*Lucky Millinder, 1941–1942,* Classics

*Lucky Days (1941–1945),* MCA

*Jumpin' at the Savoy,* Epm Musique

**SKEETS TOLBERT**

*Skeets Tolbert, 1931–1940,* Classics

*Skeets Tolbert, 1940–1942,* Classics

**NAT "KING" COLE**

*Hit That Jive, Jack, 1940–1941,*
Decca/MCA

*Nat "King" Cole, 1941–1943,* Classics

*Nat "King" Cole, 1944–1945,* Classics

**ANDY KIRK**

*Andy Kirk, 1936–1937,* Classics

**THE FOUR BLAZES**
*Mary Jo,* Delmark *(1952–1954)*

**THE THREE PEPPERS**
*The Three Peppers, 1937–1940,* Classics

**PUTNEY DANDRIDGE**
*Putney Dandridge, 1935–1935,* Classics

**HOT LIPS PAGE**
*Hot Lips Page, 1940–1944,* Classics

**JONAH JONES**
*Swingin' on Broadway,* Capitol (1957)
*Jumpin' with Jonah,* Blue Note (1958)

**COMPILATIONS**
*Black California, Volume 2,* Savoy Jazz
    (with Slim Gaillard, 1946–47)
*East Coast Jive,* Delmark (with Loumell
    Morgan, Artie Simms, and The Four
    Blues)
*52nd Street Swing: New York in the '30s,*
    Decca (with Stuff Smith, The Spirits
    of Rhythm, and Hot Lips Page)
*The Savoy Story, Volume 1: Jazz,*
    Savoy Jazz/Atlantic (includes Slim
    Gaillard's "Slim's Jam" and Hot Lips
    Page's "Uncle Sam's Blues")

## CHAPTER 3

# JUMP BLUES 'N' JIVE

**T-Bone Walker, Amos Milburn, Roy Milton,**

**Floyd Dixon, Joe Liggins, Jimmy Liggins, Tiny Bradshaw,**

**Big Joe Turner, Wynonie Harris, Roy Brown,**

**Tiny Grimes and His Rockin' Highlanders,**

**Clarence "Gatemouth" Brown**

Another tributary off the River Jive, jump blues was crucial to the birth of both R&B and rock 'n' roll. Infectiously swinging, full of good humor, and hugely popular for its time, the jump blues movement of the postwar years produced hits by Tiny Bradshaw ("The Train Kept A-Rollin'"), Big Joe Turner ("Shake, Rattle & Roll"), Big Mama Thornton ("Hound Dog"), and Wynonie Harris ("Good Rockin' Tonight") that were later revived to become rock 'n' roll classics.

Developed from a crossbreeding of jazz combos and the urban blues bands of Texas, Los Angeles, and Chicago, jump blues was marked by a swinging rhythmic pulse and was frequently sung by raucous, hard-driving vocalists who shouted about partying, drinking, and jiving. Notable forerunners of the jump blues sound would include boogie-woogie pianists like Meade Lux Lewis, Albert Ammons, and Jimmy Yancey, and the jazz bands led by Count Basie and Bennie Moten, along with such '30s jivesters as Cab Calloway and Slim Gaillard.

Kansas City was a key incubator for the jump blues scene of the late '30s, producing such prominent figures as bandleader Jay McShann and blues shouters Walter Brown and Big Joe Turner. Los Angeles became a breeding ground for jump blues after World War II, producing a bevy of charismatic saxophonists who were dubbed "honkers and shouters" for their piercing, squealy tones and frantic showmanship. Among these were Big Jay McNeely, Chuck Higgins, and Joe Houston. Some of the key independent labels that cropped up in Los Angeles and specialized in the genre during that time include Aladdin, Modern, and Specialty, which produced such jump blues stars as Roy Milton, Wynona Carr, and Jimmy and Joe Liggins.

One of the giants of jump blues is electric guitar pioneer T-Bone Walker, who emerged on the Los Angeles scene in the late '30s and later became a prominent figure on the strength of his massive 1947 hit, "Call It Stormy Monday." Walker's agile, hornlike approach to guitar influenced both jazz and blues players of the day and generations of aggressively swinging, blues-drenched players who followed in his wake.

Johnny Otis became a force in West Coast jump blues during the '40s and '50s as a bandleader, performer, songwriter, producer, and talent scout. Boogie-woogie pianists who were also prominent on the jump blues scene included Amos Milburn, Albert Ammons, and Floyd Dixon, whose "Hey Bartender" was resurrected decades later by The Blues Brothers.

The peak years for jump blues, commercially, were between 1945 and 1955. With the rise of Little Richard, Chuck Berry, and Elvis Presley in the mid-1950s, jump blues was on the wane. Because of its blatant good-timey nature, jump blues has not received the kind of extensive critical analysis that Delta blues or even Chicago blues has. But its influence can still be felt today in an endless string of blues bar bands and the resurgence of retro-swing bands since the late '90s.

# T-BONE WALKER

BORN: May 28, 1910, in Linden, Texas
DIED: March 16, 1975, in Los Angeles, California

IN A FOUR-NOTE BURST from his stinging guitar, T-Bone instantly identi-fied himself. Whether it was the opening salvo of earthy gems like "Papa

Ain't Salty," "T-Bone Shuffle," the brilliant slow blues "Mean Old World," or his enduring classic "Call It Stormy Monday," that full-bodied signature grabbed ears in the 1940s and still rings true to blues fans today.

Widely recognized as a pioneer of modern electric blues, the immensely gifted singer-guitarist was a seminal jump blues figure in the early 1940s. His swinging, hornlike guitar lines and sly vocal phrasing influenced generations of singer-guitarists.

A fabulous singer with a mellow, burnished vocal style as well as a mean guitar picker, T-Bone was also known for his flamboyant showmanship. Doing splits while playing the guitar behind his head was one of his neat little tricks. He also had a penchant for holding the body of his guitar outward, parallel to the floor.

His inherent soulfulness and jazzy dexterity on guitar—perhaps best exemplified by blazing up-tempo instrumentals like "Strollin' with Bone," "T-Bone Jumps Again," and "Two Bones and a Pick"—influenced everyone from bluesmen like B. B. King, Lowell Fulson, and Pee Wee Crayton to proto-rocker Chuck Berry to blues-rock hotshots like Duane Allman, Johnny Winter, Eric Clapton, Mike Bloomfield, and Jimi Hendrix. T-Bone's patented licks were carried on through the '70s and '80s via modern blues players like Stevie Ray Vaughan, Robert Cray, Charlie Baty, and Duke Robillard and continue to be quoted today by blues youngbloods like Jonny Lang, Kenny Wayne Shepherd, and Sean Costello.

Born in Linden, Texas, on May 28, 1910, Aaron Thibeaux Walker had a storybook blues apprenticeship as a teenager, leading Blind Lemon Jefferson from bar to bar as the older, sightless man played for tips. He later worked in touring carnivals and medicine shows with the likes of Ida Cox and Bessie Smith before forming his own group in 1928 and recording his own first 78 single for Columbia a year later—"Wichita Falls Blues"/"Trinity River Blues," billed as Oak Cliff T-Bone (named for the section of Dallas where he grew up).

The Texas bluesman moved to Los Angeles in 1934, vacating a position in the Dallas-based Lawson Brooks Band (which was then filled by a younger Texas guitarist named Charlie Christian). By 1936 he found a job dancing with the band of Big Jim Wynn at the Little Harlem Club. As Billy Vera

**T-Bone Walker, 1944. Note his trademark positioning of the guitar.**
**Frank Driggs Collection**

reveals in his insightful liner notes to *The Very Best of T-Bone Walker:* "The climax of his act was to pick up a table with his teeth and twirl it around."

In 1939 he was hired as a singer for Les Hite's Cotton Club Orchestra. (The band's 1939 recording of "T-Bone Blues" features Frank Pasley, not Walker, on guitar.) After striking out on his own, Walker signed on with Capitol Records in 1942 and cut "Mean Old World" and "I Got a Break Baby" for the fledgling label. The momentum of his recording career was halted by the American Federation of Musicians recording ban, which lasted until 1944. During the war years, Walker relocated to Chicago where he became a star attraction at The Rhumboogie, a nightclub co-owned by heavyweight boxing champion Joe Louis. He returned to Los Angeles in 1946 and signed with Black & White Records. His third session for the label, the anthemic "Call It Stormy Monday," became an immediate and huge hit in 1947, leading to a string of other successful recordings, including "T-Bone Shuffle" and "West Side Baby."

**"They call it stormy Monday, but Tuesday's just as bad."**
—*T-Bone Walker*

In 1950 Walker signed with Imperial Records. Over the course of the next four years he recorded fifty important sides, including several sessions made in New Orleans with composer-bandleader Dave Bartholomew and members of his and Fats Domino's band. In 1955 he joined Atlantic Records and cut some tracks in Chicago with some mainstays on the Windy City blues scene, including harpist Junior Wells, guitarist Jimmy Rogers, and bassist Ransom Knowling. Those tracks were combined with a separate session cut in 1956/1957 with a crew of Los Angeles musicians (including jazz guitar master Barney Kessel) and ultimately released in 1959 as *T-Bone Blues.*

By the '60s his career (and health) were in decline, though he did make a particularly fine showing in Paris in 1967 on a jazz-tinged date for the French Black & Blue label entitled *I Want a Little Girl,* which was later released stateside by Delmark. His follow-up, a 1970 release on Polydor entitled *Good Feelin',* earned him a Grammy Award but was far less representative of Walker's jump blues prowess.

Recurring ulcers caused him to curtail his activities in the early '70s. By late 1974 he entered Vernon Convalescent Hospital in Los Angeles for treatment of pneumonia. He ultimately succumbed to the illness on March 16,

1975, at the age of sixty-four. A masterful performer and true innovator, T-Bone Walker's influence carries on through the ages.

# AMOS MILBURN

BORN: April 1, 1927, in Houston, Texas
DIED: January 3, 1980, in Houston, Texas

JOVIAL BOOGIE-WOOGIE PIANO MASTER Amos Milburn specialized in good-natured upbeat romps about booze and its effects (both positive and negative), imbued with a vibrant sense of humor, double entendre, and vivid, down-home imagery in his lyrics. His best-recorded work came during the postwar years for the Los Angeles–based Aladdin label and produced hits that presaged rock 'n' roll.

> "Hello cat, I just got back and I'm looking for that place they call the Chicken Shack."
> — *Amos Milburn*

After serving three years in the Navy from 1942 to 1945, Amos put together a combo that played around the Houston–San Antonio area. He headed to Los Angeles in the summer of 1946 and ended up signing with Aladdin Records shortly thereafter. His first session for the R&B label came in September of that year and produced the infectious "Down the Road Apiece," a driving boogie number that would be revived in 1960 by Chuck Berry and again in 1965 by The Rolling Stones.

Milburn's first smash hit came in 1948 with his party classic "Chicken Shack Boogie" and he continued in that rollicking vein with "Roomin' House Boogie" and "Sax Shack Boogie." His subtler, Charles Brown–influenced side comes across on velvety-smooth numbers like "Bewildered," "It Took a Long, Long Time," "Blues at Sundown," and his own take on Brown's hit "Driftin'."

A decidedly jivier side to the irrepressible Milburn style is showcased on hipster offerings like the romping 1947 number "Wolf on the River":

> *I'm a gas head daddy and I wear my loud, loud plaids.*
> *I can sweet talk you honey and drive you simply mad.*

More Milburn jive can be heard on 1949's "Jitterbug Fashion Parade," a kind of hepcat's answer to his "Chicken Shack Boogie":

*Everyone's saying "all root, McVout,"*
*that guy on the saxophone just knocks me out.*
*He comes on in with a mellow riff,*
*makes you want to jitterbug 'til your joints get stiff.*

The success of 1950's "Bad, Bad Whiskey" spawned a whole string of paeans to booze, including "Thinking and Drinking," "Let Me Go Home Whiskey," and "One Scotch, One Bourbon, One Beer." Ironically, Milburn's career was seriously scuttled by a bout with alcoholism, which curtailed his activities in the '60s. He recorded *Return of the Blues Boss* in 1964 for Motown and his final outing came twelve years later for Blues Spectrum.

# ROY MILTON

BORN: July 31, 1907, near Wynnewood, Oklahoma
DIED: September 18, 1983, in Los Angeles, California

IN THE TRADITION OF CHICK WEBB, bandleader Roy Milton swung his combo, The Solid Senders, from behind the drums. His steady backbeat and infectious, Jo Jones–styled energy provided the kinetic pulse behind such mid-1940s jump blues hits as "R. M. Blues," "Milton's Boogie," and "Hop, Skip and Jump."

Originally a singer with the Ernie Fields Orchestra, a popular territory band of 1928, Milton later sang lead vocals in a slick, exuberant fashion from behind the kit in his own band, hinting at the influence of everybody from Louis Armstrong to Leo "Scat" Watson, Jimmy Rushing, Louis Jordan, and Nat "King" Cole along the way. Some of his most agile vocal work can be heard on buoyant, swinging interpretations of Tin Pan Alley themes like "On the Sunny Side of the Street," "My Blue Heaven," and Irving Berlin's "Marie" as well as covers of Louis Prima material like "Oh Babe" and "Oh Marie." His most urgent and gritty blues shouter persona comes across on jumping proto-rock 'n' roll originals like "Tell It Like It Is," "Waking up Baby," "Bye Bye Baby Blues," and "Playboy Blues." And his jive style is best represented by early '50s tunes like "If You Don't Know" and "Make Me Know."

**Amos Milburn, 1948. Frank Driggs Collection**

Born on an Indian reservation (his maternal grandmother was a full-blooded Chickasaw) near Wynnewood, Oklahoma, on July 31, 1907, he grew up in Tulsa from the age of four. After his stint with the Fields organization, Milton moved to Los Angeles in 1933 and began leading his own sextet around town, blending the sophisticated big-band blues of the territory bands (such as those led by Bennie Moten, Count Basie, Jay McShann, Alphonso Trent, and Walter Page) and traditional country blues, but with a touch of Southwestern swing feeling. This music was first presented on small labels that sprung up in 1944/1945 after the settlement of the Musicians Union recording ban (from 1942 to 1944). Milton's first recordings came in 1945 for Lionel Hampton's Hamp-Tone label. A year later he had the number one R&B hit in the country with "R. M. Blues," which stayed on the charts for six months.

**"Hoy, hoy hop.**
**Hoy, hoy skip . . .**
**now jump."**
— *Roy Milton*

By late 1947 Roy was signed with Specialty Records and his band, The Solid Senders, became one of the most popular groups in the country, second only to jump blues 'n' jive icon Louis Jordan & His Tympany Five. Pianist Camille Howard, an outstanding boogie-woogie player, was the secret weapon in the Solid Senders's arsenal and was heavily featured in the band through the Specialty years, which ended in 1954. She also appeared occasionally as lead vocalist, as on "Tain't Me" and the novelty number "That's the One for Me," in which she engages in some jivey repartee with Milton. But it was Milton's own crisp, driving sense of swing and personable vocal style that provided the forward momentum and sparkle behind the blues 'n' boogie formula of The Solid Senders.

Though his popularity waned with the rise of rock 'n' roll, Roy continued to record for various small labels based in California. He appeared as part of Johnny Otis's all-star revue at the 1970 Montreux Jazz Festival and later summoned up some of the old jump blues magic on 1977's *Instant Groove* for the French Classic Jazz label, covering his former hits alongside classy jazz veterans like George Kelly on tenor sax, Billy Butler and Roy Gaines on guitars, Ram Ramirez on piano, Al Hall on bass, and Eddie Locke on drums. He died six years later at his home in Los Angeles.

---

**Roy Milton, 1949, with Bill Gaither on tenor sax. Frank Driggs Collection**

# FLOYD DIXON

BORN: February 8, 1929, in Marshall, Texas

THE L.A.–BASED PIANIST became a bona fide R&B star in the early 1950s on the strength of his energetic jump blues 'n' jive fare like 1952's "Wine, Wine, Wine" and 1954's "Hey Bartender" (later popularized by Dan Aykroyd's and John Belushi's alter egos, The Blues Brothers).

A Texas émigré, Dixon arrived in Los Angeles at the age of thirteen and was soon swept up by the postwar R&B boom, particularly the jump blues of Louis Jordan and Amos Milburn along with the more refined blues stylings of Charles Brown, who became a key mentor figure for the boy. He began recording at the age of seventeen for the Supreme label in 1947 before signing in 1949 with Modern Records and cutting "Dallas Blues" and "Mississippi Blue," both of which charted favorably in 1949. That same year Dixon joined up with Eddie Williams & His Brown Buddies and recorded the original version of "Saturday Night Fish Fry," which was quickly covered by Louis Jordan.

> "My grandmother loved Manechevitz so much, it even took her off her crutch."
>
> — *Floyd Dixon*

In 1950 Dixon switched to Aladdin, where he cut his first sides with Johnny Moore's Three Blazers. He scored big for the label in successive years with "Sad Journey Blues," "Telephone Blues," and his 1952 smash hit, "Call Operator 210."

Up-tempo jump blues like "Wine, Wine, Wine," "Too Much Jelly Roll," and "Baby, Let's Go Down to the Woods" showcase his more raucous, playfully ribald side, while originals like "Real Lovin' Mama" and "Long Distance Telephone Blues" have him engaging in spirited, colloquial repartee with frequent foil Mari Jones. His 1952 recording of the buoyant yet risqué "Red Cherries" sounds directly inspired by jivemaster Slim Gaillard's early '40s original "Potato Chips."

After Aladdin, Dixon recorded for Specialty in 1953, for Atlantic's Cat subsidiary in 1954 (where he recorded "Hey Bartender"), for Ebb in 1957, and later for Checker. The jump blues star of the '50s made a comeback some forty years later with a 1996 Alligator Records release, *Wake up and Live!*

# JOE LIGGINS

BORN: July 9, 1915, in Guthrie, Oklahoma
DIED: July 26, 1987, in Los Angeles, California

THIS TALENTED PIANIST-SINGER emerged at that pivotal time in jive history—between the early '40s big bands and the late '40s R&B combos. His music often straddled that dividing line, but he ultimately made his mark in the latter category with a string of Top 10 R&B hits in the postwar era.

After an apprenticeship with Texas honker Illinois Jacquet, Liggins moved to California, performing in bands led by Cee Pee Johnson and Sammy Franklin. He formed his own group, Joe Liggins and His Honeydrippers, in 1945 and had a huge hit that year with "The Honeydripper," which sold two million copies for the Exclusive label. In all, Liggins had ten hits for Exclusive between 1945 and 1949. After joining Specialty in 1950, Liggins scored big with "Rag Mop," "Little Joe's Boogie," and the jivey "Pink Champagne," which topped the R&B charts for two months in 1950 and was later covered by Tommy Dorsey and Lionel Hampton. His 1951 tune "One Sweet Letter" was later covered by both Patti Page and The Ravens. After his stint with Specialty, Liggins cut tracks with Mercury and Aladdin, but by the end of the 1950s he was reduced to playing weddings and small clubs around L.A. He returned to Mercury in 1962 and later recorded for his own label, Honeydripper Records, and brother Jimmy Liggins's Duplex Records. Joe Liggins remained active through the '70s and '80s, putting down his smooth brand of R&B until his death in 1987.

> "Pink champagne that stole my love from me. Pink champagne, where can my lover be?"
> — Joe Liggins

# JIMMY LIGGINS

BORN: October 14, 1922, in Newby, Oklahoma
DIED: July 18, 1983, in Durham, North Carolina

THE YOUNGER and more frantic brother of original Honeydrippers bandleader Joe Liggins, Jimmy was driving the Honeydrippers's band bus before he taught himself to play guitar and branched off on his own career. A onetime prizefighter and disc jockey, Jimmy jumped into the recording business in 1947 after signing with Specialty. His "Hepcat Boogie" and "That Song Is Gone" are two obscure jive gems from 1947, but it wasn't until hitting with "Tear Drop Blues" and "Cadillac Boogie" the following year that Jimmy Liggins and His Drops of Joy came to more widespread attention.

**"Boy, that song is gone. It's a frilly-dilly, all reet, a swinging rhythm treat."**

— *Jimmy Liggins*

His raucous offerings from the early 1950s, like "Cadillac Boogie," "Saturday Night Boogie Woogie Man," and the hilarious novelty number "Drunk," are direct precursors to rock 'n' roll. After leaving Specialty in 1953, he cut some sessions for Aladdin, including the rousing "I Ain't Drunk," a jumping novelty number that was later covered by blues great Albert Collins. Unlike his tamer big brother Joe, who stretched out his career another three decades after the hits stopped rolling in, Jimmy had an antic career that came to a halt when he was shot in the face by a demented fan.

But his wild influence carried over into the careers of rock 'n' rollers like Little Richard, Chuck Berry, Bill Haley, and Elvis Presley.

## MYRON "TINY" BRADSHAW

BORN: September 23, 1905, in Youngstown, Ohio
DIED: November 26, 1958, in Cincinnati, Ohio

THE LEADER OF A HEP BIG BAND in the 1930s and a seminal R&B outfit in the 1940s, Bradshaw penned an influential jump blues opus in 1951 ("The Train Kept A-Rollin'") that would later gain a second life as a jam vehicle for rock groups like the Johnny Burnette Trio, the Yardbirds, Twisted Sister, and Aerosmith.

Bradshaw had an apprenticeship with the Mills Blue Rhythm Band before forming his own swing orchestra in 1933 and recording with Decca. During World War II he served as bandleader of a twenty-piece Armed Forces orchestra that toured abroad. His popularity increased after the war via some jump blues sessions for Savoy, in which he show-cased his Cab Calloway–influenced vocal stylings.

Between 1949 and 1952 Bradshaw scored hits with R&B offerings for Cincinnati's King Records, including the jivey smash hit "Well Oh Well," "Gravy Train," "I'm Gonna Have Myself a Ball," and the anthemic "The Train Kept A-Rollin'." Bradshaw's bands were also noteworthy for hav-ing spawned the tenor sax titans Syl Austin and Red Prysock, who scored a hit in 1956 with the fran-tic instrumental "Hand Clappin'." Bradshaw's career was curtailed by a series of strokes in the mid-1950s. His legacy continues through the faithful cover versions of his most popular songs.

> **"Whoa,**
> **bot-doo-day,**
> **bot-doo-day.**
> **Hoo-dow, hoo-day,**
> **bot-doo-day."**
> — *Tiny Bradshaw*

# BIG JOE TURNER

BORN: May 18, 1911, in Kansas City, Missouri
DIED: November 24, 1985, in Englewood, California

THREE RAUCOUS BLUES SHOUTERS emerged in the 1940s and early 1950s to help pioneer the jump blues/R&B hybrid that ultimately led to rock 'n' roll. The first and most imposing of these was Big Joe Turner. The pre-mier blues shouter of the postwar era, Turner paved the way for popular blues shouters Roy Brown and Wynonie Harris while also pioneering the first wave of rock 'n' roll.

A product of the swinging, wide-open Kansas City scene of the early 1930s, he began working in gin joints as a teen, simultaneously tending bar and singing the blues before finally hooking up with boogie-woogie piano master Pete Johnson. Together they rocked patrons with their rollicking jump blues chemistry at places like the Backbiters' Club, the Black and Tan Club, and the Cherry Blossom. As Turner told jazz critic Whitney Balliet (for the liner notes to *Have No Fear, Big Joe Turner Is Here*): "They didn't have no microphones in them days. People would sing through them big long pasteboard things—megaphones. I didn't own one of those but I didn't need one, anyway. You could hear me 10 blocks away. I shook the joint up. I always had a big voice."

After three years at the Cherry Blossom, where Turner also tended bar, the singer left town with Pete Johnson's band and toured the Midwest before returning home to Kansas City. Their partnership would endure for thirteen years, including several classic recordings and an appearance together at John Hammond's Spirituals to Swing concert at Carnegie Hall on December 23, 1938, in which Johnson and Turner appeared on a bill with the likes of Big Bill Broonzy, Sonny Terry, the Golden Gate Quartet, boogie-woogie pianists Meade Lux Lewis and Albert Ammons, and the Count Basie Orchestra. Shortly after that landmark concert, Turner began an engagement at Barney Josephson's chic new club, Cafe Society, where he performed with all three boogie-woogie piano masters—Johnson, Lewis, and Ammons—playing simultaneously. That novelty was a great draw, ensuring Big Joe and company a run of four years at the popular nightspot. Nearly forty years later Turner would have an extended engagement at Barney Josephson's other New York club, The Cookery, where he still knocked audiences out with his power and exuberance.

**"I'm like a one-eyed cat, peeping in a seafood store."**

— *Big Joe Turner*

Near the end of 1938 Turner and Johnson recorded the classic "Roll 'Em Pete" for Vocalion and followed with their seminal blues "Cherry Red," featuring trumpeter Hot Lips Page and a full combo in support. In 1940 Turner jumped to Decca and cut "Piney Brown Blues" with Johnson tickling the ivories. In 1947 Big Joe hit with the risqué jump blues "My Gal's a Jockey," then he jumped around to a number of small West Coast labels like RPM and Down Beat/Swing Time before landing with Imperial in 1950. But it was his association with Atlantic Records (and Ahmet Ertegun) that would prove to be most lucrative. His first hit for the label came in 1951 with the world-weary "Chains of Love." He followed that up with hits like "Sweet Sixteen," "Chill Is On," and "Don't You Cry" before cutting the rough-edged "T.V. Mama" with Elmore James and the raucous "Honey Hush," which topped R&B charts in 1953. But his biggest smash hit of all would come the following year with Jesse Stone's "Shake, Rattle and Roll," a tune that has been subsequently covered by dozens of artists and literally thousands of working bar bands over the years. On a roll, Big Joe quickly followed up with other seminal rockers like "Flip, Flop and Fly," "Corinna, Corinna,"

"Lipstick Powder and Paint," and the Doc Pomus tune "Boogie Woogie Country Girl," recorded with Van "Piano Man" Walls.

Big Joe continued performing and recording with fierce authority through the '80s, releasing a noteworthy collaboration in 1983 with Roomful of Blues, *Blues Train* for Muse. The Boss of the Blues checked out two years later, leaving his formidable recorded legacy behind for jump blues connoisseurs to savor through the ages.

# WYNONIE HARRIS

BORN: August 24, 1915, in Omaha, Nebraska
DIED: June 14, 1969, in Los Angeles, California

ROWDY BLUES SHOUTER Wynonie Harris had already put in time fronting the Lucky Millinder Orchestra in 1944 ("Who Threw the Whisky in the Well") and hitting in 1946 as a solo act with "Wynonie Blues" and "Playful Baby" for Apollo Records before breaking the Top 10 in 1948 with a cover of Roy Brown's urgent "Good Rockin' Tonight" for King Records.

Hugely influenced by Kansas City blues shouter Big Joe Turner and his Oklahoma City counterpart Jimmy Rushing, Harris was on the ground floor of the emerging jump blues movement that swept the West Coast in the post-war years. After releasing records on a number of smaller labels—including Philo, Apollo, Lionel Hampton's Hamp-Tone, Bullet, and Aladdin (where he dueled it out with his idol Big Joe Turner on *Battle of the Blues*)—Harris signed up with Cincinnati's King Records in 1947 and scored successes through the early 1950s, first with the anthemic "Good Rockin' Tonight," followed by a string of rollicking, ribald tunes like "I Want My Fanny Brown," "Lollipop Mama," "Sittin' on it All the Time," "I Like My Baby's Pudding," and "Lovin' Machine." He even had success with a country tune that he reinvented as an infectious jump blues number, "Bloodshot Eyes" (the title of his 1993 anthology on Rhino).

In 1956, at the age of forty-one, he hit again with the hard-driving rocker

> "Don't roll your bloodshot eyes at me."
> — *Wynonie Harris*

"Destination Love" for Atco/Atlantic but by 1960 the hits had dried up for Wynonie Harris. The hard-drinking chick-chaser and money-waster—a prototypical bad boy of rock 'n' roll—succumbed to throat cancer in 1969.

# ROY BROWN

BORN: September 10, 1925, in New Orleans, Louisiana
DIED: May 25, 1981, in San Fernando, California

POSSESSING A SET OF PIPES that had a smooth yet emotionally penetrating quality that truly cut to the bone, New Orleans–born jump blues pioneer Roy Brown exerted a primary influence on rock 'n' roll with his first hit in 1947, "Good Rockin' Tonight," a seminal rock anthem that was later covered by everyone from Elvis Presley to Jerry Lee Lewis, Ricky Nelson, and Pat Boone.

As Jeff Hannusch states in his excellent *I Hear You Knockin': The Sound of New Orleans Rhythm and Blues:* "It isn't overstating the fact to say that Roy Brown was America's first soul singer. A true master of 'the slow burn,' Roy sang the blues with a passion matched by no one. Roy Brown was one of the first singers to adapt the untamed vocal approach of gospel singers to the twelve-bar blues format."

Or as colleague Mr. Google Eyes put it (in Hannusch's book): "Nobody would 'worry' a word or a phrase quite like he could. Roy Brown could make you laugh and cry during the same song. He just had that kind of emotion when he sang."

While Brown originally recorded his signature tune "Good Rockin' Tonight" for DeLuxe Records, it was a version by powerful blues shouter Wynonie Harris that later rose to the top of R&B charts in 1948. Nevertheless, Brown had a powerful style of his own that immediately registered with jump blues fans and remains the preferred version to this day by connoisseurs. As Bill Dahl pointed out in the *All Music Guide to the Blues:* "Brown's melismatically pleading, gospel steeped delivery impacted the vocal styles of B. B. King, Bobby Bland and Little Richard (among a plethora of important singers)."

Born in the Crescent City, Brown grew up in rural Eunice in Western Louisiana, moved to Houston, Texas, at the age of fourteen and to Los Angeles at the age of seventeen. It was there that he entered an amateur show, winning first prize for singing "I've Got Spurs That Jingle, Jangle, Jingle" in a style that imitated his favorite singer of the time, crooner Bing Crosby.

After returning to Houston in 1943, Roy began to work as a singer around clubs in the Sixth Ward. A nine-month stint at Billy Riley's Palace Park in Shreveport, Louisiana, exposed him to blues for the first time. As Hannusch writes: "Up until then, Brown was content to do all of Bing Crosby's material. It wasn't until he was spurned by his band, The Coot Lewis Combo, that he began to really concentrate on singing blues. Roy maintained that he just didn't like singing the blues." But after seeing the audience throw money on the bandstand when the other singers on the show sang blues, Roy quickly learned "When My Man Comes Home" and Billy Eckstine's "Jelly Jelly."

It was in 1946, while fronting the Mellowdeers at Mary Russell's Club Grenada in Galveston, Texas, that Roy conjured up "Good Rockin' Tonight." While dead broke in 1947 Brown approached Wynonie Harris at the Dew Drop Inn in New Orleans about recording his tune, but the celebrated "Mr. Blues" rejected the notion. Meanwhile, Brown recorded the tune himself for the DeLuxe label. The impact of "Good Rockin' Tonight" was immediate in New Orleans, although it didn't enter the national charts until early the following year. (Wynonie Harris's version of the same tune came out in April of 1948 and hit bigger, rocketing to the number one slot and remaining on the R&B charts for six months, establishing him as a major star.) Roy soon became a hot item in the Crescent City. Demand for appearances increased, along with his asking price. In the wake of that initial burst of success, Roy was rushed back into the studio at the end of 1947 to cut "Mighty Mighty Man" and "Miss Fanny Brown," which also hit big in the charts, leading to some lucrative road work for Roy Brown and his touring band, The Mighty Mighty Men.

> **"I heard the news, there's good rockin' tonight."**
> — *Roy Brown*

Although Wynonie Harris would later ace him out of the Top 10 with his own hellacious version of "Good Rockin' Tonight" in 1948, Brown would register hits in later years with such party-time rockers as "Rockin' at Midnight," "Boogie at Midnight," and "Miss Fanny Brown." He had the number one R&B hit during the summer of 1950 with his impassioned "Hard Luck Blues." And "Cadillac Baby" rose to number six in November of 1950.

By 1952 Cincinnati's King Records had bought up DeLuxe Records and Brown's contract along with it. He continued to record for the label until 1957, at which point he jumped ship to Imperial, where he worked with New Orleans producer Dave Bartholomew on tunes like "Let the Four Winds Blow" (which charted at number thirty-eight nationally), "Diddy-Y-Diddy-O," "Saturday Night," and "Ain't Gonna Do It." In 1957 Roy found himself heading R&B package shows with the likes of Larry Williams, Ray Charles, Etta James, and Big Joe Turner. By 1959 he was back at King, trying desperately to fit into the new rock 'n' roll equation. He responded with the Chuck Berry-ish "School Bell Rock," but it was too little too late.

During the 1960s Roy recorded for a number of labels, including ABC-Bluesway, Gert, Summit, and Tru-Love. In 1970, he performed at the Monterey Jazz Festival with the Johnny Otis Revue. The performance was recorded and later released on Epic Records. He subsequently recorded for Friendship and Route 66 Records and in 1978 made a triumphant tour of Europe, where audiences had rediscovered the great blues shouter of the '40s and '50s. His last performance was in May of 1981 at the New Orleans Jazz & Heritage Festival, just two weeks before he died of a heart attack.

# TINY GRIMES AND HIS ROCKIN' HIGHLANDERS

BORN: July 7, 1917, in Newport News, Virginia
DIED: March 4, 1989, in New York, New York

ORIGINALLY A PIANIST AND DANCER, Lloyd "Tiny" Grimes taught himself to play guitar after hearing the great Charlie Christian. Developing his own hard-swinging, blues-oriented style on a four-string tenor guitar, he would secure himself a spot in the Jive Hall of Fame through his work in the early 1940s with popular jivesters The Cats & The Fiddle before going on to establish himself as a respected jazz guitarist with the likes of piano legend Art Tatum, saxophonist Ike Quebec, trumpeters Hot Lips Page and Buck Clayton, drummer Cozy Cole, alto saxophonist Johnny Hodges, and tenor sax legend Coleman Hawkins. His stint leading the jump blues contingent the Rockin' Highlanders introduced Tiny to a whole new audience of seminal rock 'n' rollers.

Starting out in 1935 playing piano in amateur shows around Washington, D.C., Grimes relocated to New York City in 1937, where he played piano and danced at the Rhythm Club. The following year he played tipple in a group called The Four Dots, but switched to guitar when he saw a unique four-stringed guitar in a pawnshop for sale at five dollars.

Drawing inspiration from Charlie Christian's revolutionary guitar playing with the Benny Goodman Sextet and Orchestra and also from Snags Allen, a well-respected guitarist within musician circles around New York who did not share the same profile as Christian, Grimes progressed rapidly on his four-string guitar. In later years, when asked why he played a four-string instrument, he would laugh and say, "'Cause I couldn't afford the other two strings."

> **"Romance without finance is a nuisance."**
> — *Tiny Grimes*

Along with his hard-driving single-note lines, Tiny also incorporated full chordal voicings and lush harmonies that were heavily influenced by Count Basie's horn arrangements.

In the fall of 1940 Grimes replaced Herbie Miles in the lineup of The Cats & The Fiddle, a popular jive-style recording act on the Bluebird label. He made his recording debut with the Cats on January 20, 1941. Tiny's muscular, swinging lines had an immediate impact on the group and he also contributed several affecting originals to the band's repertoire, including ebullient anthems like "I'm Singing (So Help Me)" and "One Is Never Too Old to Swing" along with the rockin' "Stomp Stomp" and "Sighing and Crying," which features Tiny's two-fisted boogie-woogie piano work. His forceful guitar signature is also apparent on a hepcat remake of Irving Berlin's "Blue Skies" and on "Lawdy-Clawdy," in which he shares vocal jive bantering up front with Austin Powell.

Feeling a need to change musical direction, Grimes left the Cats in 1942. Years later he would also cite the relatively low pay as another factor in his decision to split from the popular jive act. "I wasn't making any bread in that band," he said in a 1980 interview. "The group was making money, but we never saw any of it. It was crooked management."

---

**Following pages** Rockin' Highlanders, 1950 (from left to right): Herb Cordy, bass; Jerry Potter, drums; George Kelly, tenor sax; Tiny Grimes, guitar; Joe Sewell, tenor sax. Frank Driggs Collection

After relocating to the West Coast, Tiny hooked up with bassist Slam Stewart in 1943. They formed a trio with the legendary jazz pianist Art Tatum and eventually moved back East, where their incendiary improvisation took New York by storm.

Following his stint with Tatum, Grimes recorded for Blue Note with the Ike Quebec Quintet and also as a leader for Savoy with a young Charlie Parker (a September 15, 1944, session that yielded the bluesy "Tiny's Tempo," the boppish "Red Cross," and the jivey "Romance without Finance" with a good-natured vocal by Tiny). Grimes found regular work in the emerging postwar R&B scene, recording with the likes of popular alto saxophonist Earl Bostic, tenor sax honker Paul Bascomb, and blues shouters Gatemouth Moore and Walter Brown (he appears on a version of "Open the Door Richard" for Atlantic). In 1948 his Tiny Grimes Quintet mutated into the R&B–oriented Rockin' Highlanders with Wilbur "Red" Prysock's powerful tenor-sax honking serving as an integral part of the band. In a nod to novelty, Grimes outfitted the Highlanders in matching tam-o'-shanters, kilts, and plaid shoes. Prysock balked at wearing the garb and left the band before its first recording in late 1949.

From 1949 to 1953, various editions of Tiny Grimes and His Rockin' Highlanders cut tracks for the Gotham label with a rotating cast of lead vocalists fronting the band, including the Wynonie Harris–inspired blues shouter J. B. Summers, the mysterious bluesman Haji Baba (aka George Grant, who performed in Middle Eastern robes and a turban), a young female singer from Philadelphia named Claudine Clark, and wildman Jalacy "Screamin' Jay" Hawkins, who would go on to rock 'n' roll infamy with his 1956 hit "I Put a Spell on You," a tune that has been covered frequently (most effectively by Nina Simone) and that helped Hawkins gain an ardent cult following throughout the world. Following in the long and rich tradition of jive, Hawkins blended theatrics, entertainment, and music. Adopting a bizarre voodoo/cryptic image, he wore cloaks, was carried on stage in a coffin, and held a skull with flashing eyes. His music was a mixture of rock 'n' roll, R&B, and blues, sung in a resonantly deep, husky-tinged voice.

Grimes discovered Screamin' Jay in Atlantic City in 1951 and had him fronting the Rockin' Highlanders in their headlining appearance at Alan Freed's Moondog Coronation Ball, the first-ever rock 'n' roll show presented in Cleveland in 1952.

Grimes would later switch to strictly jazz and continue working around the New York area with his own quartet (occasionally augmented by tap dancer Jimmy Slyde) up until his death in 1989.

# CLARENCE "GATEMOUTH" BROWN

BORN: April 18, 1924, in Vinton, Louisiana

THE "SWINGING-EST" of the modern blues guitar pioneers, Clarence "Gatemouth" Brown is second only to T-Bone Walker in terms of influence, chops, and pure showmanship. A multi-instrumentalist (he also is adept on fiddle, harmonica, mandolin, and piano), he straddles many musical idioms from jump blues and Cajun to country, bluegrass, and Basie-styled swing arrangements, and he imbues each with undeniable soul and good humor.

Growing up in Orange, Texas, Gatemouth was exposed to the music of his father, a locally popular musician who specialized in country, Cajun, and blue-grass. He later came under the spell of the big bands of Duke Ellington, Count Basie, and Lionel Hampton. "I've always favored that sound of Hamp's band, the Basie band, the Duke Ellington Orchestra, Louis Jordan and His Tympany Five," says Gate. "I've been using horns on everything I recorded in my life. When I first started out back in 1947, I had a 25-piece band and was using horn arrangements. I was one of the only entertainers out there doing that. There were other people using horns too, but they didn't know how to voice them. My instrumentation was arranged differently from anybody's."

Brown may have picked up a tip or two about arranging horns from watching T-Bone Walker at Don Robey's Bronze Peacock Lounge in Houston's Fifth Ward back in the mid-1940s. In fact, Gate's big break came when he filled in for an ailing T-Bone Walker at the Bronze Peacock, thrilling the crowd with his crowd-pleasing boogie-woogie and blistering finger-picked riffs. It wasn't long before he arrived at a distinctive style of his own, heard on early Peacock record-ings like 1949's smash hit "My Time Is Expensive," 1954's influential "Okie Dokie Stomp," and 1955's jump blues gem, "Rock My Blues Away."

> **"Rock me fast, rock me slow, rock me 'til I can't stand no more. Hey babe, rock my blues away."**
>
> — Clarence "Gatemouth" Brown

In the mid-1960s Brown had a stint as house bandleader for *The!!!Beat,* a groundbreaking syndicated R&B television show (a black alternative to *American Bandstand*) that was broadcast out of Dallas and hosted by WLAC deejay Bill "Hoss" Allen. In 1973, while on tour in France, Gate recorded a casual yet heartfelt tribute to one of his biggest influences, *Sings Louis Jordan* (reissued stateside in 1993 by Evidence as *Just Got Lucky*). This swinging collection includes Jordan staples like "Choo Choo Ch'Boogie," "Let the Good Times Roll," "Salt Pork, West Virginia," and "Caldonia" and features an excellent band of big-name jazz players like Arnett Cobb and Hal "Cornbread" Singer on tenor saxophones, Jay McShann on piano, Milt Buckner on organ, Milt Hinton on bass, Al Grey on trombone, and J. C. Heard on drums.

He continued to diversify through the 1970s, playing more country, Cajun, and even calypso in concerts and turning up on the popular cornpone TV show *Hee Haw.* A fun-loving project in 1979 with Roy Clark (*Hee Haw's* resident picker) entitled *Makin' Music* included a rousing rendition of Louis Jordan's "Caldonia," along with a swinging rendition of Ellington's "Take the A Train." Through the 1980s and 1990s Brown continued to pay tribute to jump blues masters like Roy Milton ("Information Blues") and T-Bone Walker ("Strollin' with Bones") while indulging his passion for Louis Jordan's joyous shuffles ("Ain't That Just Like a Woman" and "Ain't Nobody Here but Us Chickens" on 1987's *Pressure Cooker* and "Early in the Morning" on 1995's *The Man*).

And yet, after all these years of scorching licks and good times, he still hesitates to call it blues. "It's American music . . . Texas style," Gate flatly insists.

––––––––•––––––––

## *Jivenotes:*

While the three kings of jump blues shouters—Big Joe Turner, Roy Brown, and Wynonie Harris—ruled the roost in their heyday, a second wave of blues shouters followed in their wake, including West Coast jivesters **Duke Henderson** ("Lucy Brown," "Country Girl"), **Herman Manzy** ("I'm Your Rockin' Man"), **Cee Pee Johnson** ("Miss Jiveola Brown"), **Marvin Phillips** ("Wine Woogie"), and **Frank Haywood** ("You Gotta Give It Up") as well as **Little Johnny Jones** ("Hoy, Hoy"), **Rudy Greene** ("Juicy Fruit"), **Nappy Brown** ("Don't Be Angry"), and **Jackie Brenston,** who hit in 1950 with "Rocket 88."

Also of note is the wildly eccentric West Coast jump blues 'n' jive stylist **King Perry,** whose comedic delivery on Specialty novelty numbers from 1950 to 1951 like "I Must've Been an Ugly Baby," "I Wonder Who's Boogin' My Woogie," and "Duck's Yas Yas Yas" would serve as a precursor to Screamin' Jay Hawkins's inspired madness.

# Recommended Listening

## T-BONE WALKER

*The Very Best of T-Bone Walker,*
  Rhino (1945–1955)
*Complete Capitol/Black & White*
  *Recordings,* Capitol (1946–1947)
*The Complete Imperial Recordings,*
  *1950–1954,* EMI
*T-Bone Blues,* Atlantic (1955–1957)
*I Want a Little Girl,* Black and Blue
  (1968)

## AMOS MILBURN

*Down the Road Apiece: The Best of Amos*
  *Milburn,* EMI America, 1946–1953
*Blues, Barrelhouse & Boogie Woogie:*
  *The Best of Amos Milburn, 1946–1955,*
  Capitol
*The Complete Aladdin Recordings*
  *of Amos Milburn,* Mosaic, 1946–1957
*The Motown Sessions, 1962–1964,* Motown
*The Return of Blues Boss,* Motown (1963)

## ROY MILTON

*Roy Milton & His Solid Senders,*
  Specialty (1945–1953)
*Groovy Blues, Volume 2,*
  Specialty (1945–1953)
*Blowin' with Roy,* Specialty (1945–1953)

## FLOYD DIXON

*Complete Aladdin Recordings,*
  Capitol, (1949–1952)
*Marshall Texas Is My Home,*
  Specialty (1953–1957)
*Rockin' This Joint Tonite,* JSP (1978)
*Wake up and Live!* Alligator (1996)

## JOE LIGGINS

*And His Honeydrippers,* Specialty
  (1950–1954)
*Dripper's Boogie, Volume 2,* Specialty
  (1950–1954)

## JIMMY LIGGING

*And His Drops of Joy,* Specialty
  (1947–1953)

## TINY BRADSHAW

*Breaking Up the House,* Charly
  (1949–1952)
*Great Composer,* King (1959)

## BIG JOE TURNER

*Big, Bad & Blue: The Big Joe Turner*
  *Anthology,* Rhino/Atlantic (1938–1983)
*I've Been to Kansas City,* Decca (1940)
*Jazz Heritage: Early Big Joe,* MCA
  (1940–1944)
*Careless Love,* Savoy (1945)
*Have No Fear, Big Joe Turner Is Here,*
  Savoy (1945–1947)
*Jumpin' the Blues,* Arhoolie (1948)
*Jumpin' with Joe: The Complete Aladdin*
  *Sessions,* EMI America (1948–1955)
*Boss of the Blues,* Atlantic (1956)
*Big Joe Rides Again,* Atlantic (1958)
*Flip, Flop & Fly,* Pablo (1972)

## WYNONIE HARRIS

*Wynonie Harris, 1944–1945,* Classics
*Everybody Boogie!* Delmark (1945)
*Wynonie Harris, 1945–1947,* King/Rhino
*Bloodshot Eyes: The Best of Wynonie*
  *Harris,* King/Rhino (1952–1957)

**ROY BROWN**

*Good Rocking Tonight: The Best of Roy Brown,* Rhino (1947–1957)

*Blues DeLuxe,* Charly (1947–1975)

*Mighty Mighty Man!* Ace (1953–1959)

*The Complete Imperial Recordings,* Capitol (1956–1958)

**TINY GRIMES AND HIS ROCKIN' HIGHLANDERS**

*And His Rockin' Highlanders, Volumes 1 & 2,* Gotham (1949–1953)

*And Friends,* Gotham (1949–1953)

*Callin' the Blues,* Original Jazz Classics (1958)

*Tiny in Swingsville,* Original Jazz Classics (1959)

*Profoundly Blue,* Muse (1973)

**CLARENCE "GATEMOUTH" BROWN**

*The Original Peacock Recordings,* Rounder (1949–1955)

*Just Got Lucky,* Evidence (1973)

*Makin' Music,* MCA (1979)

*Alright Again!* Rounder (1982)

*Pressure Cooker,* Alligator (1987)

**NAPPY BROWN**

*Night Time Is the Right Time,* Savoy (1954–1962)

**COMPILATIONS**

*Blues Masters, Volume 5: Jump Blues Classics,* Rhino

*Blues Masters, Volume 14: More Jump Blues,* Rhino

*Legends of Jump Blues, Volume 1,* Specialty

**CHAPTER 4**

# BEBOP 'N' JIVE

**Lester Young, Lionel Hampton, Dizzy Gillespie,
Eddie Jefferson, Babs Gonzales, Joe Carroll,
King Pleasure, Jon Hendricks**

While big bands held sway with the public during the war years, a small underground movement was gradually taking hold that would ultimately represent a line of demarcation between the Swing Era and the future. As early as 1940 pioneering musicians like trumpeter Dizzy Gillespie, drummer Kenny Clarke, and like-minded souls—including pianists Thelonious Monk, Bud Powell, Tadd Dameron, and Mary Lou Williams, along with transitional figures like guitarist Charlie Christian and saxophonist Lester Young—were congregating at Harlem nightspots like Minton's Playhouse and Monroe's Uptown House to work out new ideas about harmony, time, and meter. Alto great Charlie Parker helped solidify the movement in teaming with Gillespie at the end of 1944 on Fifty-second Street. Together they issued their musical manifesto in 1945 with "Groovin' High," followed soon after by other equally subversive statements like "Salt Peanuts," "Dizzy Atmosphere," and the anthemic vocal call-and-response number "Oop Bop Sh' Bam."

Although this new music was teeming with dazzling virtuosity and underscored by harmonic elaboration along with a liberating new approach to rhythm, it was widely reviled by the musical establishment. But even as Cab Calloway and other representatives of the old guard summarily dismissed "bebop" as "Chinese music," the cult spread and took hold by 1947, with the charismatic Gillespie as its unofficial ambassador.

Some other old-school cats, notably Benny Goodman alumnus and big-band leader Lionel Hampton, would make concessions to both bebop and the burgeoning jump blues movement that exploded in the postwar years. And though Parker would check out by 1955, his partner, Diz, continued waving the flag for bebop (and Latin jazz) into the early 1990s.

An offshoot of the bebop movement was vocalese, in which singers grafted lyrics onto a previously existing instrumental tune or recorded solo. This demanding exercise in lyric writing and performing was pioneered in the early 1940s by Eddie Jefferson and popularized in the early 1950s by King Pleasure and Annie Ross. Singers like Babs Gonzales and Joe Carroll matched the attitude of the bebop movement with their own gymnastic, jivey take on the art of delivering lyrics. Vocalese was solidifed as a genre by 1957 with the formation of the influential and popular Lambert, Hendricks & Ross, a trio that greatly extended the vocal tradition of The Mills Brothers, The Spirits of Rhythm, The Boswell Sisters, and The Andrews Sisters while serving as a role model for The Manhattan Transfer in the 1970s. In addition to an unparalleled virtuosity on their respective horns, all of these aforementioned artists share a life-affirming sense of joy that comes across in their music. It leaps off records and CDs and reaches to the back row in concert halls, communicating with spirited good humor, verve, and jive.

## LESTER YOUNG

BORN: August 27, 1909, in Woodville, Mississippi
DIED: March 15, 1959, in New York, New York

LIKE CAB CALLOWAY, Slim Gaillard, and jiveologist Dan Burley, tenor sax great and quintessential hipster Lester Young created an entire lexicon of Lester-speak that was at once bewildering and hep. As pianist Horace Silver, who worked with Young in 1952, put it, "He had a funny way of saying everything and you really had to learn his language in order to understand what he was saying. Like, for instance, on the bandstand whenever he wanted the bass player to take a solo he would look over at him and say, 'Put me in the basement.' And the cat would start playing the bass solo. Then if Lester wanted him to continue playing another chorus he would say, 'Don't quit now, take another helping.' He had some colorful lingo all his own."

Drummer Roy Haynes recalls the day in 1947 when Young invited him to join his band. "He didn't just come out and say, 'Do you want to join my band?' Instead he said, 'Do you have eyes for the slave?' That's the way he expressed it. He was always creative with words that way."

And he addressed everyone as Lady, regardless of gender, as in Lady Tate for fellow saxophonist Buddy Tate, or Lady Day for Billie Holiday. "When it came to a name for Lester, I always felt he was the great-est, so his name had to be the greatest," Holiday wrote in her autobiography, *Lady Sings the Blues*. "In this country kings or counts or dukes don't amount to nothing. The greatest man around then was Franklin D. Roosevelt and he was the President. So I started calling him the President. It got shortened to Prez."

**"To join the throng, you've got to make your own song."**
— *Lester Young*

Lester Young was indeed the president and the other tenor saxophonists knew it. As Al Cohn told Leonard Feather in a 1959 *Playboy* article, "When I was about 12 or 13, clarinet was THE instru-ment in jazz. I'd found nothing interesting in the saxophone. Then I began rummaging through the nine-cent bargain counters in those stores that sold used 78s and someone told me about a band—Count Basie. Well, when I heard 'Jumpin' at the Woodside' and 'Dark Rapture,' I switched overnight. Prez was the reason I became a saxophone player."

Writes Leonard Feather in that same tribute to Lester Young: "On the bandstand, Prez was his own man, and jazz was his language. Often obscure in his speech, he spoke lucidly and warmly through his horn. When he did, the musicians gathered and the critics took notice."

---

Following pages Lester Young (center), on tenor sax, at Kelly's Stables, 1941, with (from left to right): Shad Collins, trumpet; Harold West, drums; Nick Fenton, bass; Clyde Hart, piano; John Collins, guitar. Frank Driggs Collection

Lester Young's rendition of "Body and Soul" became the hipster's anthem in the 1940s; he was as playfully ornate with the melody as jive-talking jitterbugs were with the English language. Young, whose unique approach to the tenor saxophone charted a new course for that instrument, always maintained that the secret to one's musical success in jazz was to embrace one's own individuality. Or to put it in Lesterese: "To join the throng, you've got to make your own song."

Everything was unique about Lester Young. He read comic books and drank gin with a sherry chaser. He consumed buttermilk and whiskey or sardines with ice cream. For years he could sleep only in a room filled with light and the sound of a radio at full volume. And his speech was positively otherwordly.

"His idiosyncrasies were part of the masquerade, the massive characterization," wrote Leonard Feather in *Playboy* shortly after Young's death in 1959. "Prez used an almost entirely personal language that's become standard jazz argot. 'Bells!' and 'Ding-dong!' signified approval. 'No eyes' indicated reluctance. He sprinkled his speech with double-talk words, punctuating with 'oodastaddis!' or 'vout' or the suffix 'oreeny' [which he no doubt lifted from Slim Gaillard]. 'I feel a draft' was his signal flag for racial discomfort, when Jim Crow was watching him. White musicians were not 'ofays' to Prez but 'gray boys.' He greeted strangers with 'How are your feelings?' The more Prez declined in his battle with the forces of life, the more he depended on such hip talk to help him exclude any intruders."

Whitney Balliet expounded on Young's uniqueness in a 1981 *New Yorker* article: "Very little about the tenor saxophonist Lester Young was unoriginal. He had protruding, heavy-lidded eyes, a square, slightly Oriental face, a tiny mustache, and a snaggletoothed smile. His walk was light and pigeon-toed and his voice was soft. He was something of a dandy. He wore suits, knit ties and collar pins. He wore ankle-length coats and porkpie hats pulled down low and evenly. When he played, he held his saxophone in front of him at a 45-degree angle, like a canoeist about to plunge his paddle into the water. He had an airy, lissome tone and an elusive, lyrical way of phrasing that had never been heard before. He spoke a coded language, about which the pianist Jimmy Rowles has said, 'You had to break that code to understand him. It was like memorizing a dictionary.'"

In Lesterese "Bing and Bob" were the police, a "hat" was a woman, and a "needle dancer" was a heroin addict. "To be bruised" was to fail and "startled doe, two o'clock" meant that a pretty girl with doelike eyes was seated in the right side of the audience. A "tribe" was a band and a "molly trolley" was a rehearsal. "Can Madam burn?" meant "Can your wife cook?"

Regarding his horn work, Lester was also in a class by himself. As one sideman told Leonard Feather: "Prez got that soft tone—so different from Coleman Hawkins—because that's the way he wanted everything in life. Why, I even got him a pair of shoes once and one day I came in and found them in the wastebasket. Then I realized—they were hard-soled shoes and he would always wear moccasins or slippers. It had to be soft and gentle or Prez wanted no part of it."

His father was a multi-instrumentalist who had played in traveling minstrel shows before heading up his own family band. Lester started playing drums in his family's band when he was ten (which also included his brother Lee and sister Irma), touring the country with them for five years. Deeming the drums too much trouble to carry around, he switched to alto sax when he was thirteen. At the age of eighteen, Prez fled the family band, which at that point was based in Minneapolis, and joined Art Bronson and His Bostonians, a band based in Salina, Kansas. During the early '30s, he wandered through Kansas, Missouri, Oklahoma, and Minnesota with Bennie Moten's band, King Oliver's Creole Jazz Band, Walter Page's Blue Devils and other territory bands. In Kansas City he acquired a tenor saxophone and played his first job with Count Basie's band. As Basie told Leonard Feather: "When Prez first came to me at the Reno Club in Kansas City, it was like nothing we'd ever heard. And it was consistent. In all the years he was with our band he never had a bad night. No matter what happened to him personally, he never showed it in his playing. I can only remember him as being beautiful."

Young left Basie to accept an offer of more money from Fletcher Henderson in 1934, replacing the iconic Coleman Hawkins in the band. But Prez's unique approach to the tenor sax could not erase Hawkins's image. As he told Feather (in quintessential Lesterese): "I came to New York with the band and I got bruised because I didn't play like Hawkins. They rang the bell on me. So I really did a lot of teardrops there, you know. Some people just didn't have eyes for certain things. I was rooming at Fletcher's house and Mrs. Henderson would come in every morning and start playing me them records with Hawkins and everything, to show me what to do. And I would listen because I didn't want to hurt nobody's feelings."

Prez returned to Kansas City and after a six-month stint with Andy Kirk's band, he rejoined Basie's band in time to appear on the first Basie big-band date, cut in New York in 1937. During those landmark years with Basie, Prez reached his peak as a player and would have a huge impact on younger boppish players like Dexter Gordon and Sonny Rollins. As Gordon told Feather: "Hawk had done everything possible and was the master of the horn, but when Prez appeared we all started listening to him alone. Prez had an entirely new sound, one that we had been waiting for. He was the first one to really tell a story on the horn."

Whitney Balliet praised Prez's playing in the same *New Yorker* article: "He was an adept embellisher and a complete improviser. He could make songs like 'Willow Weep for Me' and 'The Man I Love' unrecognizable. He kept the original melodies in his head, but what came out was his dreams about them. His solos were fantasies—lyrical, soft, liquid—on the tunes he was playing, and probably on his own life as well."

Aside from his wonderfully expressive playing and unique conception, Prez attracted attention for other nonmusical eccentricities. He kept a small whisk broom in his top jacket pocket that he used to sweep away insults or anything that upset him. He kept a little bell on the bandstand beside him and would ring it whenever anybody hit a bad note or made a mistake. His porkpie hat became a visual symbol (just as Dizzy Gillespie's beret and horned-rimmed glasses would a generation later) and his eccentric lingo caught on with other musicians. As John Lewis told Whitney Balliet in *The New Yorker:* "He was a living, walking poet. He was so quiet that when he talked each sentence came out like a little explosion. His speech and dress were natural things he picked up. They weren't a disguise—a way of hiding. They were a way to be hip—to express an awareness of everything swinging that was going on. Or course, he never wasted this hipness on duddish people, nor did he waste good playing on bad musicians."

After leaving the Basie band (for the second time) in 1940, Prez headed up his own combo on Fifty-second Street that also featured his drummer brother Lee Young. He went on the road with Al Sears's band in 1942 and returned to the Basie outfit in 1943. The following year he was drafted into the Army, a terrifying experience for him that lasted fifteen months, culminating in a dishonorable discharge. He returned to the jazz world in 1946, signing up for some Jazz at the Philharmonic tours, but his spirit had been so depleted at that point that his heart was barely in it. Physical and artistic decay followed. "Lester had already reached the point of no return by 1946," said his manager Charlie Carpenter to Leonard Feather. "He was tired of the responsibilities of the world and was looking for an escape."

There were trips to the hospital—once for liquor consumption leading to malnutrition and a nervous breakdown. There were failed marriages—his third produced two childen. His drinking resumed and his physical condition deteriorated rapidly. In early 1959, though in a weakened condition, he booked a four-week engagement at the Paris Blue Note. During the engagement he drank heavily. Back in New York, broken and hopelessly depressed, he drank himself to death in his room at the Alvin Hotel just across the street from Birdland, where a year before they had held a celebratory birthday jam session in his honor.

"Lester's approach to everything he did in life was concerned with beauty," said pianist Billy Taylor to Feather. "He liked things pretty, and the word had a special meaning for him. The highest compliment he could pay anyone was, 'That was real pretty.'"

# LIONEL HAMPTON

BORN: April 12, 1909, in Louisville, Kentucky

A PRODUCT OF THE SWING ERA, having attained fame in the 1930s with Benny Goodman's orchestra and quartet, vibist-drummer-bandleader Lionel Hampton flirted with bebop after 1944. But he had exhibited a fondness for jive early on with ebullient recordings like "Jivin' the Vibes" in 1937, "Jumpin' Jive" in 1939, "Jivin' with Jarvis" in 1940, and "Give Me Some Skin" in 1941.

Hamp, who addressed nearly everyone with the jivey moniker "Gates," was raised in Chicago and began his phenomenal musical career at an early age while attending Holy Rosary Academy in Kenosha, Wisconsin, where he studied under the strict supervision of the Dominican Sisters. His first instrument was a set of drums and his idol during these formative years was drummer Jimmy Bertrand, who tossed his sticks in the air as lights blinked away from inside his bass drum (a showstopping trick that Hamp adopted in later years).

**"Hey ba-ba-re-bop."**

— *Lionel Hampton*

As a teen he played in the Chicago Defender Newspaper Boys Band. In 1928 he moved to Los Angeles and played around as a drummer with Curtis Mosby's Blue Blowers, Reb Spikes, and Paul Howard's Quality Serenaders, with whom he made his recording debut in 1929. The following year Hamp joined the Les Hite big band, which accompanied Louis Armstrong on recordings of Eubie Blake's "Memories of You" (on which Hampton made his recording debut as a vibist) and "Shine" before disbanding. Through the early 1930s he had a long-standing engagement in Los Angeles at the Paradise Cafe, where he was discovered in 1936 by Benny Goodman. That year he recorded with a quartet consisting of Goodman on clarinet, Teddy Wilson on piano, and Gene Krupa on drums and soon after joined the ranks of Goodman's orchestra. Hampton remained with Goodman until 1940, also recording sessions as a leader for Victor during that time.

In 1942 Hampton formed his own big band and scored a huge hit with "Flying Home," which featured saxophonist Illinois Jacquet in what is considered the first R&B–styled tenor sax solo. Hamp's extroverted showmanship—dancing on his drums and attacking the vibes with over-the-top ebullience—dismayed purists and critics but caught on with fans, who seemed thrilled to join in on catchy audience participation numbers like "Hey Ba-Ba-Re-Bop" and "Hamp's Boogie Woogie." He remained a vital force and lively performer well into his eighties and continued performing into his nineties. Over the years hundreds of name players have gone through the ranks of Hampton's bands, including Betty Carter, Dexter Gordon, Dinah Washington, Aretha Franklin, Arnett Cobb, Quincy Jones, Charles Mingus, Jonah Jones, Clark Terry, Cat Anderson, Fats Navarro, Joe Newman, Ernie Royal, Earl Bostic, Wes Montgomery, Art Farmer, Gigi Gryce, Benny Bailey, Clifford Brown, Al Grey, Milt Buckner, and Dizzy Gillespie.

# DIZZY GILLESPIE

BORN: October 21, 1917, in Cheraw, South Carolina
DIED: January 7, 1993, in Englewood, New Jersey

SOMETIMES CALLED "The Clown Prince of Jazz," trumpeter Dizzy Gillespie revolutionized jazz along with alto sax legend and kindred spirit Charlie

Lionel Hampton, 1942. Courtesy the Institute of Jazz Studies at Rutgers University

Parker, whom he once referred to as "the other half of my heartbeat." Their pioneering experiments with rhythm and harmony in the mid-1940s—christened "bebop" by Gillespie himself—set a new course for the music that continues to have a profound influence on jazz musicians to this day.

Aside from his unprecedented virtuosity as a trumpeter, John Birks Gillespie was also a beloved showman in the great tradition of Louis Armstrong, Fats Waller, and Cab Calloway (who was also one of his early employers). But his onstage ebullience was sometimes at odds with the more serious intent of the music. As Ira Gitler pointed out in *Jazz Masters of the Forties:* "Diz's sense of humor—and the various paths it takes—is one of the things that set him apart from the other musical giants of his circle," further noting that, "sometimes his antics have caused people to lose sight of his prodigious talent."

In a 1960 interview with Gene Lees for *Down Beat,* Dizzy complained that many of his men lacked showmanship and said, "If you got enough money to play for yourself, you can play anything you want to. But if you want to make a living at music, you've got to sell it."

In his small band setting Dizzy may have tried "selling it" with vocal novelty numbers like "Umbrella Man," "Hey Pete! Let's Eat More Meat," "Cool Breeze," "Jump Did-Le Ba," "I'm Beboppin' Too," "Ool-Ya-Koo," "Oo-Shoo-Be-Doo-Be," and "Oop-Bop Sh' Bam," though his critics often claimed he was actually selling out. When British journalist Michael James questioned Gillespie about this while on a European tour in the early '50s, the godfather of bebop replied: "I'm not interested any more in going down in history. I want to eat!"

Starting on trombone at the age of fourteen, Gillespie took up trumpet the following year. His first major job was with the Frank Fairfax band in Philadelphia. In 1937 he joined Teddy Hill's Orchestra, filling a spot formerly held by his trumpet-playing idol Roy Eldridge and making his first records with the band on "King Porter Stomp" and "Blue Rhythm Fantasy." Then in September of 1939 Dizzy found himself in fast company on a Lionel Hampton all-star date for Victor, which featured Benny Carter on alto sax, and Ben Webster, Chu Berry, and Coleman Hawkins on tenor sax. His muted trumpet work on "Hot Mallets" from that session shows a distinct departure from Roy Eldridge's influence with a stride down a new path.

In the fall of 1939 he joined Cab Calloway and for the next two years was one of three featured instrumentalists in the group. During this time he began developing his own style of playing, planting the seeds of what was to become bebop. The rhythmic and harmonic daring that Dizzy exhibited in his solos infuriated Calloway, a perfectionist who prided himself on running a tight ship. Invariably, he would chastise the upstart trumpeter for his chance-taking solos, cautioning him not to play "any of that Chinese music in this band," as Gitler reports in *Jazz Masters of the Forties.*

**"Oop-bop sh' bam, a-kluga-mop."**
— *Dizzy Gillespie*

Dizzy ultimately departed Cab's big band on particularly bad terms. After the infamous Spitball Incident of September, 1941, (someone mischievously hit the bandleader, who wrongly accused Dizzy, who then retaliated by slashing Cab's buttocks with a knife, requiring ten stitches on his posterior), Dizzy was summarily fired from the ranks of the Calloway orchestra.

For the next few years he worked with bands led by Ella Fitzgerald, Benny Carter, Coleman Hawkins, Charlie Barnet, Les Hite, Lucky Millinder, Duke Ellington (for three weeks), and Earl Hines. In January of 1944 Dizzy put together the first bop-oriented jazz group for an engagement at the Onyx Club on Fifty-second Street. Known as The Hepsations, it included bassist Oscar Pettiford, drummer Max Roach, tenor saxophonist Don Byas, and pianist George Wallington. Budd Johnson later replaced Byas and Clyde Hart replaced Wallington. This group grew out of a combo that had played at the Onyx Club in December of 1943 featuring Gillespie with tenor sax great Lester Young, bassist Pettiford, and pianist Thelonious Monk. And all of these cutting-edge musical ideas had actually been fermenting since Gillespie's participation in the Earl Hines Orchestra of 1943.

In June of 1944 Dizzy joined Billy Eckstine's new big band, which also included such future jazz stars as Charlie Parker, Gene Ammons, and Sarah Vaughan. By the end of 1944 Dizzy's name and the word "bop" were both well known among musicians. By the spring of 1945 he teamed up with Charlie Parker at the Three Deuces. The two virtuosos would soon after unleash their rapid-fire unisons on such revolutionary recordings as "Groovin' High," "Shaw 'Nuff," and "Salt Peanuts" on Guild and "Dizzy Atmosphere" on Musicraft. The harmonically and rhythmically advanced

music confused swing fans while elevating Gillespie to heroic status among the hipper set. Gillespie's beret, goatee, and black horn-rimmed "bop glasses" soon became synonymous with the bop movement.

As *Down Beat* magazine reported at the time: "Never before in the history of jazz has so dynamic a person as Dizzy Gillespie gained the spotlight of acclaim and idolization. Wherever you go in jazz circles you are reminded of Dizzy in at least one of several ways, for few musicians have escaped the aura of Dizzy's influence."

At the end of 1945 Gillespie and Parker traveled to the West Coast to play a lengthy gig at Billy Berg's in Los Angeles. Their participation in the now-legendary "Slim's Jam" session of December 29, 1945, for the L.A.–based Beltone label (with Slim Gaillard acting as a kind of sly master of ceremonies) stands as an important landmark in jive lore. Following their engagement at Billy Berg's, Gillespie returned to New York while Parker cashed in his plane ticket and remained in Los Angeles (ultimately checking into the psychiatric ward of Camarillo State Hospital for a six-month stay following a complete mental breakdown).

Back in New York Gillespie put together a big band and began pioneering Latin jazz with such Afro-Cuban masterworks as "Manteca" and "Cubana Be/Cubana Bop," which featured the exciting percussionist Chano Pozo. Due to economic pressures, Gillespie was forced to split up his groundbreaking orchestra in 1950, at which point he scaled down his band and began engaging in wildly entertaining scatting battles with effervescent vocalists like Joe Carroll.

In 1956 he was tapped by the U.S. State Department to lead the first in a series of world tours as an unofficial goodwill ambassador. Dizzy tried mounting a big band once again in 1957, which was well documented on *Dizzy Gillespie at Newport* on Verve. Around that time critic Ralph J. Gleason commented on Dizzy's penchant for joking and jiving on the bandstand in his article "Humor in Jazz" for the *Philadelpia Bulletin*: "Humor and Dizzy Gillespie are inseparable. Although some of Gillespie's bits and routines have been standard with him for years, his humor is improvisatory to a considerable degree and it is, in the same sense as the humor of Mort Sahl and Lenny Bruce, jazz humor. Gillespie's greatest attributes as a comedian are timing and a natural ability to observe, discuss and comment in a manner direct, childlike and natural."

Dizzy Gillespie, 1946. Frank Driggs Collection

And then there was his mock run for the presidency in 1964 (depicted on the November 5 cover of *Down Beat* magazine as "Dizzy's Dream Inauguration Day"). Part of his platform called for naming Malcolm X his minister of justice and appointing Miles Davis as head of the CIA. Gillespie actually made it to the White House in 1978 for a celebration of the twenty-fifth anniversary of the Newport Jazz Festival, in which President Jimmy Carter (the onetime peanut farmer) sang along to a boppish rendition of Dizzy's "Salt Peanuts."

In 1974 he signed with Pablo and began recording prolifically in small band settings, including 1975's *The Trumpet Kings at Montreux,* featuring fellow trumpeters Roy Eldridge and Clark Terry backed by the Oscar Peterson trio. In the late 1980s Dizzy put together his multicultural United Nations Orchestra, which featured such a diverse cast of players as saxophonist Paquito D'Rivera (Cuba), pianist Danilo Perez (Panama), trumpeter Arturo Sandoval (Cuba), saxophonist David Sanchez (Puerto Rico), and trumpeter Claudio Roditi (Brazil). This lineup toured the world through 1991. Dizzy's final recording was the live *To Diz with Love* on Telarc, taken from a month (January, 1992) he spent at the Blue Note in New York with a revolving cast of characters who came to pay him homage, including protégé Jon Faddis, Wynton Marsalis, Wallace Roney, Red Rodney, Charlie Sepulveda, and the elder Doc Cheatham. He died at the age of seventy-five in January of 1993 from complications of pancreatic cancer, nearly forty years after his "worthy constituent" Charlie Parker had passed away.

Dizzy's innumerable breakthroughs, triumphs, setbacks, exploits, honors, travels, gags, pranks, and jokes throughout his fabulous career have been cataloged in his entertaining memoirs, *To Be, or Not . . . to Bop.*

Leonard Feather best summed up Gillespie's contribution to jazz: "Dizzy's role in jazz history is not fully understood nor adequately acknowledged by the younger jazz students, many of whom see him as a clown, a humorous singer and monologist whose trumpet playing sometimes seems secondary to his role as entertainer. Though he is among those who feel that art and entertainment are compatible, and that communication with his audiences is vitally important, Gillespie remains first and foremost a musical giant. He has remained, in the opinion of most trumpet players and many music experts, the greatest living jazz trumpet player, a composer of superb melodies and one of the four or five most important figures in the entire history of jazz."

And an absolute gas to boot.

# EDDIE JEFFERSON

BORN: August 3, 1918, in Pittsburgh, Pennsylvania
DIED: May 9, 1979, in Detroit, Michigan

LIKE THE TITLE OF A 1976 ALBUM on Muse says, Eddie Jefferson was the undisputed "Godfather of Vocalese." Though he didn't have a great voice, in the conventional sense of tone and range, he did convey passion and ultimate hipness in every syllable he managed to squeeze into pre-existing jazz solos.

Starting out as a tap dancer, he appeared at the 1933 World's Fair in Chicago at the age of fifteen with the original Zephyrs and continued working in various tap dance teams through the '30s. Around 1938 Eddie and his dancing partner Irv Taylor first got the idea of adding lyrics to recorded improvisations. Jefferson credits Leo "Scat" Watson with inspiring him to put words to improvised instrumental solos. "We were talking about scat singing," he recalled in a 1978 interview with Carol Crawford for *Jazz Magazine.* "He had taken that about as far as it could go and he advised me to sing lyrics. You know, like you could still improvise but do it with lyrics."

Jefferson's first experiment in vocalese was a rendition of a 1939 Count Basie recording of "Taxi War Dance." As he told jazz critic Leonard Feather for the liner notes to *The Jazz Singer:* "I set lyrics to the Lester Young and Herschel Evans solos. I sang it for friends but nothing ever came of it and I don't know what became of the lyrics. Not long after, I wrote words to Chu Berry's solo on Cab Calloway's record of 'Ghost of a Chance.' But I was a dancer during those days and I did those things strictly for kicks."

> **"Come on in James Moody and blow if you want to, I'm through."**
> — *Eddie Jefferson*

A live session from 1949 finds him pioneering vocalese by singing his own lyrics to "Parker's Mood" and Lester Young's solo on "I Cover the Waterfront." His classic lyrics to "Moody's Mood for Love" were, however, recorded first by King Pleasure in 1952, who also had a hit the following year with "Parker's Mood." Pleasure, who had heard Jefferson sing his version at the Cotton Club in Cincinnati, went back to New York and sang it at the Apollo Theatre Amateur Hour. It was a rave success. Besides winning the prize, Pleasure landed a contract to record the song for Prestige. Years later a disgruntled Jefferson said, "Yeah, he copped those lyrics. But in a way it opened it up for me."

Jefferson's first studio recording came in July of 1952 for the Hi-Lo label. The following February he recorded four sides for Prestige. After meeting James Moody later in 1953, while both were working at the Apollo Theater, he joined the saxophonist's group as a vocalist, doubling as road and band manager. He remained with Moody until 1962, when the saxophonist broke up his band and joined Dizzy Gillespie's group. Jefferson and Moody were later reunited from 1968 to 1973.

Over the years Eddie Jefferson created scores of witty and fresh lyrics to jazz classics like Lester Young's "Lester Leaps In," Miles Davis's "So What" and "Bitches Brew," Horace Silver's "Filthy McNasty" and "Sister Sadie," Charlie Parker's "Now's the Time" and "Yardbird Suite," Eddie Harris's "Freedom Jazz Dance," Herbie Hancock's "Chameleon," Joe Zawinul's "Mercy Mercy Mercy," and, perhaps most impressively, to Coleman Hawkins's solo on "Body and Soul," all of which he conveyed with contagious joy. As Ira Steingroot wrote in the liner notes to the 1980 posthumous Prestige reissue, *There I Go Again:* "He welded the disparate elements of black speech—jive talk, slang, musical diction, story-telling, rhythmic genius—into a powerful instrument for musical poetry. He was one of the great scat singers with a thick, reedy intonation that matched the sax sounds he loved and an unerring sense of pitch. The way he accented his lines, the shape of his phrases and his sense of rhythm were all on par with the work of the saxophonists he admired and paid homage to in his songs."

The vocalese pioneer described his creative process to *Jazz Magazine:* "First, I learn the solo really well (off records). I might play around with a Charlie Parker or a Trane solo for two months so that I know it asleep or awake. And then I'll hear a story somewhere in there and I'll write. Later on I'll write the lyrics because I already know the solo. Usually the music tells a story of its own. There's got to be something where I can hear the story or I don't write. Bird was always melodic to me and so is James Moody. I would hear stories from them. But I never did write anything off Sonny Stitt, who's an excellent saxophone player, or Stan Getz. I never did hear stories from them. I like their music but I never heard anything for me to work with. That's where it's at."

After a few years of working with drummer Roy Brooks, Jefferson teamed up with young alto saxophonist Richie Cole in 1976. They were working together at Baker's Keyboard Lounge in Detroit when after a gig Jefferson was shot to death outside the club by an acquaintance who held a serious grudge.

# BABS GONZALES

BORN: October 27, 1919, in Newark, New Jersey
DIED: January 23, 1980, in Newark, New Jersey

A WILDLY ENTHUSIASTIC SCAT SINGER, exuberant personality, and quintessential hipster on the '40s scene, Babs Gonzales helped popularize bebop through his recordings and writings. In his *Be-Bop Dictionary*, Babs (aka Lee Brown) expounded on the pioneers of this modern music while also providing his own thumbnail biography:

"It began in 1939. I, fresh out of high school, formed my first group. This group didn't stay together long due to non-employment. In 1942, while in California, I was urged to form another group which again didn't last but three months. In December 1945, the present group [Three Bips & a Bop] was presented at Minton's Play House and we were fortunate to stay there 16 weeks. For the next year we gigged up and down the East Coast from Boston to Washington with occasional locations in Newark and New Haven. Finally while doing a guest shot at the 1280 Club, Alfred Lions of Blue Note heard us and gave us our long awaited first record date." In addition to the biographical sketch in the *Be-Bop Dictionary,* his life story is detailed in not one but two autobiographies, 1967's *I Paid My Dues* (a book as colorful and outrageous as Mezz Mezzrow's revealing tome *Really the Blues*) and 1975's *Movin' on Down de Line,* both by Expubidence Publishing.

**"Oop-pop-a-da"**

— *Babs Gonzales*

In a 1965 interview with Ira Gitler on radio station WBAI in New York he explained the genesis of the Three Bips. "I formed the Bips because I felt bebop needed a vocal bridge to the people. The fire was there. Bird was cooking and Oscar Pettiford and Dizzy with their little group, but it wasn't really the people. I had been doing some solo work with Lucky Thompson around

New Haven, as a solo vocalist, but it was more or less a real imitation of Billy Eckstine, to tell you the real truth. Everybody was going behind B [Eckstine] in those days."

Born in Newark, Babs went to Newark Arts High School with Sarah Vaughan and Ike Quebec. He took up piano and after finishing school in 1939 formed a six-piece combo featuring Dizzy Gillespie and Don Byas. In 1941 Babs joined Charlie Barnet's big band and stayed with him for six months. There followed a five-month stint with Lionel Hampton. "I learned a lot from Gates," he told writer Valerie Wilmer in *Jazz People*. "He's a great showman."

Regarding the choice of his nickname, he told Wilmer: "My real name is Lee Brown and I picked Gonzales when I was with Charlie [Barnet] because they was Jim Crowing me in ofay hotels on the road and so I said if it's just simple enough to change my last name—why not? Get in the crazy hotels and sleep with the ofays. They think I'm Cubano and I can speak the language too. So it stuck and only my real close people know my expubidence." ["Expubidence" was one of Gonzales's own words, meaning "inherent talents, charm, and personal charisma."]

In 1943 Babs formed a four-girl vocal group that included Nadine Cole, first wife of Nat "King" Cole. The quartet performed around Hollywood for about five months that year and it was during this time that Babs wrote "Oop-Pop-A-Da." During an eight-month stint in 1944 with Benny Carter's band he wrote "Prelude to a Nightmare" and "Lullaby of the Doomed." During his stay in Hollywood he also worked (wrapped in a turban and calling himself Ram Singh) as a chauffeur for screen idol Errol Flynn.

By 1945 he was back in Harlem, gigging at Minton's Playhouse with a group comprised of Max Roach on drums, Bud Powell on piano, and Rudy Williams on alto saxophone. "They hired me for four weeks and I stayed for 37," he told *Melody Maker* in a 1951 interview.

In May of 1946 he began rehearsing Babs's Three Bips & a Bop with pianist Tadd Dameron, Art Phipps on bass, the Charlie Christian–inspired guitarist Pee Wee Tenny, and Babs on a scaled down drum set, which he played standing up. As he reports in his *I Paid My Dues* (which is revealingly subtitled "Good Times . . . No Bread, A Story of Jazz . . . And Some of Its Followers, Shyster Agents, Hustlers, Pimps and Prostitutes"): "I copped a gig at Minton's and one night [Blue Note record label founder] Alfried Lions came in to dig us. He said we gassed him but we were too far out for the people."

Nearly a year later, in February of 1947, Lions relented and they finally went into the WOR studios to cut their first sides for Blue Note. That session was augmented by Rudy Williams on alto sax and Charles Simon, who replaced Babs on drums. They recorded the frantic "Pay Dem Dues," an ethereal interpretation of "Stompin' at the Savoy" and two scat vehicles in "Lop-Pow," which sounds heavily influenced by both Leo "Scat" Watson and Slim Gaillard, and Babs's best-known opus de jive, "Oop-Pop-A-Da," which was later covered by Dizzy Gillespie. In a bit of controversy, Gillespie put his own name as composer of the tune on his RCA/Victor version of "Oop-Pop-A-Da," which well outsold Babs's original. Babs later sued Victor, but ultimately settled with the company. As he told Wilmer: "The bread was cool from my point of view, but I'm glad that Birksy [an affectionate name for John Birks Gillespie] could get his big band behind it instead of scuffling."

Babs and the Bips returned to the studio in May of 1947 to cut "Runnin' Around," "Babs' Dream," the scat-happy, riff-oriented "Dob Bla Bli," and the haunting "Weird Lullaby," which features Babs singing in a minor key in some strange, imaginary language. In January of 1949, with a new lineup, he cut "Capitolizing," a briskly scatted salute to his new record label, and the autobiographical "Professor Bop." In March of that year he traveled to Los Angeles, where he recorded a wacky Latin-flavored cover of "The Continental" and the hypercharged scat romp "Prelude to a Nightmare" with a group consisting of pianist Wynton Kelly, trombonist J. J. Johnson, tenor saxophonist Herbie Steward, and alto saxophonist Art Pepper. Back in New York on April 27, 1949, for a session with Kelly, Johnson, drummer Roy Haynes, and tenor saxophonist Sonny Rollins, he cut "Real Crazy," "When Lovers They Lose" (which later showed up as "Lullaby of the Doomed"), and the anthemic "Then You'll Be Boppin' Too," a primer on the art of bop singing. A frantic version of "St. Louis Blues" from that same session bears the surreal, stream-of-consciousness stamp of scat pioneer Leo "Scat" Watson.

A hip humorist and social commentator as well as a raucous-voiced singer, Gonzales worked as vocalist and road manager for James Moody from 1951 to 1953. Later Babs sessions included a 1956 recording with the Jimmy Smith trio—yielding a soulful "'Round about Midnight" with Babs's original lyrics and the jivey "You Need Connections" and two jams from a 1958 date featuring pianist Sonny Clark and bassist Paul Chambers.

Like Leo Watson and Slim Gaillard before him, Gonzales was an extravagant individualist. As Ira Gitler wrote in his liner notes to the Blue Note compilation *Weird Lullaby:* "Babs was nothing if not colorful. Anyone who shows up wearing a Mexican sombrero, Scottish plaid overcoat and Dutch wooden shoes can only be described in those terms. His personality was equally flamboyant. 'Jive' in both its swing and bop era connotations fits him."

In her book *Jazz People*, Valerie Wilmer referred to Gonzales as "Jester to the court of King Diz" and went on to describe his unique sartorial splendor in one memorable passage: "Babs is said to have once caused a minor furor on the Champs Elysées by appearing in an orange, brown and purple check coat of excessive length, a black shirt and chrome-yellow bowtie, with a grey and red check beret topping the whole confection like the cherry on a trifle."

## JOE CARROLL

BORN: November 25, 1915, in Philadelphia, Pennsylvania
DIED: February 1, 1981, in Brooklyn, New York

AN INVENTIVE SCAT SINGER, great jazz vocalist, and comedic foil for Dizzy Gillespie from 1949 to 1953, Joe Carroll is best remembered for scat-infested material like "In the Land of Oo-Bla-Dee," "Hey Pete! Let's Eat More Meat," and "Jump Did-Le Ba," his bop version of "Lady Be Good," and the bop anthem "Oo-Shoo-Be-Do-Be." A direct descendant of Leo "Scat" Watson's frantic approach to swinging nonsensical syllables and stream-of-consciousness verbiage, Carroll remained on the fringes of the scene until Gillespie took him under his wing in 1949 and began promoting his unique scat prowess on record and in concert.

"Oo-shoo-be-do-be-oo-oo."
— *Joe Carroll*

"I would go to different clubs," he was quoted in a 1981 *New York Times* obituary, "and I would go in and sing my little thing. I wasn't working there but they would always bring me on stage. And I'd do my thing and nobody listened. But it was so beautiful after I met Diz and joined him." Carroll is prominently featured scatting and jiving his way through *School Days,* Gillespie's 1951 recording for his own Dee Gee label. Joe highlights here include his aforementioned hepization of "Lady Be Good," a dead-on imitation of Satchmo on "I'm Confessin' (That I Love You)," which is appropriately retitled "Pop's Confessin'," and the jivey children's rhyme "School Days" (a tune previously recorded in 1949 by Louis Jordan). Carroll also turns in a suave reading of "I'm in a Mess" and swings hard on Kenny Clarke's boppish lament "Nobody Knows."

After his stint with Dizzy, Carroll worked as a leader, releasing his self-titled debut on Epic in 1956 and *Man with a Happy Sound* in 1962. He toured with Woody Herman in 1963 and again in 1965. He continued performing through the 1970s and in 1980 he made appearances at the Chicago Jazz Festival, the Monterey Jazz Festival, and at the Highlights in Jazz series in New York City. He gave his final performance in Morristown, New Jersey, just a few days before he was felled by a heart attack.

# KING PLEASURE

BORN: March 24, 1922, in Oakdale, Tennessee
DIED: March 21, 1982, in Los Angeles, California

BORN CLARENCE BEEKS, this ultrahip singer took the name King Pleasure after winning a talent competition in November of 1951 at Harlem's Apollo Theatre, where he wowed the audience by singing Eddie Jefferson's original lyrics to a recording of James Moody's "I'm in the Mood for Love." Prestige quickly signed up this hot property and released his 1952 debut recording *Moody's Mood for Love*, which was named Record of the Year in 1953 by *Down Beat* magazine. At that time he told *DB's* Leonard Feather: "I believe that there is a sound, there is a mood which can be interpreted into words, at least in a general way. And it is my ambition to interpret a full band arrangement into words with individual voices replacing individual instruments expressing into words what the instruments expressed in mood."

Pleasure had a minor hit in 1953 with "Parker's Mood," which was based on a famous Charlie Parker alto sax solo. As he told *Metronome* in 1954: "I always loved music. I've been blowing all my life. They call my singing every kind of thing, but to me it's blowing. Almost all musicians try to sing through their instruments and I do the same thing. Only my instrument is a voice to start off with."

The King, however, had a short reign. After making a few appearances on the touring scene (performing seated in a throne with a microphone attached) and recording a few sessions, King found his singing career curtailed due to personal problems, leaving it to Lambert, Hendricks & Ross to pick up the torch that had initially been lit by vocalese pioneer Eddie Jefferson. He made something of a comeback in the early '60s recording for Aladdin, Jubilee, and United Artists before retiring to obscurity, though he remains a major influence on singers like Al Jarreau and contemporary groups like Manhattan Transfer and New York Voices.

# JON HENDRICKS

BORN: September 16, 1921, in Newark, Ohio

A FACILE RHYMER, prolific lyricist, and agile, imaginative scatter, Jon Hendricks has been called "The Poet Laureate of Jazz." Critic Ralph J. Gleason praised his skills in a 1959 article: "Nothing any formal poet has yet written carries the drama for a jazz musician (or any member of the ever-widening jazz culture) that these lines about Charlie Parker by Jon Hendricks carry: Lack of acceptance is less like something to hide from, and more like something Bird died from."

> "Get a record
> that'll play
> a week."
> — Jon Hendricks

With his gift for verse and an uncanny rhythmic sensibility, Hendricks helped revolutionize the world of jazz singing in the mid-1950s with the popular vocalese group Lambert, Hendricks & Ross.

A preacher's son—the seventh son of seventeen children—Hendricks began entertaining at an early age. By eleven he was singing live on the radio and by fourteen he was gigging at jazz clubs and after-hours joints up and down Toledo's Indiana Avenue–like the Waiters and Bellman's club, where he was accompanied by pianist Art Tatum, a friend of the family. "One night," Hendricks told the *Washington Post* in a 1980 interview, "Fats Waller came by and heard me. He wanted to take me on the road but my mother wouldn't let me go. She said he drank too much."

At the age of sixteen, Hendricks joined a group called the Swing Buddies, which gave him his first taste of group singing. Following a hitch in the service, during which time he got his first look at Europe, he returned to the States in 1946 and was musically transformed by hearing Dizzy Gillespie's "Salt Peanuts." As he told writer Stanley Crouch in a 1984 *Village Voice* interview: "The music opened up things that were already inside me. It was a continuation of what I had heard from Art Tatum back home in Toledo. I had been scatting in that direction but the people thought I was crazy. This music proved to me that I had been right all along."

Hendricks struggled for a couple of years in a local bebop band before joining a group led by bassist Harold Jackson while by day he attended the University of Toledo, where he studied law. In 1950 Charlie Parker came to Toledo and gave a concert at the Civic Auditorium. Hendricks went up on stage and scatted about eight choruses of "The Song Is You." Parker later asked him his name and seemed surprised to learn that Hendricks was a law student. "You're not a lawyer," Bird admonished him, "you're a singer," and persuaded him to leave Toledo and come to New York. Two years later, Hendricks would seek Bird out when he arrived in the Big Apple, ultimately finding him in Harlem, where he was performing at the Apollo Bar on 125th Street and Seventh Avenue. Instead of taking up Parker's offer to stay with him, Hendricks moved into a hotel, where he worked as a clerk while writing lyrics in his free time.

In 1952 Hendricks penned the tongue-twisting lyrics to "I Want You to Be My Baby," a boogie-woogie vehicle for Louis Jordan. That same year he heard a recording of King Pleasure's vocalese hit "Moody's Mood for Love." It was a major revelation to him. "I was mesmerized by that song," he recalled in a 1982 *New York Times* interview. "It was so hip; you didn't have to stop at 32 bars. You could keep going."

For his first effort in this new vocalese direction, he joined forces in 1955 with Dave Lambert, a pioneering arranger and bebop vocalist who had worked in Gene Krupa's orchestra in the mid-1940s and had led a vocal choir on a Charlie Parker session for Clef in 1953. Lambert and Hendricks's radical reworking of Jimmy Giuffre's "Four Brothers"—which had lyrics by Hendricks and note-for-note duplications of the original solos by Herbie Steward, Zoot Sims, Stan Getz, and Serge Chaloff—was recorded for the small Avalon label and got little distribution, but it came to the attention of Milt Gabler, a producer at Decca records, who asked Hendricks to repeat the recording for his label. That record didn't make much noise either, though the flip side, a vocalese rendition of "Cloudburst" set to Sam "The Man" Taylor's saxophone solo, became a big hit in England.

For their next project, Lambert and Hendricks endeavored to tackle the Count Basie book. But after a frustrating, failed attempt at recording the material with a vocal choir, they decided to regroup. As Hendricks told *Village Voice* writer Stanley Crouch: "Dave hired his own group, which he called the Dave Lambert Singers—eleven very white people, which means that they were totally removed from swing. They couldn't swing at all! So there we were with nothing. It was awful. They couldn't do it. We sent all the singers home and were at a loss. In my characteristically blunt way, I said, 'I think we better get some Negroes. No offense but those people couldn't swing if you hung 'em.'"

In 1957 Lambert and Hendricks ended up cutting all the tracks with the help of just one extra person—Annie Ross, a singer from England who had recorded a stirring and supremely hip vocalese rendition of Wardell Gray's "Twisted" for Prestige a few years earlier. Using multitracking methods and working into the wee hours in the studio for a period of three months, striving to re-create the rich textures of the classic Basie ensemble sound, Lambert, Hendricks & Ross finally emerged with what became *Sing a Song of Basie,* a collection of Count classics like "One O'clock Jump," "Little Pony," "Down for Double," and the jivey "Avenue C" with additional lyrics by Hendricks. A few months after the album's release on ABC Records in 1958, LH&R became the most sought-after singing group in jazz.

Perhaps realizing that multitracking was a bit of a gimmick, Lambert, Hendricks & Ross then recruited a straight rhythm trio and began touring and recording that way. The first studio effort—1959's *The Swingers!*—represented a leap in quality and musicianship, leading to a contract with Columbia later that year. The trio recorded three albums for the label during the next two years, including a tribute to Duke Ellington.

All three had pursued separate solo projects during the trio's run. After constant touring began to wear her out, Ross left the group in 1962. [See separate entry on Annie Ross in chapter seven.] Lambert and Hendricks replaced her with Yolande Bavan, and switched to the RCA label. However, it was nearly impossible to replace a soloist of Ross's caliber, and the three albums Lambert, Hendricks & Bavan recorded between 1962 and 1964 were decidedly below par. The group broke up in 1964 and Lambert's death in a traffic

---

**[Dave] Lambert, [Jon] Hendricks & [Annie] Ross, 1958.**
**Courtesy the Institute of Jazz Studies at Rutgers University**

accident just two years later quashed any hopes of a reunion. Both Hendricks and Ross continued to perform and record, with Ross doing much theater and film work as well.

In the mid-1960s Hendricks was commissioned by the Monterey Jazz Festival to write *Evolution of the Blues,* in which he traces the history of black music from Africa to modern times. The production was later staged in San Francisco and ran for five years before moving on to Chicago.

After living in London with his family for five years in the 1970s, he returned to the States and began performing with a vocal group consisting of his wife, Judith, daughter, Michelle, and son, Eric, who was later replaced by a then-unknown Bay Area singer named Bobby McFerrin. The Hendricks family returned to New York in 1981 and Jon later became a significant force behind Manhattan Transfer's 1985 tribute recording, *Vocalese,* for which he penned lyrics and also performed.

In 1996 Jazz at Lincoln Center held a gala seventy-fifth anniversary celebration for Hendricks before a packed house at Avery Fisher Hall, with trumpeter Wynton Marsalis conducting the Lincoln Center Jazz Orchestra. There he reprised all his old vocalese numbers alongside such colleagues as James Moody, Al Jarreau, Bobby McFerrin, Dianne Reeves, daughter Michelle, and Manhattan Transfer. Then in 1999 he had a reunion with Annie Ross at the Blue Note, the first time the two had performed together in a nightclub since the Kennedy administration. As Gene Seymour wrote about that nostalgic show in *Newsday:* "Was it exactly like old times? Of course not. Neither of them is as capable of great vocal leaps as they once were. But their articulation was still fast and clear enough to inspire awe and laughter at those witty, inventive lyrics applied to classic jazz improvisations. So what if Hendricks occasionally lost his way in the exact order of songs. Nothing was wrong with his memory when he tore through the extended lick on 'Cloudburst.'"

The ageless Jon Hendricks is still turning a hip phrase and scatting up a storm after all these years.

———————————•———————————

### Jivenotes:

Two other noteworthy bop 'n' jivesters are **Buddy Stewart** and **Dave Lambert,** who pioneered bop vocals together in the mid-1940s with Gene Krupa's band. Their recording of "What's This?" with Krupa first brought their duetted vocal skills to wide attention. Lambert, a singer-arranger who had also worked with Johnny Long, Stan Kenton, and Harry James, was a singer-actor in the Broadway musical *Are You with It?* and also provided vocal backgrounds for such artists as Charlie Parker, Teresa Brewer, Tony Bennett, Al Hibbler, Chris Connor, Carmen McCrae, and Neal Hefti. He recorded with his vocal group for Capitol in 1949 and teamed up with Jon Hendricks in 1955 for a recording of "Four Brothers," which led to the formation of Lambert, Hendricks & Ross in 1957. He also did a solo record, *Dave Lambert Sings and Swings Alone* for United Artists in 1959. He died tragically in Westport, Connecticut, on October 3, 1966, hit by a car while changing a tire. Stewart toured with Charlie Ventura's band in 1947, with Kai Winding in 1948, and Charlie Barnet in 1949. He was killed in an automobile accident in New Mexico on February 1, 1950.

Two singers who follow in their wake—although a generation apart from each other—are **Mark Murphy** (born March 14, 1932), whose 1981 recording *Bop for Kerouac* on Muse made him an icon in hipster circles, and Chicago-based **Kurt Elling** (born November 2, 1967), whose 1995 debut on Blue Note, *Close Your Eyes,* jump-started his career. Both singers combine extravagant scatting, hip wordplay, and an unrelenting sense of swing.

## Recommended Listening

**LESTER YOUNG**

*The Lester Young Story, Volumes 1-5,*
  Columbia (1936–1941)
*The Complete Aladdin Recordings,*
  Blue Note (1942–1948)
*The Complete Savoy Recordings,*
  Savoy (1944–1949)
*Lester Swings,* Verve (1945–1951)
*Jazz Immortal Series: The Pres,*
  Savoy (1950)

**With Count Basie:**
*The Complete Decca Recordings,*
  Decca/GRP (1937–1939)
*Essential Count Basie, Volume 2,*
  Columbia (1939–1940)

**LIONEL HAMPTON**

*Hot Mallets,* Bluebird (1937–1939)

*The Complete Lionel Hampton,*
  Bluebird (1937–1941)
*Lionel Hampton's Jumpin' Jive,*
  Bluebird (1939)
*Steppin' Out,* MCA (1942–1944)
*Midnight Sun,* GRP (1946–1947)
*The Blues Ain't News to Me,* Verve
  (1951–1955)

**DIZZY GILLESPIE**

*Groovin' High,* Savoy (1945–1946)
*The Complete RCA Recordings,*
  RCA/Bluebird (1947–1949)
*Dizzy's Diamonds,* Verve (1950–1964)
*School Days,* Savoy (1951)
*Birks Works: Big Band Sessions,*
  Verve (1956–1957)
*At Newport,* Verve (1957)

*The Ebullient Mr. Gillespie*, Verve (1959)
*Swing Low Sweet Cadillac*, MCA (1967)
*Musician-Composer-Raconteur*,
  Pablo (1981)

**EDDIE JEFFERSON**
*Come Along with Me*, Prestige (1952–69)
*The Jazz Singer*, Evidence (1959–1960)
*Body and Soul*, Prestige (1968)
*Godfather of Vocalese*, Muse (1976)

**BABS GONZALES**
*Weird Lullaby*, Blue Note (1947)
*Voila!* Hope (1958)
*Tales of Manhattan*, Jaro (1959)
*Sundays at Small's Paradise*,
  Dauntless (1961)
*The Expubident World of Babs Gonzales*,
  EXP (1968)
*The Ghettosburg Address*, Expubidence
  (1970)

**JOE CARROLL**
*Joe Carroll*, Epic (1956)
*Joe Carroll with Ray Bryant*,
  Columbia (1956)
*Man with a Happy Sound*,
  Charlie Parker (1962)
**With Dizzy Gillespie:**
*The Complete RCA Recordings*,
  RCA/Bluebird (1947–1949)
*School Days*, Savoy (1951)
*The Champ*, Savoy (1951)

**KING PLEASURE**
*The Original Moody's Mood*, Prestige (1952)
*The Source*, Prestige (1952)
*King Pleasure Sings/Annie Ross*,
  Prestige (1952–1954)

*King Pleasure*, Prestige (1955)
*Golden Days*, Original Jazz Classics (1960)
*Mr. Jazz*, Hi Fi (1962)
*Moody's Mood for Love*, Blue Note (1962)

**JON HENDRICKS**
*A Good Git-Together*,
  World Pacific (1959)
*New York, N.Y.*, Decca (1959)
*Fast Livin' Blues*, Columbia (1961)
*In Person at the Trident*, Smash (1963)
*Cloudburst*, Enja (1973)
*Tell Me the Truth*, Arista (1975)
*Love*, Muse (1981)
*Freddie Freeloader*, Denon (1990)
*In Person*, Polygram (1991)
*Boppin' at the Blue Note*, Telarc (1996)

**DAVE LAMBERT**
*Dave Lambert Sings and Swing Alone*,
  United Artists (1958)

**BUDDY STEWART**
*The Young at Bop*, Emarcy (1948)

**MARK MURPHY**
*Bridging a Gap*, Muse (1973)
*Mark 2*, Muse (1975)
*Satisfaction Guaranteed*, Muse (1979)
*Bop for Kerouac*, Muse (1981)
*Some Time Ago*, High Note (1999)
*The Latin Porter*, High Note (2000)

**KURT ELLING**
*Close Your Eyes*, Blue Note (1995)
*The Messenger*, Capitol (1997)
*This Time It's Love*, Blue Note (1998)
*Live in Chicago*, Blue Note (2000)

**CHAPTER 5**

# N'AWLINS JIVE

**Danny Barker, Professor Longhair, Huey "Piano" Smith,
James Booker, Dr. John, Mr. Google Eyes, Lloyd Price, Ernie K-Doe,
James "Sugar Boy" Crawford, Jessie Hill, Lee Dorsey, Eddie Bo,
Clarence "Frogman" Henry, Kermit Ruffins**

Given its location, geography, and history, it is easy to understand how New Orleans came to cultivate its own unique sense of jive. It is in the Deep South on the mouth of the Mississippi River, is easily accessible to the Caribbean, and was successively occupied by the Spanish and the French before being annexed to the United States with the Louisiana Purchase of 1803. The city is also imbued with the hoodoo spirit of Marie Laveau, Creole voodoo queen from the 1820s who made her living selling hexes, charms, and spell-casting gris-gris dust to blacks and whites.

Add up all these factors—along with the omnipresent heat and humidity and funk of this place, the decadence and lure of Mardi Gras, the constant pulse of brass bands and second-line beats, the juxtaposition of sweet-smelling jasmine that permeates most neighborhoods with the stanky aroma of alcohol and vomit on Bourbon Street—and then you better appreciate the unique sensibility of this lush gumbo of culture that exists literally below sea level. Then you may come to understand why the locals say "Yeah, you right" rather than "All reet" or greet each other with "Where y'at?" instead of the more Yankee-fied "What's happening?" It will also help to explain the musical climate that has produced generations of drummers who play so far behind the beat.

New Orleans guitarist Phil deGruy once noted that New Orleans has three speeds: slow, stop, and mildew. *Yeah, you right, Phil.*

The colorful history of New Orleans's music is rich with lore—the almost-mythic Buddy Bolden playing his trumpet so loud and brilliantly that you could hear it for miles; pianist-composer Ferdinand "Jelly Roll" Morton entertaining clients in the whorehouses of Storyville; Louis Armstrong getting his chops together on riverboat gigs and French Quarter nightclubs before departing town to join his mentor Joe "King" Oliver in Chicago in 1922; The Boswell Sisters creating a new twist on the vocal harmony tradition; Louis Prima tearing it up in the French Quarter with his hot jazz; on and on through piano masters like Isadore "Tuts" Washington, Champion Jack Dupree, Professor Longhair, James Booker, Dr. John, Tommy Ridgley, and Eddie Bo; singers and irrepressible showmen like renowned jump blues-man Roy Brown, Joe "Mr. Google Eyes" August, Jessie "Oop Poo Pah Doo" Hill, Lloyd "Lawdy Miss Clawdy" Price, and Ernie "Mother-in-Law" K-Doe; guitarists like Eddie "Guitar Slim" Jones, and Earl "Trick Bag" King, Walter "Wolfman" Washington, and a whole lineage of great artists and showmen that followed in their wake.

That unique spirit of second-line syncopation—where eager paraders literally follow behind marching brass bands in a second line—and that laid-back aesthetic of "laissez les bon temps rouler" (let the good times roll) continue to this day and is unveiled each spring at the New Orleans Jazz & Heritage Festival. There you can soak up this unique southern-fried brand of jive in all of its glorious facets.

## DANNY BARKER

BORN: January 13, 1909, in New Orleans, Louisiana
DIED: March 14, 1994, in New Orleans, Louisiana

A BELOVED FIGURED IN NEW ORLEANS, guitarist-banjoist Danny Barker was a humorous personality, colorful storyteller, and tireless educator who greatly helped to preserve New Orleans musical traditions in the '70s,

'80s, and '90s. Early in his career Barker played banjo with the Boozan Kings and also toured Mississippi with pianist Little Brother Montgomery. In 1930 he moved to New York and went straight to Broadway in a show called *The Constant Sinner* starring Mae West. "She played the part of a swinging madam, a downtown, big-time chick who frequented Harlem. There was a cabaret scene in the show and I was in the band," recalls Danny in his memoirs. "The show lasted about eight weeks. Broadway wasn't ready for it. Mae West had a black lover, supposedly, in the play—a little advanced for the time for the attitudes of the Whites on Broadway." So advanced, apparently, that it never found an audience.

> "'Cause if you feel my thigh, you're gonna go up high, so don't you feel my leg."
> — *Danny Barker*

Following that flop, Barker worked in a string of bands, including Dave Nelson's Harlem Highlights, Buster Bailey and His Seven Chocolate Dandies, Henry Allen and His Orchestra, Billy Kyle and His Swing Club Band, Albert Nicholas, James P. Johnson, Chu Berry and His Stompy Stevedores, and the Mills Blue Rhythm Band led by Lucky Millinder. In 1937, while working with his wife, Blue Lu Barker, as a duo in a Harlem nightspot, Danny was discovered by Cab Calloway, who enlisted him into the ranks of his orchestra. The following year, while still employed with Cab, Blue Lu Barker, accompanied by Danny Barker's Fly Cats, cut the risqué tune "Don't You Feel My Leg" for Decca.

Danny remained a fixture in Cab's band through 1946, appearing on several recordings with the King of Hi-De-Ho. During his stint with Calloway, Barker also recorded with Ethel Waters, Lionel Hampton, Teddy Wilson, and Wingy Manone. By 1947 Barker was involved with the Dixieland revival, playing banjo with New Orleans trumpeter Bunk Johnson. He continued to play in that context around New York through the 1950s and then returned to New Orleans in 1965. During the period that Barker worked as the assistant curator of the New Orleans Jazz Museum, from 1965 to 1975, he also led the Onward Brass Band (his granduncle was a clarinet virtuoso who played with the Onward Brass Band at the turn of the century) and began encouraging younger players to investigate their own roots.

In 1986 he penned his entertaining memoirs, *A Life in Jazz.* Two years later he recorded the definitive unaccompanied solo set, *Save the Bones* (Orleans),

which included a jocular, jivey extrapolation on "St. James Infirmary" with Barker improvising his own lyrics throughout. Some of his last recordings were on records by Wynton Marsalis and the Dirty Dozen Brass Band. His funeral in 1994 was a major event in New Orleans music circles.

# PROFESSOR LONGHAIR

BORN: December 19, 1918, in Bogalusa, Louisiana
DIED: January 30, 1980, in New Orleans, Louisiana

ONE OF THE FOUNDING FATHERS of New Orleans R&B, Professor Longhair (nicknamed Fess) combined a singular rhumba-boogie piano style with second-line rhythms for a wholly infectious, kinetic blend that influenced every Crescent City pianist who followed in his wake—James Booker, Fats Domino, Huey "Piano" Smith, Dr. John, and Allen Toussaint, who describes Longhair as "the Bach of Rock."

Albert Goldman wrote of Fess's quirky style in a 1978 *Esquire* article: "His endless series of hesitations, feints, change-ups, drops, shoots, curves and knuckle balls made him the Satchel Paige of the piano. Like the legendary pitcher, he was a type of witch doctor or conjure man, fallen into an alien world but still practicing his tricks, spells, illusions and black arts."

Roeland Henry Byrd grew up on the streets of the Big Easy, tap dancing for tips on Bourbon Street with his running partners. After a brief fling with drums and then guitar, he started playing piano in 1936, inspired by local piano aces like Sullivan Rock, Kid Stormy Weather, and Isadore "Tuts" Washington. But the young Byrd eventually brought his own unorthodox conception to the 88s. As Mac Rebennack said in an interview: "Fess didn't even think of the piano like it was a piano. He looked at it for what it really is, a percussion instrument. But he looked at it like he was playing all the Caribbean stuff in one thing. There was something real magic about his concept. When I first saw Fess I was really into [boogie-woogie pianist] Pete Johnson. But when I heard Fess on that gig. . . . It must've been like when guys tell me when they heard Art Tatum, like they're looking at God or something. That thing of his was so different. Everybody who heard him at the

**Danny Barker, 1947. Frank Driggs Collection**

time was blown away, had no idea what the hell he was doing. But Fess changed everything—the way people felt grooves, the way people just moved to the changes."

Pianist Eddie Bo made the point more emphatically to Jonathan Foose in *Up from the Cradle of Jazz:* "I don't know if I can find words to describe his talent. Professor Longhair was not from the earth. I think he came from another planet. I've never heard anyone from this earth play like that."

**"Looky there,**

**she ain't got no hair**

**. . . bald head!"**

— *Professor Longhair*

A natural-born cardsharp and gambler, Byrd began to take his playing seriously in 1948, eventually earning a gig at the Caldonia Club. It was there that club owner Mike Tessitore bestowed Byrd with his professorial nickname (due to Byrd's shaggy coiffure). Longhair debuted on wax in 1949 for the Dallas-based Star Talent label, laying down four tracks (including "Professor Longhair's Boogie" and the first version of his signature "Mardi Gras in New Orleans," complete with whistled intro). His band was inexplicably called the Shuffling Hungarians. Union problems forced those sides off the market, but Longhair's next legit date for Mercury (recorded with union sanction) the same year produced his first and only national R&B hit in the hilarious "Baldhead," which peaked at number five in *Billboard*'s R&B chart in August of 1950.

Longhair recorded "Gone So Long" for Federal in 1951, then in November of 1953 he cut a session for Atlantic, which included the immortal "Tipitina" and the infectious boogie "Ball the Wall." After recuperating from a minor stroke, Longhair came back on Leola Rupe's West Coast–based Ebb Records in 1957 with a storming "No Buts—No Maybes." He revived his "Go to the Mardi Gras" for Joe Ruffino's Ron imprint in 1959.

Other than the ambitiously arranged "Big Chief" in 1964 for Watch Records, the '60s held little charm for Longhair. He hit the skids, abandoning his piano playing entirely and taking a job sweeping out a local New Orleans record store. A booking at the fledgling 1971 Jazz & Heritage Festival revived interest in his music and the tireless promotion of Allison Kaslow put him on the comeback trail. There followed a celebrated appearance at the 1973

**Professor Longhair, 1973. Frank Driggs Collection**

Montreux Jazz Festival in Switzerland. In 1977 a group of music fans and entrepreneurs bought a local New Orleans watering hole and rechristened it Tipitina's after Fess's famous song. He played there regularly when he wasn't on the road. Tipitina's remains a thriving operation to this day, bringing in national talent on regular basis.

Fess made a slew of albums in the last decade of his life, topped off by a terrific 1979 set for Alligator, *Crawfish Fiesta*. He later made appearances on the PBS-TV concert series *Soundstage* (with Dr. John, Earl King, and The Meters) and *The Today Show,* and co-starred in the documentary *Piano Players Rarely Ever Play Together* (which became a memorial tribute when Longhair died in the middle of its filming; funeral footage was included).

On the evening of January 30, 1980, Fess went to bed and never woke up. A heart attack in the middle of the night silenced one of New Orleans's seminal and most revered R&B stars. But his music remains anthemic in the Crescent City.

# HUEY "PIANO" SMITH

BORN: January 26, 1934, in New Orleans, Louisiana

HUEY SMITH began playing piano at an early age and was writing songs by the age of seven or eight. "From childhood he had taken jive phrases, children's street poems, and jump-rope rhythms to create lyrics," writes Jason Berry in *Up from the Cradle of Jazz.* "The songs were light and fun, filled with innocent exuberance." His earliest musical influences were Charles Brown, Bull Moose Jackson, Ivory Joe Hunter, Ray Charles, and Hank Williams, but Louis Jordan had the greatest sway over him. "I tried to hear all of his records," Smith said in Jeff Hannusch's *I Hear You Knockin':* "When I couldn't, me and all the kids in the neighborhood would go down to the Lincoln Theatre and see him in those shorts like 'Saturday Night Fish Fry' and 'Reet, Petite and Gone.' If you ask me, that's where rock 'n' roll started. It was with Louis Jordan."

He formed his first group, the Honeyjumpers, at the age of fourteen. Two years later, in 1950, Smith was introduced to Eddie "Guitar Slim" Jones. It was the beginning of a strong musical bond that lasted until the guitarist's mysterious death in 1959. Smith made his first recording as a member of

Eddie Jones and His Playboys, cutting "Bad Luck Is on Me" in 1952. Huey got his first chance to record as a leader in June of 1953, cutting "You Made Me Cry" and "You're Down with Me" for Savoy.

In 1955 Huey would supply the piano on Little Richard's first Specialty session, "Tutti Frutti," while also contributing to Lloyd Price's Specialty sessions and playing on Smiley Lewis's smash hit, "I Hear You Knocking." That same year he played piano on Earl King's classic debut for Ace Records, "Those Lonely, Lonely Nights," then cut the party number "We Like Mambo" for the label (though the composer credit was erroneously listed as Eddie Bo). His second session for Ace later in 1955 (which was properly credited) was "Little Liza Jane."

At the Club Tiajuana, Huey met Bobby Marchan, a singer from Youngstown, Ohio, who led a troupe of female impersonators called The Powder Box Revue. Huey penned some numbers for Marchan, including "Little Chickee Wah Wah." In 1956 Smith went out on the road with Shirley and Lee, who had a smash hit with "Let the Good Times Roll." Marchan and Huey came up with the idea of forming The Clowns, patterning their act after the successful and colorful Coasters. Marchan took over lead vocal duties. During the summer of 1957 they recorded "Rockin' Pneumonia and the Boogie Woogie Flu," with Smith playing off a line from Chuck Berry's "Roll over Beethoven": *I got rockin' pneumonia, sittin' down at a rhythm revue.* It was their breakthrough hit.

> "A-ha-ha-ha . . . haaaay-o. Gooba-gooba-gooba-gooba A-ha-ha-ha. A-ha-ha-ha . . . haaaay-o."
>
> — *Huey Smith*

Other hits followed, including 1958's "Don't You Just Know It," with its catchy call-and-response chorus of "A-ha-ha-ha . . . haaaay-o!" It remained on the Hot 100 charts for thirteen weeks. During The Clowns's tour that year, James Booker impersonated Huey in the band while the leader stayed at home in New Orleans. After a bitter dispute with Ace's founder, Johnny Vincent, over the tune "Sea Cruise" (Vincent stole the idea from him and gave it to singer Frankie Ford to record), Smith left the label and moved to Imperial. He cut eight sides there, including the catchy "Sassy Sarah," "Educated Fool," and "The Little Moron." Meanwhile Vincent released a previously recorded version of "The Popeye" on Ace. It became a surprise hit in 1962. Imperial was so infuriated by the success of that Ace record that Smith was subsequently dropped from the label.

Huey abandoned music in the late '60s, becoming a Jehovah's Witness. He came out of retirement for a reunion with Bobby Marchan at the 1979 New Orleans Jazz & Heritage Festival.

# JAMES BOOKER

BORN: December 17, 1939, in New Orleans, Louisiana
DIED: November 8, 1983, in New Orleans, Louisiana

THE PIANO PRINCE OF NEW ORLEANS was a technically gifted virtuoso who scored a national hit in 1960 for the Duke label with his rocking organ instrumental "Gonzo." He subsequently toured with Lionel Hampton, The Coasters, and B. B. King and for a time got plenty of studio work, appearing as a session player on hundreds of dates from blues and Dixieland to pop with the likes of Ringo Starr, Dr. John, Aretha Franklin, The Doobie Brothers, Bobby "Blue" Bland, Maria Muldaur, and The Grateful Dead.

A longtime heroin addict who was also openly gay, Booker lived his entire life against the grain. As Jason Berry put it in *Up from the Cradle of Jazz:* "He was a man of bizarre eccentricities whose life was a study in struggle. Thin, kaleidoscopic in moods, he appeared larger than he was by sheer force of personality. He was blind in one eye and when he wore sunglasses and a trenchcoat he looked mysterious. Booker was an outrageous, extravagantly funny man, yet a loner whose handful of friends were bar owners and booking agents who never quite knew how to handle him."

After doing time in Angola State Penitentiary on a narcotics bust, Booker came out in 1974 with a rollicking intro to "Goodnight Irene" that started: "This song was written by a dude named Leadbelly. Leadbelly and Little Booker both had the pleasure of partying on the Ponderosa, you dig? Up there at Angola."

As Michael Goodwin pointed out in a *Village Voice* review of 1989: "He sang in an inimitable, ironic, self-mocking tone—half-giggle, half-howl. Sometimes it sounded as if he were going mad." And yet, he explained himself on the title track from *Classified:*

> *Don't call me crazy, don't you dare call me all out of my name*
> *If you had my feelings, I'm quite sure you'd feel the same.*

*Some say I'm crazy, some say that I'm dumb.*
*It doesn't mean that they know where I'm comin' from.*

An idiosyncratic genius who somehow combined Chopin and Fess with touches of Jerry Lee Lewis, Erroll Garner, and Jelly Roll Morton and whose flair for melodic embellishment was unparalleled, James Carroll Booker III started off on saxophone at the age of nine before switching to piano the following year. He studied classical piano with his sister at the age of twelve, while simultaneously soaking up boogie-woogie. By fourteen he was considered a child prodigy. In 1953 he formed his first band, Booker Boy and the Rhymaries, with Art Neville and Curtis Groves, and in 1954 recorded "Doing the Hambone" for Imperial Records, under the supervision of Dave Bartholomew. In 1955 he gigged frequently with guitarist Earl King and toured with singer Joe Tex. There followed some more recording opportunities with Chess in 1956 and Ace in 1957 as well as tours backing the popular singing team of Shirley and Lee in 1958.

Booker recorded again for Ace in 1958, cutting "Open the Door" and "Teenage Rock," doubling on piano and organ. But when Ace's Johnny Vincent overdubbed Joe Tex's vocals on those tracks, Booker left the label in a huff and went out on tour with Huey "Piano" Smith's band, The Clowns, subbing for the bandleader himself. By 1960 he had signed a contract with the Duke label and hit big with "Gonzo," which climbed to number ten on the R&B charts. The surprising success of that Duke debut led to five years of sessions for the label and touring gigs with the likes of Joe Tex, Roy Hamilton, and Wilson Pickett.

**"Unique distinction has never known nor visited a more worthy servant such as myself."**

*— James Booker*

Following a dark year in Angola (he was released from prison in 1968), Booker migrated to New York and dropped off the scene for several years. But he emerged in 1975 as part of an American R&B tour in Europe. In the spring of 1976 producer Joe Boyd took him into the studio to cut his first album, *Junco Partner,* a solo piano album characterized by Booker's rollicking, rowdy keyboard style, classical flourishes, and wild sense of abandon in the vocal department.

He remained active (and still addicted to heroin) through the '70s and early '80s. Then on the night of November 8, 1983, the self-proclaimed Black Liberace quietly expired in the waiting room of Charity Hospital at the age of forty-three.

# DR. JOHN

BORN: November 20, 1941, in New Orleans, Louisiana

IN HIS AUDACIOUS 1995 AUTOBIOGRAPHY, *Under a Hoodoo Moon*— a "little book of rememberations" that stands alongside Babs Gonzales's *I Paid My Dues* and Danny Barker's *A Jazz in Life* for sheer entertainment value—Mac Rebennack expresses the everlasting hold that the Crescent City has over him: "New Orleans remains its own strange self, and more than a little bit out of synch with other places in the United States. This is one of its charms, but also a curse."

The eccentric charm that characterizes New Orleans has also been imbued in Rebennack's music since he began recording in the late 1950s, long before he adopted the *nom de funk* Dr. John. Growing up in New Orleans's Third Ward, he took piano lessons from one of the nuns at church and also picked up some boogie-woogie licks from his hip aunt Andre. And all through his childhood young Mac would spin all the latest records at his father's radio and appliance shop, which was also well stocked with "race" records by the likes of Roosevelt Sykes, Champion Jack Dupree, T-Bone Walker, Lightin' Hopkins, and Memphis Minnie.

> **"I been in the right place, but it musta been the wrong time."**
> — *Dr. John*

As a teen Mac worked as a gofer, running scag to eager clients when he wasn't hanging out at Cosimo Matassa's recording studio on Governor Nicholls Street. As Shirley Goodman told Tad Jones in *Up from the Cradle of Jazz:* "He'd run errands for Cosimo, listen to the playback and bug the musicians to show him things on their instruments. Everybody liked Mac, but sometimes Cosimo or Dave [Bartholomew] would chase him out of there."

During this time he became friends with Alvin Red Tyler and Lee Allen and began taking guitar lessons with Walter "Papoose" Nelson, the guitarist in Fats Domino's band. He later took up lessons with Roy Montrell and started playing gigs with Montrell's aunt, a sanctified gospel performer named Sister Elizabeth Eustace.

While still attending Jesuit High School, Rebennack formed his first band, The Dominos, which performed Fats Domino tunes at an annual talent show. Mac made quite an impression with his wild rock 'n' roll guitar playing and posturing. In 1957 he dropped out of Jesuit midway through his junior year to pursue music full-time. He cut his first session with saxophonist Leonard James shortly thereafter—an instrumental "Boppin' and Strollin'" under James's name.

In March of 1958 Rebennack joined the local Musicians Union and began writing songs in earnest. One his earliest successes, co-penned with Seth Davis, was "Lights Out," a risqué rocker that Jerry Byrne cut for Specialty that year:

*Standing on the front porch,*
*I grabbed her and kissed her.*
*Boy, was I surprised when I saw her little sister.*
*Lights out! Lights out!*
*I'm glad to know that the lights were out.*
*Sister knows more about*
*What to do when the lights go out.*

Over the course of 1958 and 1959, Mac gigged with Jimmy Clanton, Big Boy Myles, Joe Tex, Clyde McPhatter, Roy Brown, and James "Sugar Boy" Crawford. During this same period he released singles with Ronnie & The Delinquents ("Bad Neighborhood") and Morgus & the 3 Ghouls ("Morgus the Magnificent"). He also took a job as an A&R man for Johnny Vincent's Ace label, overseeing and playing on sessions for the likes of Huey "Piano" Smith, Lee Allen, Eddie Bo, Earl King, Frankie Ford, Paul Gayten, and a dozen others. An ugly incident in 1961 nearly ended his guitar-playing career. As he recounts in his book:

"On Christmas Eve my little band and I took a gig at a joint in Jacksonville, Florida. We was getting ready to go to the gig when we realized that [singer] Ronnie Barron, who always took forever to do hisself up for the gigs, had disappeared. I went to look for him and found him being pistol-whipped by the motel owner, who'd caught Ronnie with his old lady. I went to get the gun out of the guy's hand. We wrestled for it. I thought my left hand was

over the handle but I was actually grabbing the barrel. We started in Ronnie's room and ended up outside in a brick garden. I looked down and saw the ring finger of my left hand, my fretting hand, hanging by a thread."

New Orleans doctors were able to reconstruct the finger, but a year passed before he regained full use of it. He soon shifted his energies to piano and, with James Booker's help, learned to play organ. As Booker told Jason Berry in *Up from the Cradle of Jazz:* "I went down to Bourbon Street and played at one club called Papa Joe's, and the guy heard me play and he bought three organs because he had two other places, Madame Franchine's and Poodle's Patio. I played all three of those places every night, and when it got to taxing my body, I called on Dr. John and taught him how to play organ and let him be my understudy. That's how he started playing organ."

In 1963 New Orleans district attorney (and soon-to-be Kennedy conspiracy theorist) Jim Garrison closed down a lot of the clubs on Bourbon Street that featured music as a backdrop for such illicit activities as drug sales and prostitution. "There was no work left in New Orleans," Mac explained in an interview. "If I wanted to keep playing music, I had to leave town and go out to the West Coast." In Los Angeles Rebennack fell in with a clique of New Orleans musicians, including Alvin Robinson, Jessie Hill, and Harold Battiste, who arranged for Mac to join the Sonny & Cher band and also recommended him to other producers for session work, which came in droves.

By 1967 Rebennack was ready to reinvent himself. He had long harbored the idea of making a series of records based on the voodoo myth of Dr. John, a real-life Senegalese prince who lived and conjured in New Orleans in the 1840s. As he writes in his book: "Through my contacts with gris-gris and spiritual church people and by reading New Orleans history that my sister and others had turned me on to, I had begun to dig the importance of Dr. John as an early spiritual leader of the New Orleans community. But it was when I read a piece by the 19th century writer Lafcadio Hearn that my head really got turned seriously around. In Hearn's story, I found that Dr. John and one Pauline Rebennack were busted in the 1840s for having a voodoo operation and possibly a whorehouse. I don't know for sure, but there's a strong chance that Pauline Rebennack was one of my relatives, so I feel more than an incidental sympathy for the man whose name I took as a stage name in 1967."

The resulting album for Atlantic, *Gris-Gris,* was built on street chants,

**Dr. John, the Night Tripper (aka Mac Rebennack), 1968. Frank Driggs Collection**

words half-spoken, half-sung, and a dark, psychedelic undercurrent that was later referred to as "voodoo rock." As he told writer Jeff Hannusch for the liner notes to *Mos' Scocious: The Dr. John Anthology* (Rhino): "I knew [Atlantic president] Ahmet Ertegun was upset about it. He was stuck with another record he didn't know what the hell to do with. It wasn't exactly somethin' you could fit into a slot. You couldn't put your finger on what the hell it was. It was voodoo music, but there is not exactly a calling for that in the marketplace. It just happened that we fit into the psychedelic movement."

The tune "Gris-Gris Gumbo Ya-Ya" on that Atlantic debut also introduced Rebennack's alter ego:

> *They call me Dr. John,*
> *I'm known as the Night Tripper,*
> *Got a satchel of gris-gris in my hand.*
> *Got many clients come from miles around*
> *Runnin' down my prescriptions.*
> *I got medicines, cure all y'alls ills.*
> *I got remedies of every description.*

With the release of that bit of voodoo-inspired exotica in the early part of 1968, Rebennack began building a fervent underground following with his music and eccentric stage presence, which incorporated such ceremonial aspects of New Orleans life as second-line parading and Mardi Gras costuming. As Jason Berry/Tad Jones/Jonathan Foose wrote in *Up from the Cradle of Jazz:*

"He burned candles and incense to set the mood and, like a warrior preparing for battle, suited up in stages. On his head he wore a turban or crown laced with plumes of red, orange and aqua; he put yellow, blue and red greasepaint on his face, with sprinklings of glitter dust. He wore long robes with tassels, and around his neck hung necklaces, bones, crosses and a small drum on a cord. He cut a striking figure in all those feathers and colors—throwing glitter dust into the audience."

*Gris-Gris* sold fifty thousand copies in its initial release and spawned a series of similarly idiosyncratic N'awlins–flavored swamp-rock-voodoo outings like *Baylon* (1969), *Remedies* (1970), and *The Sun, The Moon & Herbs* (1971). Dr. John dipped heavily into a roots bag on 1972's *Gumbo*, resurrecting Fess's classics "Big Chief" and "Tipitina's," Earl King's "Those Lonely, Lonely Nights" and Sugar Boy Crawford's "Jock-A-Mo" (retitled "Iko Iko") along with a Huey "Piano" Smith medley of "High Blood Pressure"/"Don't You Just Know It"/"Well I'll Be John Brown." That landmark album brought a great deal of worldwide attention to the New Orleans R&B tradition and also marked the end of the gris-gris/voodoo-rock phase of Rebennack's colorful career.

Mac saw a commercial breakthrough in 1973 with the release of the Allen Toussaint–produced *In the Right Place,* which featured solidly funky instrumental backing from The Meters. The pubic instantly connected with the killer radioplay hit, "Right Place, Wrong Time," which led to television appearances on NBC's *Midnight Special,* Don Kirshner's *Rock Concert,* and PBS's *Sound Stage* as well as concert appearances in London, Paris, and at the Montreux Jazz Festival.

Rebennack continued to release solidly funky New Orleans–flavored material through the '70s and '80s while also teaming with songwriting partner Doc Pomus on material for a variety of other artists, including B. B. King and Johnny Adams. In 1989 he teamed with producer Tommy LiPuma (the man who helped George Benson break through to mainstream acceptance in 1976 with *Breezin'*) for a classy set of big-band arrangements of Tin Pan Alley tunes entitled *In a Sentimental Mood.* A duet with Rickie Lee Jones on "Makin' Whoopie" from that album received a Grammy Award for Best Jazz Vocal Performance the following year.

1992's *Goin' Back to New Orleans* was Rebennack's love letter to his Crescent City roots, including old anthems like "Basin Street Blues" and "Didn't He Ramble," Jelly Roll Morton's "I Thought I Heard Buddy Bolden Say," Louis Armstrong's "I'll Be Glad When You're Dead, You Rascal You," Fats Domino's "Goin' Home Tomorrow," Smiley Lewis's "Blue Monday," Buddy Johnson's "Since I Fell for You," and an inspired reading of Louis Moreu Gottschalk's "Litanie des Saints."

Following the slamming funk of 1994's *Television,* 1995's *Afterglow* repeated the formula of *In a Sentimental Mood,* this time with John Clayton providing hip big-band arrangements of Louis Jordan's "I Know What I've Got," Irving Berlin's "Blue Skies," Duke Ellington's "I'm Just a Lucky So-and-So," and Tin Pan Alley nuggets like "I'm Confessin' (That I Love You)" and "Gee Baby, Ain't I Good to You." The album also allowed Mac to stretch out on piano, flashing his considerable N'awlins chops (or as he calls it, "radiatin' the 88s").

On his most recent offering, *Duke Elegant,* Dr. John puts a decidedly personal spin on Ellingtonia, which proves the old adage: You can take the boy out of New Orleans but you can't take New Orleans out of the boy. As Mac explains in the liner notes to *Goin' Back to New Orleans:*

"Here I am, Dr. John, born and raised in New Orleans, brought up to the sounds of music. Night and day. Barrelhouse and Junkie Blues, Funky Butt, Gut Bucket, and all that Jazz . . . Music to make you dance and shake your butt until your butt is funky. The most important thing to remember is this: New Orleans music was not invented, it just kind of grew up naturally, joyously, just for fun. No deep psychological traumatic jive. Never. Just plain, down to earth, happy times music. When I was growing up in New Orleans, just a little weed-hopper from the Third Ward, I used to think, 'Oh man, this music makes me feel the best!' That's it. It's music where you can laugh at yourself, laugh at the music, knowing you're having a helluva time."

This is a perfect epitaph for this living ambassador of New Orleans good-time music.

# MR. GOOGLE EYES

———————◆———————

BORN: September 13, 1931, in New Orleans, Louisiana

AN EARLY INSPIRATION for Deacon John, Earl King, Johnny Adams, Ernie K-Doe, and Dr. John, singer Joe August (aka Mr. G, aka Mr. Google Eyes) was born in the same lower Ninth Ward neighborhood that produced Fats Domino. August began singing in public as a kid at Dooky Chase, the restaurant where he worked during the day delivering sandwiches on his bike. (The proprietor was the one who bestowed the nickname "Mr. Google Eyes" due to his propensity for ogling the ladies while he was supposed to be working.) When he was just fourteen years old, August began making the rounds of the city's clubs around 1945, singing opposite Roy Brown and working with top-notch acts like Paul Gayten and Annie Laurie. Billed as "Mr. Google Eyes—the world's youngest blues singer" he played the Downbeat Club, Dew Drop Inn, The Pelican, Foster's, and the Plum Room. He even once engaged in a celebrated "Battle of the Blues" with Billy Eckstine at the Club Desire. "In fact, he was the first one to call me Mr. G,"

**"Hey waitress . . . your name Caroline. Come on here, girl. Bring me some wine."**
— *Mr. Google Eyes*

he told Jeff Hannusch in *I Hear You Knockin'*, "because they were callin' him Mr. B."

Mr. G's first recordings in 1946 were "Poppa Stoppa's Be-Bop Blues" (named after the popular New Orleans deejay, a ploy to ensure himself some airplay) and "Real Young Boy (Just 16 Years Old)" for Coleman Records. He did four recordings for the regional label, backed by Lee Allen and Paul Gayten. Columbia bought out his Coleman contract and had him record the jivey Louis Jordan–inspired jump blues "No Wine, No Women" along with Paul Gayten's "For You My Love," backed by Billy Ford and His Musical V-8s. During this time the husky-voiced singer became one of the city's top rhythm and blues attractions. Dig Dr. John's assessment of Mr. G's panache, as described in *Under a Hoodoo Moon*:

"The first time I ever laid eyes on him, he was luxuriating outside his club in a purple Buick with leopard skin upholstery and leopard skin covering the dash and lining the trunk. It was some eye-popping car, but G had the style to drive a set of wheels like that. G played his club with his own badass, low-down, bebop scat-jazz r&b act. I used to go and watch G because I knew he knew how to work a house. I'd bring the singer with my band along and tell him to keep his eyes on Mr. Google Eyes. G would get down there, pull his coat back, rear back on the crowd, talk shit and work 'em. That's an artform; people don't know nothing about that today."

Mr. G moved to Newark, New Jersey, in the mid-1950s and worked New York clubs like Birdland, where he played opposite the likes of Miles Davis and Gene Ammons. He later cut some sessions for Savoy with the Johnny Otis Orchestra. Years after the limelight had faded, in 1980 and 1981, he hosted a Dew Drop Inn revival at the Contemporary Arts Center in New Orleans.

# LLOYD PRICE

BORN: March 9, 1932, in Kenner, Louisiana

A SELF-DESCRIBED "COUNTRY BOY" from Kenner, Louisiana, Lloyd Price was writing songs in grade school and by the age of thirteen he was playing both trumpet and piano as well as singing in his Sunday school choir. At the age of eighteen he put together his first band, The Blue Boys, and took a job at a nightclub called The Top of the Town in suburban Kenner. Around that time a popular disc jockey on WBOK named Okey Dokey used an expression, "Lawdy Miss Clawdy," which inspired Price to write the song of the same name. Produced by local big-band leader Dave Bartholomew (and featuring the signature piano work of Fats Domino), the tune became a hit for Art Rupe's Specialty label in 1952 and was named Record of the Year in both *Billboard* and *Cashbox*.

The flip side of that megahit, which paved the way to early rock 'n' roll, was "Mailman Blues," a jump blues inspired by Lionel Hampton's hit "Flying Home" from ten years earlier.

Price toured extensively in 1952 on the strength of his million-seller jukebox hit "Lawdy Miss Clawdy," appearing at large venues like the Apollo Theatre in New York, the Howard Theater in Washington, D.C., and the Royal Theater in Baltimore. A March 1953 review in *Color* magazine describes a typical Price show at the time: "When Lawdy Lawdy Mr. Clawdy gets hot, they stop dancing and swoon all around him. He stampedes 'em. He must have had rhythm in his nursery rhymes because he rocks the crowd. The police often have to come in and pull the ladies arms from around him for they hug him and kiss him. They usually stop dancing and make a huge circle and pile all around him to watch the members of his combo do their stuff."

**"Oh now lawdy, lawdy, lawdy Miss Clawdy, girl what you done to me."**

— *Lloyd Price*

Price followed up his initial burst of success with tunes like "Chee Koo Baby," featuring some great second-line drumming by Earl Palmer, and "Oo-Ee Baby." He continued churning out popular recordings for Specialty, including "Froglegs" and the quintessentially N'awlins "Where You At?"—both recorded in 1953—and "Night and Day Blues," recorded in 1954, at which point he was drafted. After a two-year stint in the Army, which included a tour of duty in Korea, Price cut three more sessions for Specialty in 1956—"I'm Glad, Glad," "Baby Please Come Home," and "Forgive Me, Clawdy." While he was away, Elvis Presley had cut "Lawdy Miss Clawdy" on his first album for Sun Records.

In 1958 Price formed his own regional label, KRC Records, and released the plaintive ballad "Just Because." The record was later picked up for national distribution by ABC-Paramount. Price's canny updating of an age-old Crescent City blues number "Stagger Lee" became a number one R&B hit the following year, prompting an appearance on Dick Clark's popular

*American Bandstand* TV show. Over the next couple of years he had a string of hits under the auspices of ABC-Paramount, including "I'm Gonna Get Married," "Where Were You (On Our Wedding Day)," and "Personality," which shot up the pop charts in 1959.

Price left ABC-Paramount in 1962 to launch his own Double L Records (Wilson Pickett made his solo debut for the label in 1963). In the late '60s he formed an all-star big band that featured James Booker, then in 1969 he started up Turntable Records and had a sizable hit with "Bad Conditions." In subsequent years he recorded for Monument, Encore, Jac, and Wand before joining forces with notorious boxing impresario Don King to launch the LPG label in 1976.

After living in Africa during the latter part of the '70s, Price returned to America in the early '80s. He largely resisted performing until a 1993 European tour with Jerry Lee Lewis, Little Richard, and Gary U. S. Bonds convinced him there was still a market for his bouncy, upbeat oldies.

# ERNIE K-DOE

BORN: February 22, 1936, in New Orleans, Louisiana

THE NINTH OF ELEVEN CHILDREN fathered by a Baptist preacher, Ernest Kador came up emulating the volatile gospel-drenched vocal stylings of Archie Brown Lee, lead singer of The Five Blind Boys of Mississippi. He went on to sing as a boy with such spiritual groups as the Golden Choir Jubilees of New Orleans and the Divine Travelers. At the age of fifteen he won a talent contest for dancing and singing. At the age of seventeen he moved to Chicago with his mother and began going around to clubs that sponsored amateur shows. In the Windy City he was introduced to the music of such secular singing groups as The Four Blazers, the Moonglows, and the Flamingos.

"The worse person
I know . . .
mother-in-law."
— *Ernie K-Doe*

While still in Chicago, K-Doe did a blues session on November 30, 1953, for United Records. He returned to New Orleans in 1954 and formed his own group, The Blue Diamonds. They became a regular attraction at the Tiajuana Club, where K-Doe also acted as master of cere-monies. In June of 1954 Kador cut "Honey Baby" backed with "No Money" at Cosimo's studio for the Savoy label. That record made some noise region-ally and Kador's reputation spread during the mid-1950s through frequent performances at the Dew Drop Inn and Sho Bar on Bourbon Street along with his regular appearances at the Tiajuana.

In 1955 Specialty Records recorded his "Do Baby Do" and "Eternity," neither of which scored nearly as big as Little Richard's "Tutti Frutti," which the label had also released around the same time. In 1955 he cut "Tuff Enough" for New York's Ember label and then in 1960 he jumped to Minit Records and debuted with "Make You Love Me" backed with "Where There's a Will, There's a Way." His second Minit release, "Hello My Lover" backed with "Tain't It the Truth," sold eighty thousand copies. It was at that point that Kador switched the spelling of his name to K-Doe.

His third single for Minit, cut in March of 1961, became the hit of a life-time. "Mother-in-Law," a catchy number aided by Benny Spellman's authori-tative bass vocal and background vocals by Willie Harper and Calvin LeBlanc of The Del Royals, is the song with which K-Doe will forever be associated. Written by Allen Toussaint, it rose to number one on the R&B charts and the pop charts just a month after it was issued. ("Mother-in-Law" was subsequently revived by Herman's Hermits in 1966, by Clarence Carter in 1973, and by Huey Lewis in 1994.)

In the wake of that smash hit K-Doe embarked on a national whirlwind tour, headlining with the likes of Sam Cooke, Jerry Butler, Joe Tex, James Brown, and Little Willie John. His follow-up recording, "Te-Ta-Te-Ta-Ta," was penned by K-Doe himself while its flip side, "Rub-Dub-Dub," was co-penned with Robert Parker. Also in 1962 K-Doe released "Popeye Joe" to sat-isfy the demand for the Popeye dance craze, which had outstripped the Twist for local popularity.

K-Doe's 1962 showdown with James Brown at the Municipal Auditorium in New Orleans was legendary. As he told Jeff Hannusch in *I Hear You Knockin'*: "It was the biggest battle of my life. You see, it was a dressing thing . . . New Orleans against Macon, Georgia, and I sure wasn't gonna let New Orleans down. I had a royal blue smoking jacket on but under that, nobody knew. Then James Brown came out in a brown suit, white shirt, brown polka dot tie. But while the announcer was talking, everybody went to screaming. You see, when I pulled off that smoking jacket, guess what? Everything else I had on was ice blue. And on 'Certain Girl' I changed suits nine times! I had a clothes rack and a valet backstage. Every time I'd get to a certain part in the song, I'd just run straight around to the side, change my suit and come back out the other side."

A dynamic showman who is given to splits and spins and acrobatic microphone work, K-Doe continued to entertain crowds through subsequent decades, even though he was never again able to break into the Hot 100. After a successful association with the Imperial-distributed Minit Records, K-Doe switched to the Duke label in 1964 and tried going the sequel route with "Mother-in-Law (Is in My Hair Again)" for the Duke label. In 1967 he had moderate success with "Later for Tomorrow" and a remake of "Until the Real Thing Comes Along" for Duke. Then in 1970 he reunited with hit-maker Toussaint for an album that was released on the Janus label.

In 1982 K-Doe began hosting a radio show on WWOZ, a popular community-sponsored FM station. His on-air antics and constant brags like "I'm cocky, but I'm good" made it perhaps the most popular underground program of its type in the city. In 1995 the singer-deejay expanded his horizons by opening his Ernie K-Doe Mother-in-Law nightclub, where he appears regularly on weekends. He continued to record a host of jive-laden funk albums into the '80s and '90s for various local New Orleans labels.

At the age of sixty-four, Ernie K-Doe still has a strong desire to perform. He says he enjoys singing because it gives him a feeling of happiness and joy. Plus he still gets a special kick from hearing audiences yell out, "Burn! K-Doe, burn!"

# JAMES "SUGAR BOY" CRAWFORD

BORN: October 12, 1934, in New Orleans, Louisiana

ONE OF THE MORE NOTEWORTHY practitioners of New Orleans–flavored jive during the 1950s was singer-pianist Sugar Boy Crawford. Best-known for his explosive "Jock-A-Mo," Crawford led the bands The Chapaka Shawee, The Cane Cutters, and The Sugar Lumps. Crawford remained active up until the early '60s. His career ended prematurely after he was permanently injured and nearly killed by an overzealous police officer in Monroe, Louisiana, at which point he found solace in the church.

James Crawford Jr. started out in music when he formed a high school band called The Chapaka Shawee. After their first job in 1952 the Shawee youngsters developed a good local following. In November of 1952 they cut their first and last session for Aladdin, "One Sunday Morning" and "No One to Love Me," which featured a weeping monologue by Sugar Boy. In 1953 they recorded "I Don't Know What I'll Do" as Sugar Boy Crawford and The Cane Cutters for the Chess label.

By early 1954 guitarist Snooks Eaglin joined The Cane Cutters and together they cut the anthemic "Jock-A-Mo," among the first records to capture the festive spirit of Carnival (the entire season of merry-making that permeates the Crescent City beginning January 6 and culminating with Mardi Gras Day). The record sold heavily in New Orleans during the Carnival season of 1954 and was subsequently covered by a host of New Orleans musicians, including Professor Longhair and Dr. John. "We used to see the Indians a lot because we lived near the Battlefield [Claiborne and Poydras Streets]," Crawford told Jeff Hannusch in *I Hear You Knockin'*. "I never was interested in being an Indian, because to tell you the truth I was afraid of them. Back then they used to carry real hatchets that they decorated. On Mardi Gras Day they'd be running around the neighborhood singing and shouting. If they ran into another tribe that they didn't like, somebody was gonna get hurt."

**"Talkin' 'bout hey now, hey now, Iko Iko ande."**
— *Sugar Boy Crawford*

In 1956 Crawford recorded four singles for Imperial, all supervised by Bartholomew. "She's Got a Wobble (When She Walks)" made some noise regionally along with "Morning Star." But by 1958, when Imperial turned its attention almost exclusively to rising star Ricky Nelson, the black artists on the roster got lost in the shuffle.

Crawford continued to record for small labels, and had some success with "Have a Little Mercy" in 1961. Then in 1963 the tragedy struck that nearly ended his life. As he recalled to Jeff Hannusch in *I Hear You Knockin'*: "It was in '63, when everybody was upset because of the freedom marches. We were driving to a job and the police pulled us over in Monroe, Louisiana. They said I was drunk and speeding. The police pulled me out of the car and hit me with a pistol. They knocked a hole in my head and I ended up in the hospital in Monroe for three weeks before I was transferred back home. I was paralyzed for about a year. I was just like an infant. I had a blood clot on the brain. I couldn't hear, I couldn't see or walk. I was almost dead. They had to operate on me to put a plate in my head. I came back gradually but I had to be constantly watched for two years. The first time I looked at a piano, I knew what it was, but I didn't remember how to play it." Since 1969 Sugar Boy's performing has been confined to singing spirituals in church.

# JESSIE HILL

BORN: December 9, 1932, in New Orleans, Louisiana
DIED: September 17, 1996, in New Orleans, Louisiana

A ONE-TIME DRUMMER for Professor Longhair, Jessie Hill attained stardom with his wild call-and-response novelty number from 1959, "Ooh Poo Pah Do," the first hit for Joe Manashak and Larry McKinley's Minit Records. The tune grabbed listeners with its funky N'awlins calypso rhythm and its foreboding line: *I won't stop trying 'til I create a disturbance in your mind.* After a period of regional popularity, it broke nationally in 1960 and was later covered by everyone from Wilson Pickett, Rufus Thomas, Ike & Tina Turner, Paul Revere & The Raiders, and The Righteous Brothers to Mitch Ryder & The Detroit Wheels. But Hill, who came to be known as "Mr. Ooh Poo Pah Do," cut the definitive version that lives on through time.

> **"I wanna tell you about Ooh Poo Pah Do."**
> — *Jessie Hill*

Hill hailed from the same Ninth Ward neighborhood that produced Fats Domino, Prince La La, and Walter "Papoose" Nelson, as well as Popee, David, Melvin, and Betty Ann Lastie. He also befriended Eddie Bo and Oliver Morgan as a youth. His first group was The House Rockers, formed in 1952 with David and Melvin Lastie. Popular New Orleans singer Mr. Google Eyes also remembers using the same group to back him at the Club Desire around that time.

In 1954, after touring the Midwest with The House Rockers, Hill began working a steady gig as the drummer with Professor Longhair. In the late '50s he took over the drummer's stool for a short time with Huey "Piano"

Smith's The Clowns, which also featured pianist James Booker and singer Bobby Marchan. Then in 1958 he left The Clowns and got The House Rockers back together with Alvin "Shine" Robinson on guitar, Richard Payne on bass, and John Boudreaux on drums.

Allen Toussaint produced the 1959 session that produced "Ooh Poo Pah Doo." Hill's follow-up releases like "Highhead Blues," "Scoop Scoobie Doobie," "I Got Mine," and "Oogzey Moo" couldn't capture the magic of his first release and he bowed out of Minit in 1962 with the sequel number, "I Can't Get Enough of That Ooh Poo Pah Doo."

After relocating to Los Angeles in 1963, Hill formed a songwriting partnership with Mac Rebennack (their publishing company was called I Found It). Together they penned songs for everyone from Aretha Franklin and Tina Turner to Sonny & Cher, Junior Parker, and Willie Nelson. He made a disappointing album for Blue Thumb in 1970 (*Naturally*) before returning to his Crescent City home in 1977. In subsequent years, he maintained a presence around town at the New Orleans Jazz & Heritage Festival and local clubs like Tipitina's, always concluding his sets with his four-million-seller, "Ooh Poo Pah Do." He remained active up until his death in 1996.

# LEE DORSEY

BORN: December 24, 1926, in New Orleans, Louisiana
DIED: December 2, 1986, in New Orleans, Louisiana

A FORMER UNDEFEATED lightweight boxing contender known as Kid Chocolate, Irving Lee Dorsey quit the fight game in 1955, returned to his native New Orleans from Portland, Oregon, and became a body and fender repairman. He married in 1957 and would eventually become the father of eleven children. But along the way, through a twist of fate, Dorsey took a detour out of the body and fender business. As he recalled to Jeff Hannusch in *I Hear You Knockin'*:

"I used to sing to make my work go easier, but I wasn't thinking of making no records. Then one day this guy came in to get his car fixed [independent producer Reynauld Richard] and he said, 'Hey, you wanna make a record?' I said, 'Sure.' I didn't think he was serious but he was. That evening he left $50 and told me to come down to Cosimo's studio on Govenor Nicholls. I went down that evening after I cleaned up from work. I didn't have any songs but Richard asked me if I could write a poem. 'Sure,' I said, 'I can come up with that.' So I wrote, 'Rock, Pretty Baby' and 'Lonely Evening,' and as it turned out they made a little bit of noise."

That single came out on Cosimo's Tex label in 1957. Next up was "Lottie-Mo," which got him booked on Dick Clark's *American Bandstand*. It did so well on the local charts that ABC-Paramount picked it up for national distribution. Then in 1961 Dorsey hit big with "Ya Ya," an infectious ditty that reached number one on the R&B charts and number seven on the Hot 100 in late 1961, ultimately going gold. That year Dorsey went out on package tours with such big names as Big Joe Turner, Chuck Berry, T-Bone Walker, and James Brown with his Famous Flames. His next release, "Do-Re-Me," written by Earl King, incorporated the same nursery rhyme approach of "Ya Ya" and scored with listeners once again ("Do re me fa so la ti, forget about the dough and think about me").

**"Sittin' here la la, waitin' for my ya ya."**
— *Lee Dorsey*

In 1965 he did "Ride Your Pony" for Amy Bell Records. It was his first hit in four years. On a roll, he continued the momentum in 1966 with "Get out of My Life Woman" and "Workin' in a Coal Mine," his second gold record (covered in the '80s by the new-wave provocateurs Devo). Dorsey's last recordings to make the charts were 1967's "Go Go Girl" and "My Old Car."

In 1969 in a catch-up bid to try to sound "with it," he released the single "Everything I Do Gonna Be Funky." Dorsey's *Yes We Can* from 1970 featured "Sneaking Sally thru the Alley," which would later be covered by British pop star Robert Palmer. The album's title track and single, "Yes We Can," made it to number forty-six but inspired a more successful version by the Pointer Sisters a few years later.

Dorsey continued recording in the '70s, releasing *Night People* in 1977 on ABC-Paramount. A 1979 motorcycle accident (he was broadsided by a car being chased by the police) brought his career to an abrupt halt. He worked the 1980 New Orleans Jazz & Heritage Festival from a wheelchair and passed away in 1986.

# EDDIE BO

BORN: September 20, 1937, in New Orleans, Louisiana

EDWIN JOSEPH BOCAGE, known to music lovers around the world as Eddie Bo, was born in New Orleans, raised in Algiers and the Ninth Ward. His family was legendary in the traditional jazz community; cousins Peter, Henry, and Charles had all made important contributions playing with the finest jazz orchestras prior to World War II. After graduating from Booker T. Washington High School and spending time abroad in the Army, he returned to New Orleans to study composition and arranging at the Grunewald School of Music. It was here that Eddie Bo developed a unique style of piano playing and arranging that incorporated complex bebop voicings, influenced by his

**"You better check Mr. Popeye 'cause Olive's in the danger zone."**

— *Eddie Bo*

love of jazz piano greats Art Tatum and Oscar Peterson, and also blended in the rhumba-boogie of New Orleans own piano legend Professor Longhair. Ultimately the combination of styles that became Eddie Bo's trademark was an uptown, jazz-tinged take on New Orleans R&B that was more relaxed and laid-back than that of most New Orleans pianists.

As singer-guitarist-producer and prolific composer, Bo was a versatile session musician and recording artist in New Orleans. Through the '50s and '60s he recorded for various labels, including Ace, Ric, Scram, Apollo, Rip, Seven B., Blue Jay, Chess, and At Last Records. On Ric Records, Bo scored a monster hit in 1962 with "Check Mr. Popeye," a salute to one of New Orleans's periodic dance crazes that was perhaps inspired by the Crescent City's favorite fried chicken chain. He later acted as a producer for Rip and Instant Records, for which he had a Top 40 R&B hit in 1969 with the funky "Hook & Sling—Part I." In a career that spans more than forty-five years, Bo has made more 45s than any artist has in New Orleans other than Fats Domino. He has produced records for Irma Thomas, Robert Parker, Art Neville, Chris Kenner, Al "Carnival Time" Johnson, and Johnny Adams.

During the 1950s Eddie Bo led a group of stellar New Orleans sidemen around the country, backing such vocalists as Ruth Brown, Big Joe Turner, Lloyd Price, Smiley Lewis, Earl King, the Wild Magnolias, Algiers Brass

Band, Treme Brass Band, Johnny Adams, and The Platters. As a vocalist he is one of a kind, as a pianist he transcends categories.

From May 28 to 30, 1997, Eddie explored new territory by performing in Karachi, Pakistan, at the American Food & Music Festival at the Karachi Sheraton. As a prelude to that groundbreaking adventure, Mayor Marc Morial declared May 22, 1997, as Eddie Bo Day in New Orleans and named Eddie New Orleans's Ambassador to Pakistan. Still busy performing and recording, Eddie does a happy-hour set with his band at Tipitina's French Quarter every Friday and Saturday and he frequently rocks the house at Storyville on Bourbon Street.

# CLARENCE "FROGMAN" HENRY

BORN: March 19, 1937, in New Orleans, Louisiana

ON THE STRENGTH OF A NOVELTY SONG in which he alternately sings like a girl and like a frog, the aptly-named Clarence "Frogman" Henry hurtled to international stardom in 1957. Paul Gayten produced the froggy feature "Ain't Got No Home" for the Argo label. It quickly became a novelty smash hit. Henry's vocal trickerations turned "Ain't Got No Home" into a number three R&B hit and a number twenty pop hit late in 1956. That trademark bullfrog croak has helped him endure as an entertainer along the Gulf Coast to this day.

Naturally, Fats Domino and Professor Longhair were young Clarence Henry's main influences while growing up as an aspiring pianist in the Big Easy. He played piano and trombone with Bobby Mitchell & the Toppers from 1952 to 1955 before catching on with saxist Eddie Smith's band. Henry improvised the basic idea behind "Ain't Got No Home" on the bandstand one morning in the wee hours; when the crowd responded favorably, he honed it into something unique. Paul Gayten (New Orleans A&R man for Chess Records) hustled Henry into Cosimo Matassa's studio (J&M Recording) in September of 1956. Local deejay Poppa Stoppa (Clarence Hayman) laid the "Frogman" handle on the youngster when he spun the 45 on his popular WWEZ radio show. As Henry told *Offbeat,* "Back then, everybody called Fats Domino the 'Fatman.' Poppa Stoppa told me, 'Clarence you got this song about a frog, we'll have to start calling you 'Frogman.' And it stuck."

Despite some energetic follow-ups like "It Won't Be Long," "I'm in Love," and the inevitable froggy sequel "I Found a Home," Henry didn't hit the charts again until he covered Bobby Charles's warm swamp pop ballad "(I Don't Know Why) But I Do," which reached number four on the national charts in early 1961. That same year he turned in a Domino-tinged version of the old Mills Brothers song "You Always Hurt the One You Love," which climbed to number twelve on the charts.

> **"I ain't got no home, no place to roam."**
>
> — *Clarence "Frogman" Henry*

Henry continued to record New Orleans–styled standards and catchy originals for Argo but the hits dried up after 1961. In 1964 he opened eighteen concerts for the Beatles across the U.S. and Canada, but his main source of income after that whirlwind tour came from Bourbon Street clubs. "I played nearly every club on the strip, six hours a night, six nights a week," he told Jeff Hannusch of *Offbeat*. "I had the best band in town. But I just got burned out. I enjoyed the work, but I was becoming a physical wreck. I needed the change."

Henry takes it easier these days. He doesn't play the piano on shows much any more, but he stays busy during the New Orleans Jazz & Heritage Festival and especially around Mardi Gras. He's also become a popular attraction at the area's casinos. Meanwhile, his biggest hit, "Ain't Got No Home," can be heard on the soundtrack to the hit movie *Forrest Gump*. "Paramount Pictures was very generous with me," Henry told *Offbeat*. "It's been in several other movies too. My man Rush Limbaugh plays it all the time. You can't buy publicity like that. I get fan mail (often addressed 'Frogman, New Orleans USA') every day of the year."

# KERMIT RUFFINS

BORN: December 18, 1964, in New Orleans, Louisiana

A CHARTER MEMBER of the ReBirth Brass Band from 1982, trumpeter Kermit Ruffins has become a capable and talented bandleader, writer, singer,

**Kermit Ruffins, 1999. Courtesy Basin Street Records**

musician, and showman in his own right. Clearly touched by the spirit of Louis Armstrong, the modern day disciple has charmed audiences with his easy grin and gravelly voiced interpretations of Pops fare like "Big Butter and Egg Man," "When It's Sleepy Time Down South," "Struttin' with Some Barbecue," and the jive anthem "When You'se a Viper."

Since 1992 Ruffins has led his Barbecue Swingers, a high-spirited quintet of young jazzbos with a decidedly N'awlins flavor. (Ruffins even dishes up his own recipe for red beans and rice, turkey necks, or filé gumbo between sets at his long-standing Thursday night gig at Vaughan's in the Ninth Ward.) He released three CDs on the Texas-based Justice Records, debuting in 1992 with *World on a String,* a swinging affair that featured special guest appearances by trad jazz giant Danny Barker on banjo, Walter Payton on bass, and jazz patriarch Ellis Marsalis on piano. Local radio responded to Ruffins's vocal charms and he followed up in 1994 with *Big Butter and Egg Man,* another obvious homage to Satchmo. He also exhibited his growing skills as a songwriter with the jivey "I'll Drink ta Dat" and the romantic "Leshianne," a tribute to his wife. That sophomore outing employed Kermit's former ReBirth bandmate Philip Frazier on sousaphone to great effect.

**"She wants a great big butter and egg man."**

*— Kermit Ruffins*

With the release of 1996's *Hold on Tight,* Ruffins continued to win accolades for his performing skills and engaging onstage personality. That swan song for Justice included effervescent readings of "Pennies from Heaven" (another Armstrong staple) along with the self-penned title track, the buoyant ditty "Ding Dong the Wicked Witch Is Dead" from *The Wizard of Oz,* and another viper anthem in "Light Up."

More recently Ruffins has released *The Barbecue Swingers Live* (1998) and *Swing This!* (1999) for the hometown Basin Street label. The Kermit Ruffins Big Band, a seventeen-piece ensemble conducted by legendary composer-arranger Wardell Quezerque, is another project that this modern traditionalist and heir apparent to Louis Armstrong's legacy is exploring from time to time.

New Orleans writer John Sinclair summed up Ruffins's appeal in this perceptive review in *Offbeat:* "The Barbecue Swingers have also evolved into a perfect vehicle for Kermit's completely distinctive vocal stylings and an effective foil for his earthy, equally distinctive personality, which works well to sell the band's unique repertoire and its penchant for straight-ahead swinging. Kermit exudes down-home New Orleans charm and loves to clown onstage, infusing the band's performances with humor and good feeling."

—•—

## Jivenotes:

Two mysterious figures came out of the flush years of New Orleans R&B/jive. One is **Prince La La** (Lawrence Nelson, younger brother of guitarist Walter "Papoose" Nelson, onetime guitarist for Fats Domino and early guitar teacher of Mac Rebennack). A cousin of the famous Lastie brothers—David, Walter ("Popee"), and Melvin—Prince La La is generally credited as the guy who turned Dr. John on to the world of voodoo. His one notable recording for AFO in 1961 was "She Put the Hurt on Me." He died under mysterious circumstances and was later eulogized in song by Oliver Morgan, who recorded "Who Shot the La La" in 1963 for Crescendo Records. The other anomaly is **Eskew Reeder** (aka Equerita), the flamboyant pianist-singer who was a major influence on a young Little Richard. A South Carolina native, Reeder came to New Orleans decked out with wild hair and rhinestone sunglasses. He cut a group of frenzied rock 'n' roll sides for Capitol, including 1956's "Green Door" and "I Waited Too Long."

## Recommended Listening:

**DANNY BARKER**
*Save the Bones,* Orleans (1988)
**With Cab Calloway:**
*Cab Calloway and Company,*
  RCA (1931–1949)
*The Hi-De-Ho Man,* RCA (1935–1947)
*Cab Calloway,* Epic (1939)
*Are You Hep to the Jive?* Sony/Legacy
  (1939–1947)

**PROFESSOR LONGHAIR**
*Fess: Professor Longhair Anthology,*
  Rhino (1950–1985)
*New Orleans Piano,* Atlantic (1972)
*Rock 'n' Roll Gumbo,* Dancing Cat (1977)

*Live on the Queen Mary,*
  One Way (1978)
*Crawfish Fiesta,* Alligator (1980)
*Mardi Gras in New Orleans,*
  Nighthawk (1981)
*The Last Mardi Gras,* Atlantic (1982)
*House Party New Orleans Style,*
  Rounder (1987)

**HUEY "PIANO" SMITH**
*Rockin' Pneumonia and the Boogie*
  *Woogie Flu,* Ave 9 (1957–1959)
*The Imperial Sides,* Pathe Marconi
  (1960–1961)
*Rockin' and Jivin',* Charly (1978)

## JAMES BOOKER

*Junco Partner,* Hannibal (1976)

*New Orleans Piano Prince: Live!*
   Rounder (1977)

*Resurrection of the Bayou Maharaja,*
   Rounder (1977–1982)

*Spiders on the Keys,* Rounder (1977–1982)

*Classified,* Rounder (1982)


## DR. JOHN

*Mos' Scocious: The Dr. John Anthology,*
   Rhino (1959–1989)

*Gris-Gris,* Atco/Atlantic (1968)

*Babylon,* Atco/Atlantic (1969)

*Remedies,* Atco/Atlantic (1970)

*The Sun, Moon & Herbs,* Atco/Atlantic
   (1971)

*Gumbo,* Atco/Atlantic (1972)

*In the Right Place,* Atco/Atlantic (1973)

*Desitively Bonnaroo,* Atco/Atlantic (1974)

*Hollywood Be Thy Name,*
   United Artists (1975)

*City Lights,* Horizon/A&M (1978)

*Tango Palace,* Horizon/A&M (1979)

*Brightest Smile in Town,* Clean Cuts (1983)

*In a Sentimental Mood,*
   Warner Bros. (1989)

*Goin' Back to New Orleans,*
   Warner Bros. (1992)

*Television,* GRP (1994)

*Afterglow,* Blue Thumb (1995)

*Trippin' Live,* Surefire/Wind-Up (1997)

*Anutha Zone,* Pointblank (1998)

*Duke Elegant,* Blue Note (2000)


## LLOYD PRICE

*Lawdy!* Specialty (1952–1956)

*Heavy Dreams,* Specialty (1952–1956)

*Lloyd Price Sings His Big Ten,*
   Capitol (1952–1959)

*Greatest Hits,* MCA (1957–1960)

*Mr. Personality,* ABC-Paramount (1959)

*Mr. Personality Sings the Blues,*
   ABC-Paramount (1960)

*Lloyd Price Sings the Million Sellers,*
   ABC-Paramount (1961)


## ERNIE K-DOE

*Mother-in-Law,* EMI America (1961)

*Burn! K-Doe, Burn!* Charly (1989)

*I'm Cocky but I'm Good,* Dubat (1996)

*Fever,* Dejan (1996)

*Building Is Shakin' & the Walls Are
   Tremblin',* Aim (1999)

*The Best of Ernie K-Doe,*
   Mardis Gras (1999)


## JAMES "SUGAR BOY" CRAWFORD

*Sugar Boy Crawford,* Chess (1985)

*The Chicago Years,* Vogue (1988)


## JESSIE HILL

*Y'all Ready Now . . . Plus,*
   Charly (1956–1959)

*Golden Classics,* Collectables (1957–1965)

*Naturally,* Blue Thumb (1972)

*Hurts So Bad,* Capitol (1982)


## LEE DORSEY

*The Best of Lee Dorsey,*
   Fire/Island (1961–1963)

*All Ways Funky,* Charly (1961–1978)

*The New Lee Dorsey,* Amy (1965–1967)

*Yes We Can,* Polydor (1970)

*Night People,*
   ABC-Paramount (1977)

## EDDIE BO

*Check Mr. Popeye,* Rounder (1962–1964)

*Vippin and Voppin,* Charly (1962–1969)

*If It's Good to You It's Good for You,*
Scram (1969)

*Check Your Bucket,* Bo-Sound (1970)

*Another Side of Eddie Bo,* Bo-Sound
(1979)

*Watch for the Coming,* Bo-Sound (1984)

*New Orleans Piano Riffs,* Tuff City (1993)

*Back up This Train,* Bo-Sound (1996)

*New Orleans Solo Piano,* Night Train
International (1996)

*Hook & Sling,* Tuff City Records (1997)

*A Shoot from the Root,* Soulciety (1997)

*Nine Yards of Funk,* Bo-Sound (1998)


## CLARENCE "FROGMAN" HENRY

*Ain't Got No Home,* MCA (1956–1964)

*But I Do,* Charly (1956–1964)

*Alive and Well,* Pye (1970)

*New Recordings,* CFH (1979)

*Bourbon Street,* Maison de Soul (1985)

*The Legendary Frogman Henry,*
Silvertone (1999)


## KERMIT RUFFINS

*World on a String,* Justice (1992)

*Big Butter & Egg Man,* Justice (1994)

*Hold on Tight,* Justice (1996)

*Barbecue Swingers Live,* Basin Street
(1998)

*Swing This!* Basin Street (1999)

**With the ReBirth Brass Band:**

*Here to Stay,* Rounder (1984)

*Feel like Funkin' It Up,* Rounder (1989)

*Kickin' It Live,* Rounder (1991)

*Take It to the Street,* Rounder (1992)

*Rollin',* Rounder (1994)


## COMPILATIONS

*Crescent City Soul: The Sound of New
Orleans,* EMI (1947–1974)

*Creole Kings of New Orleans, Volumes
1 & 2,* Specialty (1950–1958)

*Chess New Orleans,* MCA/Chess
(1953–1965)

*New Orleans Party Classics,*
Rhino (1954–1990)

*Gumbo Stew: Original New Orleans
R&B,* AFO (1961–1970)

CHAPTER 6

THE

# WHITE CONNECTION

The Rhythm Boys, Cliff Edwards, Emmett Miller, Mezz Mezzrow,

Louis Prima, Harry "The Hipster" Gibson, Johnny Otis, Bob Dorough,

Mose Allison, Ben Sidran, Tim Hauser, Dan Hicks

Throughout the history of America there have been countless examples of white entertainers assimilating, emulating, and in some cases appropriating black performance qualities. From the rise in popularity of minstrelsy in the 1830s to Stephen Foster's plantation songs of the 1850s; from Al Jolson's and Emmett Miller's blackface routines of the 1920s to George Gershwin's *Porgy and Bess* in 1933; from Louis Prima aping Louis Armstrong in the 1940s to Elvis Presley imitating Otis Blackwell in the 1950s to Mick Jagger imitating Amos Milburn and Muddy Waters in the '60s; from K. C. & The Sunshine Band in the '70s to Stevie Ray Vaughan in the '80s and rapper Vanilla Ice in the '90s, the pattern is clear. And with mega-selling white rapper Eminem currently imitating hardcore black rappers to great success and a plethora of white retro-jivesters getting over quite well with

Caucasoid renditions of Cab Calloway and Louis Jordan fare, the two-hundred-year-old tradition of minstrelsy continues into the new millennium.

As Louis Jordan told Arnold Shaw in *Honkers and Shouters:* "There is nothing that the white artist has invented or come along with in the form of jazz or entertainment. Rock 'n' roll was not a marriage of rhythm and blues and country and western. That's white publicity. Rock 'n' roll was just a white imitation, a white adaptation of Negro rhythm and blues."

Indeed.

Sam Phillips, who in the early 1950s recorded black bluesmen and R&B artists from Junior Parker to Rufus Thomas for his Sun Records label, had long predicted that if he could get a white boy with "the Negro look and the Negro feel," he would make a million dollars. Elvis fit the bill and the rest is history.

While minstrelsy reigned supreme in the American entertainment world from about 1845 to 1900, it contributed no particularly outstanding characteristics to the development of jazz. Yet, as Marshall Stearns points out in *The Story of Jazz:* "[Minstrelsy] is of vast importance to the history of jazz because it served as a vehicle for the spread of American Negro music. [It] furnished an introduction to the general public of a type of entertainment based upon Negro elements of story, dance and song. Minstrelsy educated the general ear, preparing the way for the introduction of jazz."

And so, white Americans (by proxy) were able to pick up on what black Americans were putting down. More burlesque than truthful, minstrelsy was an imitation of Negro life, but its appeal was enormous through the late 1800s. Big minstrel companies continued to tour in 1919 and small companies were still playing the South as late as 1955.

White men in blackface impersonating Negroes began appearing as entertainment between plays as early as 1800. One, Thomas Dartmouth Rice (professionally known as Daddy Jim Crow Rice), began performing around 1829. His routine consisted of blackening his white face with burnt cork and copying the "Negro songs" he had overheard a deformed stable groom sing in Louisville, Kentucky. The act was hugely successful with white audiences. Daddy Rice became so popular that by 1840 he spawned Daddy Rice imitators who were inserted in every type of playbill in the country. In January of 1843 many of these performers were combined by the Virginia Minstrels into one big show in New York. The troupe performed to wildly enthusiastic audiences at the Chatham Theatre until disbanding in July of 1843. A year later the Christy Minstrels organized, continuing the momentum of this American pastime.

As Eileen Southern explains in *The Music of Black Americans:* "For more than four decades, Ethiopian minstrelsy was the most popular form of theatrical entertainment in the United States and to the rest of the world, and was America's unique contribution to the stage. To obtain material for their shows, the minstrels visited plantations, then attempted to recreate plantation scenes on the stage. They listened to the songs of the black man as he sang at work in the cotton and sugarcane fields, on the steamboats and river docks and in the tobacco factories. The melodies they heard served as bases for minstrel songs, and they adapted the dances they saw to their needs."

They also incorporated the "Ethiopian instruments" they saw at plantation frolics—banjos, tambourines, fiddles, and bone castanets. These shows generally consisted of three parts: jokes, specialty acts and ensemble numbers, and a "Walk Around Finale"—an act in which some of the performers sang and danced up front while the remainder of the company gave support from the back (not unlike the dance line in "Soul Train"). Essentially, as the minstrel E. P. Christy pointed out (as quoted in Eileen Southern's book), white minstrels tried "to reproduce the life of the plantation darky" and to imitate the "Negro peculiarities of song."

During this time, Stephen Foster's music made a deep impression on the public. Often referred to as "America's Troubadour," Foster's most enduring melodies from the late 1840s and early 1850s—"Old Black Joe," "Massa's in the Cold, Cold Ground," "Camptown Races," "Old Folks at Home," and "Swanee River" (Foster was from Pittsburgh and had never even seen the Swanee River)—show a strong camp-meeting influence with lyrics in Negro dialect. (Foster was brought up by a mulatto nurse and as a child loved Negro music.)

Negro minstrel troupes did not appear until after the Civil War. One Negro minstrel, William Henry Lane, who billed himself as "Juba," was universally conceded to be the greatest minstrel dancer of all time and shared top billing with white companies. By 1842 Master Juba, as he came to be known, was so famous that English novelist Charles Dickens identified him as "the greatest dancer known." With his celebrated status Juba was a precursor to the great dancer Bill "Bojangles" Robinson, who enjoyed regal status among blacks in the 1920s.

Minstrelsy and the beginnings of jazz collided in the 1890s. Besides carrying American Negro music to the public, minstrelsy also served as a training ground for early jazzmen. "All the minstrel shows like The Rabbit Foot Minstrels [where a young Louis Jordan got his start] and the Georgia Minstrels used New Orleans musicians year in and year out," says guitarist Danny Barker, a mainstay of Cab Calloway's band in the 1930s, as quoted in Marshall Stearns's *The Story of Jazz*.

W. C. Handy joined Mahara's Minstrels in 1896 and the following year became cornet soloist and leader of the troupe. Pianist Clarence Williams, who would become a key figure during the Harlem Renaissance of the 1920s, ran away from home at the age of twelve to join a minstrel troupe. Jelly Roll Morton worked with McCabe & Young Minstrels in 1910. Pianist James P. Johnson played ragtime with an amateur minstrel group in New York City. Trumpeter Bunk Johnson was on tour with various minstrel shows beginning in 1903. Hot Lips Page and Lester Young played with minstrel shows when they were first starting out. "A lot of men came up through the minstrel shows," drummer Jo Jones told Nat Hentoff in *Hear Me Talkin' to Ya*.

By 1920 minstrel shows met stiff competition from vaudeville, cabarets, talking movies, and from jazz itself. The minstrel dance was siphoned off into social dancing by the dance team of Vernon and Irene Castle, who developed the popular fox-trot. The Charleston soon became a dance craze, popularized by the 1923 revue *Runnin' Wild*. And by the time the Suzy-Q, the Lindyhop, and the Shim-Sham-Shimmy came along in the 1930s, minstrelsy was already ancient history.

In his 1957 essay "The White Negro: Superficial Reflections on The Hipster," which originally appeared in *Dissent* magazine and was later published by City Lights books, Norman Mailer identifies a new existentialist character that emerged in post World War II American culture. "The hipster, the man who knows that if our collective condition is to live with instant death by atomic war, relatively quick death by the State as *l'univers concentrationnaire*, or with a slow death by conformity with every creative and rebellious instinct stifled . . . then the only life-giving answer is to accept the terms of death and to divorce oneself from society, to exist without roots, to set out on that uncharted journey into the rebellious imperatives of the self."

Or as Louis Jordan so succinctly put it in song, "Let the good times roll."

In his treatise Mailer identifies "the Negro" as the ultimate hipster and further speculates why many alienated young white Americans emulate him. "In such places as Greenwich Village, a menage-a-trois was completed—the bohemian and the juvenile delinquent came face-to-face with the Negro, and the hipster was a fact in American life. If marijuana was the wedding ring, the child was the language of hip for its argot gave expression to abstract states of feeling which all could share, at least all who were Hip. And in this wedding of the white and black it was the Negro who brought the cultural dowry." Mailer further identifies this new breed of urban adventurers who drift out at night looking for action with a black man's code, "the White Negro."

Mailer's concept of "the White Negro" has persisted over time—from Emmett Miller, the humorous "Minstrel Man from Georgia," who entertained audiences in the 1920s by inhabiting the character of black people he had observed, on to Bing Crosby, whose early idol was another minstrel man, Al Jolson, and who even performed in blackface himself on the silver screen (see his "Abraham" bit from 1942's *Holiday Inn*). Other quintessential hipsters include clarinetist and fabled Harlem pot peddler Mezz Mezzrow, New Orleans jivesters Louis Prima and Wingy Manone, stride pianist and novelty songster Harry "The Hipster" Gibson, R&B bandleader Johnny Otis, '30s big-band leader and beloved hepcat radio comedian Phil Harris, and other enigmatic figures like Cliff Edwards, Tom Waits, Dan Hicks, Leon Redbone, and Ray Benson of Asleep at the Wheel. They are all part of the great Circle of Jive.

## THE RHYTHM BOYS

FORMED: April 1927 in Los Angeles, California

ULTRAHEP AND CUTTING-EDGE in 1927, the three Rhythm Boys—Al Rinker, Harry Barris, Bing Crosby—emerged from the ranks of Paul Whiteman's orchestra to become full-fledged stars in their own right for a brief spell in 1930. By blending tight vocal harmonies, uninhibited scatting, and onstage hijinks, The Rhythm Boys's hot new sound greatly appealed to young flappers and hepcats alike in the Roaring Twenties and laid the groundwork for swinging vocal harmony groups like The Spirits of Rhythm. Among their dozens of records were popular hits like "I'm Coming Virginia," "My Blue Heaven," "Them There Eyes," and wild scat vehicles like "Wa-Da-Da."

A former drummer with The Musicaladers (a six-piece band he put together with college chum Al Rinker during their law school years at Gonzaga University in Spokane, Washington), Crosby had impeccable time and a playful sense of jazzy phrasing. Rinker, a hot piano player and novelty singer, had a similarly jazzy sensibility. Together, billed as "Two Boys and a Piano," he and Bing made their professional recording debut on October 14, 1926, with Columbia Records ("I've Got the Girl"). Bandleader and talent scout Paul Whiteman caught their lively act at the Metropolitan Theater in Los Angeles in December of 1926. Impressed by their unique sound, which was marked by uncannily facile scatting, and their vibrant stage presence, Whiteman hired them to be a featured part of his touring company. The two were a hit at the Tivoli Theater in Chicago, but bombed at the Paramount Theatre in New York. Whiteman soon added another ingredient to the act in the form of scat hotshot Harry Barris, a confident and talented man whose business card read "Young Mister Show Business, Himself." And thus The Rhythm Boys were born in April of 1927.

> "Wa-da-da, wa-da-da, everybody's doing it now."
> — The Rhythm Boys

By the summer of 1927 they had become a household name, drawing raves for their performances. Bing played the cymbal with sly, rhythmic aplomb as the trio unleashed its signature brand of hep tomfoolery (i.e., jive) on Barris originals like "Mississippi Mud," "Wa-Da-Da," "So the Bluebirds and the Blackbirds Got Together," and "My Suppressed Desire" (in which Bing scats with abandon on the first chorus and then encourages Rinker on the verse with a hearty "Tell it!").

The Rhythm Boys were an immediate smash at the Palace Theatre and the Cocoanut Grove in Los Angeles as well as on national radio broadcasts. Their appearance in the 1930 Whiteman movie *The King of Jazz*—in which they sang "Happy Feet," "A Bench in the Park," and "I Like to Do Things for You"— helped elevate their profile overnight. After a "King of Jazz" tour in 1930, however, they were summarily fired by Whiteman, who cited Crosby's frequent drunken episodes as "conduct unbecoming a professional entertainer." The Rhythm Boys went on to record "Three Little Words" with the Duke Ellington Orchestra and later that year sang the song with the Ellington Orchestra again—this time in blackface—in the movie *Check and Double Check*.

After a spectacular ten-month run at the Cocoanut Grove, with the Gus Arnheim Orchestra, the act broke up in 1931 and Crosby signed on as a solo with Brunswick. Under the direction of Jack Kapp, Crosby's recording career quickly exploded on the strength of major hits like "Just One More Chance," "I Surrender Dear," and "Where the Blue of the Night (Meets the Gold of the Day)," earning him the title "King of the Crooners." Crosby can also be heard expressing his jazz aspirations in uninhibited fashion on a 1932 recording of "Some of These Days," backed by jazz greats Frankie Trumbauer on saxophone and Eddie Lang on guitar, and on his scintillating scat reading from that same year of "St. Louis Blues," backed by the Duke Ellington Orchestra.

In 1932 *The Big Broadcast* (which featured cameos by Cab Calloway and his Cotton Club Orchestra, The Mills Brothers, and The Boswell Sisters) was

**The Rhythm Boys, 1930 (from left to right): Harry Barris, Bing Crosby, Al Rinker.
Frank Driggs Collection**

a starring vehicle for this new singing sensation, the Elvis Presley of his day.

After signing in 1934 as the first artist with the fledgling label Decca, Crosby continued to enhance his popularity through many appearances on radio and in the movies. He worked frequently with such jazz greats as Jack Teagarden, Wingy Manone, Eddie Condon, Matty Matlock, Joe Venuti, Bob Scobey, Red Nichols, and singer Connee Boswell and was particularly comfortable in duet settings with jive icons Louis Armstrong ("Gone Fishin'") and Louis Jordan ("Your Socks Don't Match"). He slings some stylish jive of his own on a hepcat version of "Pinetop's Boogie Woogie," from a 1946 recording with the Lionel Hampton Orchestra, and on "Bebop Spoken Here," a 1949 duet with Patty Andrews, backed by the Vic Schoen Orchestra.

The biggest-selling recording artist of all time, Crosby had an impact on the course of popular singing in America that is incalculable. As Larry Carr wrote in his liner notes to *The Bing Crosby Story* (Columbia): "Popular singing can quite literally be divided into two periods—"B.C. and A.C." [i.e., "Before Crosby and After Crosby"]. No other singer of any description ever had such a wide, far-reaching influence as Crosby did." And the cat could swing, too. Once a Rhythm Boy, always a Rhythm Boy.

## CLIFF EDWARDS

BORN: June 14, 1895, in Hannibal, Missouri
DIED: July 17, 1971, in Hollywood, California

A BROADWAY ANOMALY of the 1920s, Edwards (aka "Ukulele Ike") was an ebullient entertainer whose advanced sense of rhythm and timing allowed him to take great liberties with the tempo and lyrics. His unique scatting technique had a great impact on a young Bing Crosby, who put some of those tricks to good use with The Rhythm Boys.

Edwards played the ukulele on a series of recordings in the early 1920s, including "I'm a Bear in a Lady's Boudoir," "Hush My Mouth if I Ain't Goin' South," "Fascinatin' Rhythm," "Dinah," and "Hard Hearted Hannah." His joyful singing style was featured in a number of movies in the late 1920s and early 1930s, including 1928's *They Learned about Women,* 1929's *So This Is College,* and the 1931 Buster Keaton vehicle, *Sidewalks of New York.* Edwards would later gain mainstream fame as the voice of Jiminy Cricket in Walt

Disney's *Pinocchio.* His heart-wrenching reading of "When You Wish upon a Star" from that 1940 animated feature remains a classic. Edwards's voice appeared a year later in the Disney animated feature *Dumbo,* in which he sang the jivey number "When I See an Elephant Fly" in perfect black dialect.

Neojivester Casey MacGill, who sings, scats, and plays ukulele in the current Broadway production of *Swing!* maintains that Edwards's contribution cannot be overlooked. "He's been a big influence on me," says MacGill. "I love the way he sings. Now, he had an approach that was diametrically opposite of Fats Waller, but it was equally valid because he could turn a sow's ear into a silk purse. He could take a real corny pop song from the late '20s or mid-1930s and he had an alchemistic way of turning it into a heartfelt performance, a completely believable reading.

> **"Hush my mouth if I ain't goin' South."**
> — *Ukulele Ike*

"He wasn't really a great scat singer. He was kind of stuck in an early '20s kind of approach, but he did make some interesting sounds with his mouth . . . his little instrumental imitations. He had a really unique style. I think he's somebody that's been very tragically overlooked and I think his influence was extremely important for Bing Crosby. You've gotta give Edwards the credit for being one of the very first, if not *the* first, modern pop singers."

# EMMETT MILLER

BORN: February 2, 1903, in Macon, Georgia
DIED: March 29, 1962, in Macon, Georgia

A MISSING LINK IN POPULAR AMERICAN CULTURE, minstrel man Emmett Miller was one of the original architects of modern country music who helped merge the old and the new, the folk with the popular, the African American with the European. An obvious and huge influence on the legendary "Blue Yodeller" Jimmie Rodgers and Texas swing pioneer Bob Wills (both of whom devoted entire albums to Miller) as well as on Hank Williams, Lefty Frizell, Merle Haggard, Eddy Arnold, Roger Miller, and Leon Redbone, he was not exactly blues, not quite country, and not entirely pop.

Miller's comedic timing, especially on his hilarious blackface dialogues, also had a major impact on the young Bing Crosby.

Growing up in the Deep South at the turn of the century, young Miller became fascinated with Black speech and singing. As Charles Wolfe points out in his liner notes to the excellent sampler, *The Minstrel Man from Georgia* (Columbia/ Legacy): "Friends remember that he would spend hours in the black section of town listening and absorbing. 'He got to where he talked just like a black man,' said his friend Claude Casey."

> "Anytime you're feeling lonely, anytime you're feeling blue."
> — *Emmett Miller*

In 1919 Miller joined O'Brien's Minstrels, a company that went broke later that year. Shortly thereafter he was asked to join The Dan Fitch Minstrels and spent the next several years with them getting solid grounding in show business. In New York, the troupe packed the Hippodrome and earned enthusiastic reviews. One of the features of the show was Miller's famous "strut." As old friend and accompanist Turk McBee told Charles Wolfe in the liner notes, "He did one of the funniest walks you ever saw. He did a little shuffle. I've seen him stop the show with one of those walks."

Miller's first recordings came in 1924 for the Okeh label—his signature song "Anytime" and "The Pickaninny's Paradise," a blackface specialty from 1918. In 1926 Miller joined the legendary Al G. Field Minstrels, which had been founded in 1894. He soon became the star of the show, garnering rave reviews from Florida to New York. From 1928 to 1929 he cut thirty-one sides in New York for Okeh Records backed by The Georgia Crackers, which comprised such New York jazz stars as Tommy and Jimmy Dorsey, guitarist Eddie Lang, trombonist Jack Teagarden, and drummer Gene Krupa.

In 1930 Miller recorded "The Gypsy," a sort of rhythmic chant song that anticipated modern rap music and would influence 1930s hepcat bandleaders like Cab Calloway and Phil Harris. Miller's loose, sly patter and elastic cadence over the top of this groove is as firmly in the jive canon as Louis Armstrong's "Hobo You Can't Ride This Train." Miller made his last known recordings for Bluebird in 1936 before hitting the traveling show circuit in the 1940s, sticking to his blackface style and jokes. He scored something of a hit in 1949 with "Dixieana" and later appeared in the 1951 musical film *Yes, Sir, Mister Bones.*

# MEZZ MEZZROW

BORN: November 9, 1899, in Chicago, Illinois
DIED: August 5, 1972, in Paris, France

BORN MILTON MESIROW, Mezz was a capable Dixieland clarinetist with a deep feeling for the blues and a particularly strong affinity for Chicago and New Orleans jazz and the culture of jive. However, his constant preoccupation with black jazz players and his determination to identify with them was a source of embarrassment to many of his peers, as Digby Fairweather points out in *Jazz: The Rough Guide*. He further quotes the great soprano saxophonist Sidney Bechet as saying: "When a man is trying so hard to be something he isn't, then some of that will show in the music. The idea of it will be wrong." Or, according to James Lincoln Collier, who wrote *The Making of Jazz:* "Mezzrow was white, but he felt that there was something special about the black experience, and he made efforts to turn himself into a black man."

Nevertheless, Mezz's path was set from the time he entered "The School" (Pontiac Reformatory in Michigan) as a young boy. As Mezz writes in his colorful and somewhat fanciful memoirs entitled *Really the Blues:* "The Southerners had called me a 'nigger-lover' there. Solid. I not only loved those colored boys, but I was one of them—I felt closer to them than I felt to the whites, and I even got the same treatment they got. I remember that when Sullivan [a boyhood pal] visited our synagogue back in Chicago, the rabbi told him that Moses, King Solomon and the Queen of Sheba were all colored, and maybe the whole world was once colored.

"By the time I reached home, I knew that I was going to spend all my time from then on sticking close to Negroes. They were my kind of people. And I was going to learn their music and play it for the rest of my days. I was going to be a musician, a Negro musician, hipping the world about the blues the way only Negroes can. I didn't know how the hell I was going to do it but I was straight on what I had to do. Most of my skullbusters got solved at The School. I went in there green but I came out chocolate brown."

In 1933 Mezzrow put together a big band featuring such jazz greats as

> "Before I knew it, I was standing on The Corner pushing gauge."
>
> — *Mezz Mezzrow*

saxophonist Benny Carter, bassist Pops Foster, and pianist Teddy Wilson. On the jive side Mezzrow recorded Stuff Smith's "I'se a Muggin'" in 1935 and Cab Calloway's "Come on with the Come On" in 1936. In 1938 he participated in an all-star session in New York—with expatriate Sidney Bechet, stride piano master James P. Johnson, trumpeter Tommy Ladiner, and guitarist Teddy Bunn—which was organized by French jazz critic Hughes Panassie. The resulting record had considerable impact in Europe, though Mezzrow's playing on it was panned by Collier in *The Making of Jazz:* "He was considered something of a joke by the others. His intonation was poor, his technical skills were rudimentary, and his conception ordinary."

Despite this harsh criticism, Mezzrow did have his share of fans and longtime supporters, notably Panassie. But perhaps his biggest claim to fame was as the *numero uno* marijuana supplier in the jazz community. Louis Armstrong was a frequent customer during the 1930s and 1940s, as were innumerable potheads in Harlem. The potency of Mezzrow's marijuana was legendary in musician circles. In Cab Calloway's 1936 *Hepster's Dictionary,* the term "mezz" is defined as "anything supreme or genuine." Stuff Smith reiterated this point in his 1936 hit "You'se a Viper":

> *Dreamed about a reefer five foot long.*
> *The mighty mezz, but not too strong.*
> *You'll be high but not for long.*
> *If you're a viper.*

In *Really the Blues* Mezzrow explains how he became a pot peddler: "That mellow Mexican leaf really started something in Harlem—a whole new language, almost a whole new culture. . . . As soon as we got some of that Mexican bush, we almost blew our tops. Poppa, you never smacked your chops on anything sweeter in all your days of viping. It had such a wonderful smell and the kick you got was really out of this world. Guys used to say it tasted like chocolate candy, a brand Hershey never even thought of. I laid it on the cats in the Barbecue [a local bar], and pretty soon all Harlem was after me to light them up. . . . Before I knew it I had to write to our connection for a large supply, because everybody I knew wanted some. Before I knew it, I was standing on The Corner pushing gauge."

Here's another slice of jive from that hepcat tome. It's a scene of Mezzrow pushing his gauge to vipers in Harlem:

FIRST CAT: Hey there, Poppa Mezz, is you anywhere?

MEZZ: Man I'm down with it, sticking' like a honky.

FIRST CAT: Lay a trey on me, ole man.

MEZZ: Got to do it, slot. . . .

FIRST CAT: . . . Jim, this jive you got is a gasser.
I'm going up to my dommy and dig that new mess Pops
laid down for Okeh. I hear he riffed back on "Zackly." Pick
you up at The Track when the kitchen mechanics romp. . . .

SECOND CAT: Hey rough, give it up tough, you've had
it long enough. Knock me some of that righteous bush,
Poppa Mezz, so we can get tall and have a ball. How'm
I doin'? Am I rhymin' or am I rhymin'?

MEZZ: Solid, ole man. You ain't climbin', you're really
chimin'. If you ain't timin', a hawk can't see.

SECOND CAT: . . . This hemp that you're pushin' is
groovy studdy, so tell all the cats light up and be somebody.
Well Jim, I'm goin' to knock a fade up the main stroll and
see what's on the rail for the lizard.

You dig? If not, here's the English translation:

FIRST CAT: Hello Mezz, have you got any marijuana?

MEZZ: Plenty, ole man. My pockets are full as a factory
hand's on payday.

FIRST CAT: Let me have three cigarettes [fifty cents'
worth].

MEZZ: I sure will, pal. . . .

FIRST CAT: . . . Friend, this marijuana of yours is terrific.
I'm going home and listen to that new record Louis
Armstrong made for the Okeh company. I hear he did some
wonderful playing and singing on that number "Exactly
Like You." See you at the Savoy Ballroom on Thursday.
That is the maids' night off, when all the domestic workers
will be dancing there. . . .

SECOND CAT: Hey, you look like you're making plenty
of money, so don't treat me so rough and tough, so tell
me the secret of your success because you've been keeping
it to yourself long enough. How am I doing, Mezz?

Am I playing the rhyming game expertly or not?

MEZZ: You were doing nothing else but, you're really ringing true. If you're not coming in on time, a hawk can't see.

SECOND CAT: . . . This marijuana you're selling is wonderful, pal. Everybody ought to smoke it up and wake up. Well, I'm going to disappear up Seventh Avenue and see if there's anything interesting waiting for me.

While the lore of Mezzrow's marijuana business may have overshadowed his contribution to jazz, he continued to record prolifically through the '30s, '40s, and '50s. From 1945 to 1947 Mezzrow ran his own King Jazz label, documenting his casual sessions with Sidney Bechet, drummer Sid Catlett, pianist Sam Price, and trumpeter Hot Lips Page. After a triumphant appearance at the Nice Jazz Festival in 1948 he settled in Paris and became a big star in Europe. From 1951 to 1955 he regularly featured trumpeter Buck Clayton on his own recordings. His last sessions occurred in Paris in 1958.

# LOUIS PRIMA

BORN: December 7, 1910, in New Orleans, Louisiana
DIED: August 24, 1978, in New Orleans, Louisiana

WITH HIS WILD, BOISTEROUS STAGE PRESENCE, Louis Prima carried the torch for jive in Las Vegas during the 1950s. An ebullient entertainer, energetic trumpet, and rambunctious vocalist, Prima patterned his infectious style after his New Orleans hometown hero, Louis Armstrong. Eventually he found his own irrepressible voice and developed his unique brand of jive—part Dixieland, part jump blues, part comedy—with Sam Butera & The Witnesses. They scored a string of hits in the '50s, including "Just a Gigolo," "Oh Marie," "Zooma Zooma," "That Old Black Magic," and the anthemic "Jump, Jive an' Wail," the tune that helped launch the neoswing movement some twenty years after his death.

"Prima was a fun guy, kind of a cross between two other Louises—the later Louis Armstrong and Louis Jordan," says Casey MacGill of the Broadway musical *Swing!* "I think he makes a good entrée into swing for a lot of kids who are so far removed, age-wise, from the '30s and '40s."

Born on the edge of New Orleans's notorious Storyville district, Louis and his older trumpet-playing brother Leon soaked up the Dixieland sounds of Joe "King" Oliver and Louis Armstrong as kids. Louis dropped out of high school to become a musician and by 1930 was gigging in speakeasies around the French Quarter in a hot band.

In 1934 Prima moved to New York and was playing on Fifty-second Street with his New Orleans Gang, which included the great clarinetist Pee Wee Russell. A year later he headlined at the Famous Door, where his brand of New Orleans–flavored hepcat jive went over bigtime, and in 1937 he opened his own branch of the Famous Door in Hollywood. During his stay on the West Coast he romanced starlets, performed with a young Martha Raye, and appeared in Hollywood movies, including *Rhythm on the Range* with Bing Crosby and *Rose of Washington Square* with Tyrone Power and Alice Faye, while also racking up hits with "The Lady in Red" and "In a Gypsy Tearoom."

**"You gotta . . . jump, jive . . . then you wail."**

— *Louis Prima*

Following the success of his tune "Sing, Sing, Sing," which had become a signature piece for the Benny Goodman Orchestra in 1938, Prima broke up his Gang and formed a big band, whose repertoire turned away from jazz and moved toward pop and dance numbers.

By 1949 Prima scaled down to a six-piece combo, which featured seventeen-year-old singer Keely Smith. His heavy, bellowing delivery meshed magically with Smith's smooth phrasing and clear tones, and together they developed a special chemistry on stage. Prima and Smith married in 1952 and by the end of 1954 they found success in Las Vegas as a high-powered cabaret act that emphasized his exuberant front man shtick and his risqué banter with Keely, along with the hot, honking, rock 'n' roll–flavored tenor sax work of Sam Butera against the relentlessly hard-driving shuffle beat of The Witnesses. They signed with Capitol Records in 1956 and had hits with exuberant fare like "Oh Marie," "That Old Black Magic," and "Jump, Jive, an' Wail," the tune that resurfaced forty years later as the soundtrack to the catchy, jitterbugging Gap ad.

**Louis Prima, 1958. Frank Driggs Collection**

In 1967 Prima made an acclaimed cameo in the animated Disney classic *The Jungle Book*, providing the voice of King Louie the orangutan. His riotous scat duet with fellow jivester Phil Harris (as Baloo the bear) on "I Wanna Be like You" was a jivey highpoint of the film, sounding not unlike Slim Gaillard and His Flat Foot Floogie Boys from 1940 doing call-and-response vocals on 1940's "Broadway Jump." In the early 1970s Prima and Butera held a long residency at the Royal Sonesta Hotel in the French Quarter of New Orleans. In November of 1975 Prima underwent surgery to remove a brain tumor. He remained in a coma for nearly three years until his death on August 24, 1978, at New Orleans's Touro Infirmary.

# HARRY "THE HIPSTER" GIBSON

BORN: June 27, 1915, in New York, New York
DIED: May 3, 1991, in Northern California

A TALENTED STRIDE AND BOOGIE-WOOGIE PIANIST, eccentric vocalist, and novelty songwriter, Gibson was a favorite on Fifty-second Street during its heyday. As Chris Erikson wrote in the *New York Daily News*: "He was a high-living, piano-pounding, jive-talking hepcat on the scene in the early '40s, a perennial face on 52nd Street. Hugely influenced by Fats Waller, he mugged at the audience like a maniac, eyes rollings, eyebrows wiggling, fingers flying, suddenly jumping up and smacking the ivories with his elbows when he took a notion. He'd lay down tunes full of double-talk, cranked to the gills on reefer and pills and booze, and then he'd drive things home with his signature number":

> *They call him Handsome Harry the Hipster*
> *He's a ball with all the chicks*
> *Plays piano like mad, his singing is sad*
> *He digs those mellow kicks*
> *They call him Handsome Harry the Clipster*
> *'Cause he'll hype you for your gold*
> *He's frantic and fanatic, with jive he's an addict*
> *Well, I don't know, I was only told.*

Born in the Bronx in 1915, Harry Raab was a prodigy who was picking

out tunes on the piano at the age of three. By the age of thirteen he was playing dances with a jazz band. Then he landed a job in a speakeasy owned by
mobster Dutch Schultz, playing Dixieland with the Chocolate Bars of
Rhythm. In the late '30s he got a job as Fats Waller's
intermission pianist at The Yacht Club on Fifty-
second Street. He spent the next five years playing
every joint on the strip for union scale ($56 a
week). For a time he teamed up with singer
Ruth Gruner, billing themselves as The Gib-
sons, after Harry's favorite gin-based highball.

**"Who put the
Benzedrine in
Mrs. Murphy's
Ovaltine?"**

— *Harry
"The Hipster"
Gibson*

  After going solo he developed a wild and
zany stage act, partly patterned after his mentor
Fats Waller. While his piano playing was a mixture of ragtime, stride, blues, boogie, trad jazz, and
subtle touches of bop, his surreal stage show was marked
by the kind of uninhibited, frenetic performing style that predated Jerry Lee
Lewis and Little Richard by more than a decade.

  A restless spirit and born entertainer, Harry preferred to hang after
hours with his jive-talking cohorts than to face his domestic responsibilities.
(He had a wife and several kids at home.) After his debut record, *Boogie
Woogie in Blue,* hit in 1944 he played at Billy Berg's in Hollywood for a grand
a week. He returned to New York to headline the Onyx Club, Leon &
Eddie's, and the Three Deuces. (He wrote his jive opus "Get Your Juices at
the Deuces" for that hipster haven.) During this period he made some
"soundie" jukebox films of his most popular songs (available as the Rhapsody
Films video *Boogie in Blue*). After being introduced to the Hollywood film
crowd by Orson Welles, who had taken a liking to him, Harry also appeared
and performed in a couple of movie features.

  *Down Beat* magazine, which put him on its cover in 1945, called Harry "a
wild boogie woogie keyboarder with a froglike, frantic voice." Columnist
Earl Wilson said Gibson was "a great mad character" who "kept putting his
chewing gum and his feet on the piano and ad-libbed fantastically." But at the
same time KMPC radio in Los Angeles banned his records, denouncing them
as degenerate and a bad influence on young listeners, causing a minor scandal
that led to a major controversy. In spite of his great successes of the 1940s
Gibson led a frenetic life marked by several marriages and periods of incar-
ceration for drug offenses.

Rock 'n' roll squeezed him off the scene in the late '50s. By the '60s Harry was driving a cab while sometimes playing strip joints, eventually fading from the scene entirely. By 1968 he was living back in California and gigging occasionally around Los Angeles. In 1974 he recorded a decidedly bent Christmas album that became a favorite of syndicated novelty song radio host Dr. Demento. Gibson moved to a trailer in the California desert in 1986 and in 1989, at the age of seventy-four, the eternally high Hipster went back into the studio to cut some new tunes, including "I Flipped My Wig in San Francisco" and "Get Hip to Shirley MacLaine." The tapes didn't find an interested label in his lifetime but the sessions finally emerged on Chicago's Delmark label five years after Harry killed himself on May 3, 1991.

Gibson's definitive recordings were made for Musicraft between 1944 and 1946 and have been compiled on *Boogie Woogie in Blue,* which features guest appearances from Slim Gaillard and Tiny "Bam" Brown as well as drummers Sid Catlett and Zutty Singleton and includes such whacked-out original numbers as "Four-F Ferdinand the Frantic Freak," "While Strolling through the Park I Heard a Lark Bark," "Stop That Dancin' up There," his theme song "Handsome Harry the Hipster," and his showstopper, "Who Put the Benzedrine in Mrs. Murphy's Ovaltine?" His flair for showmanship was captured on a few "soundies" during the 1940s (compiled on the Rhapsody Films video *Boogie in Blue*).

During his run of fame in the '40s, Gibson caught the attitude, language, and mannerisms of hipsters, paving the way for underground entertainers and comedians like Lord Buckley, Lenny Bruce, and Dick Shawn.

# JOHNNY OTIS

BORN: December 28, 1921, in Vallejo, California

LIKE MEZZ MEZZROW, Johnny Otis so fervently identified with black culture that he adopted it as his own. The son of Greek immigrants, John Alexander Veliotes was brought up in an integrated neighborhood of Berkeley, California, where his father ran a grocery store. Gradually, as many of his nonblack playmates moved away, he gravitated toward the black

**Movie still from *Boogie in Blue*. Harry "The Hipster" Gibson, 1945. Courtesy of Rhapsody Films**

world, eventually changing his name to the blacker-sounding Otis when he was in his teens. As he wrote in his 1968 autobiography, *Listen to the Lambs:* "As a kid I decided that if our society dictated that one had to be either black or white, I would be black. . . . I related to the way of life, the special vitality, the atmosphere of the black community."

Starting as a jazz drummer in 1939 Otis worked with the Count Otis Matthews Combo in Oakland before moving to Los Angeles in 1943 and joining Harlan Leonard's Rockets, a Kansas City–styled band that had a residency at The Club Alabam on Central Avenue. In 1945 Otis made his first recordings as a bandleader for the Excelsior label, including two tracks with blues-singing star Jimmy Rushing. During this time he also appeared as a drummer on a string of hits for the Philo label, including "Flying Home" by Illinois Jacquet and "Drifting Blues" by Johnny Moore's Three Blazers, featuring Charles Brown.

By 1947, with the decline of big bands, Otis turned from jazz to R&B. He downsized his big band to a septet—following the example of Louis Jordan and Roy Milton—and cut tracks for Excelsior with honking tenor saxophonist Big Jay McNeely. He also began featuring such singers as Mel Walker, Little Esther Phillips, and the Robins, a vocal group that would later become The Coasters.

In 1951 Otis recorded with Dinah Washington, using Ben Webster as a guest with his band. In 1953 he signed with Don Robey's Duke/Peacock label and cut several jump blues tracks as a leader and as a backing band for some of Robey's acts, including Johnny Ace, Marie Adams, and Big Mama Thornton, whose "Hound Dog" created a stir and would cause a sensation three years later when Elvis Presley cut a cover version of the tune. Otis presided over his own short-lived Ultra/Dig label in 1956 to showcase his new discovery Arthur Lee Maye & The Crowns. Then in 1957 he signed with Capitol Records and scored a massive hit a year later with the infectious ditty "Willie and the Hand Jive."

> **"I know a cat named Way-Out Willie, he's got a cool little chick named rockin' Milly."**
> — *Johnny Otis*

In the late 1950s Otis became a radio deejay and hosted a live R&B revue on a weekly TV series shot in Los Angeles. Then in 1958 he did a guest shot in the movie *Juke Box Rhythm.* In 1970 the R&B renaissance man put together a fabulous jump blues oldies package for the Monterey Jazz Festival, which included such stars as Big Joe Turner, Roy Milton, Roy Brown, Pee Wee Crayton, and Eddie "Cleanhead" Vinson. Like Little Richard, he had a stint as a preacher in his own church. Then in 1972 he formed his own Blues Spectrum label, which was inaugurated to document living jump blues legends like Big Joe Turner, Joe Liggins, and Louis Jordan.

In the early 1990s he led an occasional big band, featuring some Swing Era veterans and his sons, guitarist Shuggie and drummer Nicky Otis.

# BOB DOROUGH

BORN: December 12, 1923, in Cherry Hill, Arkansas

BACK IN 1956 Bob Dorough introduced his classic vocalese adaptation of Charlie Parker's "Yardbird Suite" on his acclaimed Bethlehem debut, *Devil May Care*. That album caught the ear of Miles Davis, who would enlist the singer for a 1962 recording of "Blue Xmas" and in 1967 for a recording of "Nothing like You" on his landmark quintet album, *Sorcerer*.

Growing up in Texas, Dorough was exposed to small-group jazz while attending Texas Tech in Lubbock. Drafted into the Army in 1942 he initially served in an antiaircraft artillery unit before a punctured eardrum led to his transfer to a band unit, where he met jazz musicians from New York and Chicago. After his discharge in 1945 he enrolled at North Texas State (one of the first American universities to establish a jazz curriculum) where he majored in composition and minored in piano. "That's when I first heard Charlie Parker," he told Don Heckman of the *Los Angeles Times*. "I was playing a kind of primitive piano at the time when I met a couple of guys who had Parker's bebop recordings on Dial. They invited me up to the room to hear things like 'Hot House' and 'Groovin' High,' and explained how they were actually based on the chords to tunes I might know. So I learned then that 'Hot House' is actually based on 'What Is This Thing Called Love?' It was wild, a really thrilling musical breakthrough for me."

**"No cares for me, I'm happy as I can be."**
— *Bob Dorough*

After moving to New York in 1950 he became part of a jazz jam scene that included the likes of Bill Evans, Tommy Flanagan, Pepper Adams, Kenny Burrell, and Thad and Elvin Jones.

From 1952 to 1954 he worked as musical director for Sugar Ray Robinson when the ex-boxing champ tried a singing career. Following the 1956 release of his Bethlehem debut, Dorough drifted to Los Angeles and worked as a solo singer-pianist and as part of a jazz quintet. In 1962 he co-wrote the Mel Torme pop single "Comin' Home Baby" and later that year recorded with Miles Davis. His second album as a leader, *Just about Everything,* was released in 1966 on the small Focus label. Three decades passed before Dorough would record again as a leader. His 1997 debut for Blue Note, *Right on My Way Home,* marks the comeback of one of jazz's true individualists. His rollicking, reckless, and highly idiosyncratic style is show-cased on rousing renditions of the Cootie Williams classic "Fish for Supper," Dave Frishberg's "Oklahoma Toad," and the swinging novelty number "The Coffee Song (They've Got an Awful Lot of Coffee in Brazil)".

At the age of seventy-seven Dorough continues to spread joy with his eccentric, fun-loving bebop 'n' jive. As he told Joel E. Siegel of *Jazz Times* magazine in a 1997 interview: "My job is to cheer people up, baby."

# MOSE ALLISON

BORN: November 11, 1927, in Tippo, Mississippi

HIS WRY DITTIES AND DOWN-HOME SOUTHERN CHARM have enter-tained listeners for four decades. As a pianist, vocalist, and songwriter, Mose Allison has had a strong influence on two generations of musicians. And as a social commentator he ranks right up there with such acclaimed acerbic observers of the human condition as Kurt Vonnegut and Hunter S. Thompson. As Patrick W. Hinley of *Down Beat* magazine put it in his 1987 review of *Ever Since the World Ended*: "He has a way of summing things up with just enough of a twist to the dagger to make it tickle."

That sentiment goes back to Allison's 1957 debut for Prestige, *Back Country Suite,* which included the tune "Young Man Blues," later popularized in 1970 by The Who. Allison wrote a sequel to that tune forty years later entitled, appropriately enough, "Old Man Blues."

Growing up in Mississippi, Mose was exposed to a wide range of jazz and blues that was available in the South during the '30s and '40s, drawing heavily on such influences as Nat "King" Cole, Sonny Boy Williamson, Percy Mayfield, and Louis Jordan. Widely varying sources continue to spur Mose's music, from John Lee Hooker to Thelonious Monk, from Muddy Waters to John Lewis. "I always figured that you've got to be able to assimilate what normally seem to be opposing elements. That's the way reality is," he told Nat Hentoff for the liner notes to his 1962 Atlantic debut, *I Don't Worry about a Thing.*

> "Because your mind is on vacation and your mouth is working overtime."
> — *Mose Allison*

As a young man he studied piano and trumpet, then attended Louisiana State University as a literature major. Following a stint in the Army he moved to New York City in 1956 and tried to break into the scene as a trumpet player. He later got work in town as a pianist with groups led by Stan Getz, Zoot Sims, Al Cohn, Chet Baker, and Gerry Mulligan.

After drawing some initial buzz from *Back Country Suite,* Allison came into his own as a singer-songwriter in the 1960s with sharp-edged jive tunes like "Your Mind Is on Vacation (But Your Mouth Is Working Overtime)" and "I Don't Worry about a Thing ('Cause I Know Nothing's Gonna Be Alright)." He also garnered praise for his jazzy interpretation of bluesman Willie Dixon's "Seventh Son," which he continues to perform in his nightclub act.

Says Mose regarding his position in the marketplace, "In the South I'm considered an advanced bebop type. In New York I'm considered a country blues, folk type. Actually, I don't think I'm either."

Regardless of the category, Allison has made an undeniable impact on the jazz 'n' jive scene as a gifted and colorful singer-songwriter.

## BEN SIDRAN

———◆———

BORN: August 14, 1943, in Chicago, Illinois

IN HIS PH.D. DISSERTATION, *Black Talk* (which was published in 1971 by Holt, Rinehart & Winston, then reprinted in paperback in 1983 by Da Capo Press) writer-musician-producer Ben Sidran addressed the oral continuum and its impact on music over time, or as Archie Shepp referred to it in the foreword to that tome, "the social process by which black music is communicated." Among other things, Sidran concluded that the musician is the document. "He is the information itself," wrote Sidran. "The impact of stored information is transmitted not through records or archives but through the human response to life. And that response is ongoing, in the air, everywhere, an alternative constantly available to those who have ears to hear."

**"One-two-three-four-five-six-seven . . . steps to heaven."**

— *Ben Sidran*

Sidran has practiced his own sort of oral tradition through a recording career that stretches back thirty years, beginning with 1971's *Feel Your Groove* and continues to this day with his various albums and productions for other artists. A contemporary renaissance man who has written music criticism for *Rolling Stone,* published two books, and done session work as a pianist with the likes of Eric Clapton, Peter Frampton, and The Rolling Stones, Sidran has also contributed to the growing body of jive with original material that is imbued with mother wit, wisdom, and swing.

Although he holds a doctoral degree in American studies from England's University of Sussex, Ben claims "I got my real education at the University of Bob Dylan and Mose Allison." Born in Chicago and raised in Wisconsin, Ben first began playing professionally while attending the University of Wisconsin at Madison, where he met Steve Miller and Boz Scaggs, with whom he would record on the first Steve Miller Band album, *Children of the Future.*

After recording his first solo album, *Feel Your Groove,* for Capitol Records in 1971, Sidran went on to teach at the University of Wisconsin while releasing three more albums for Blue Thumb Records and a subsequent four for Arista, which featured such top-notch jazz players as saxophonist Phil Woods, trumpeter Blue Mitchell, and drummer Tony Williams. "Playing with them, I got a sense that the only way to really learn this music is to be in the same room, breathing the same air with the innovators," Sidran said. "The music's in the feeling and the expression of the moment, not in the notes."

His 1979 album for A&M, *The Cat and the Hat,* which featured vocalese versions of Miles Davis's "Seven Steps to Heaven" and Thelonious Monk's

"Ask Me Now," became an instant favorite with hip radio programmers everywhere. "Having produced a Jon Hendricks album and watching how the man works gave me a lot of insight into writing lyrics for bebop tunes," he said. "For example, he told me that you have to be able to hear the entire melody line in your head in such a way that you feel and understand the song's internal logic first before you go ahead and try to fit words into the puzzle."

Through the 1980s and 1990s, Sidran hosted National Public Radio's popular *Jazz Alive!* program while continuing to tour, record, and produce. He produced Mose Allison's last four Blue Note recordings—1987's *Ever Since the World Ended*, 1990's *My Backyard*, 1994's *The Earth Wants You*, and 1998's *Gimcracks and Gewgaws*.

# TIM HAUSER

BORN: December 12, 1941, in Troy, New York

THE FOUNDER OF MANHATTAN TRANSFER has been knee-deep in music from the time he could walk. As a youngster living on the New Jersey shore in the 1950s, Tim attended St. Rose High School in Belmar, where he was a member of the glee club. It was also the era of "classic" rock 'n' roll and doo-wop, and Tim lived it. His musical roots were heavily influenced by the black R&B music of the time.

"I must have been in my early teens when I got exposed to that whole language of jive that permeated that scene at the time," he recalls. "And I actually got exposed to it through a lot of New York radio personalities, like Jocko, The Bruce, and Jazzbo Collins, to a degree. [See the foreword for more on these cats.] But of those guys, to me, Jocko was unreal. When I first started listening to him I was thirteen and I thought, 'This is happening!' Through him I just got attuned to that kind of jive sensibility, and then just hearing fragments of those things in lot of rhythm 'n' blues records I naturally got deeper and deeper into it. You make discoveries along the way and it just kind of builds up until you realize that that is a whole genre, a thing unto itself. And then, of course, you go back and find out where those cats got it from. It's just a part of black talk that really started to proliferate in the music of the '30s and '40s. And you know how it is, you just go on in your life and as you're moving forward someone turns you onto this, someone turns you onto that . . . and the picture just gets bigger and bigger until there it is." A major jive epiphany came backstage at a rock 'n' roll show starring Frankie Lymon and The Teenagers. "I heard them warming up before the show. The sound of their harmony made me want to do the same thing."

Hauser began to sing professionally at the age of fifteen when he founded a teenage doo-wop/R&B/rock 'n' roll quintet called The Criterions. They cut several songs for the Laurie label. In 1959 "I Remain Truly Yours," a song they cut during their third session, was a mild success, reaching number twenty-four on the charts in New York. The group also performed at many R&B revues and record hops in the New York area, appearing alongside Dion & The Belmonts, The Elegants, and The Heartbeats. The Criterions also made an appearance on Alan Freed's *Big Beat* TV show. Hauser also developed his producing skills at an early age. When he was seventeen he produced a version of "Harlem Nocturne" for The Viscounts. The song reached the number three spot on the *Billboard* chart in 1959. That same year he graduated from St. Rose and entered Villanova University. His college years were a continuation of the musical involvement he had started to develop, with Tim spending much of his college time energetically expanding his musical interests. In an early interview with Manhattan Transfer that appeared in *The New York Sunday News* in August of 1975, writer Nat Hentoff describes Tim recalling his college days: "He rose suddenly, smote his forehead, and said, 'Do you know how much music meant to me when I was going to college? Do you really know? Music meant so much to me that I even gave up chicks.' Laurel Masse was sitting nearby and asked Hauser if he was serious. 'I am! I am!' he said."

Tim was involved in radio WWVV, and was active in the Villanova Singers, which included his classmates Jim Croce and former Criterion Tommy West. Tim formed a folk trio with West and another former Criterion Jim Ruf. They called themselves The Troubadours Three, and sang professionally throughout the area. In 1963 he graduated from Villanova with a BA in Economics. That summer The Troubadours Three toured the United States as performers with "Hootenanny Stars of 1963."

In 1964 Tim spent time in the Air Force and the New Jersey Air National Guard. A detour in his musical pursuits came in 1965, when he took a job as a research analyst with an advertising firm. Then in 1967 he became the manager of the market research department of the special products division of The National Biscuit Company (Nabisco). But his love for music, and his strong desire to be a musician and to sing, was still present. As Tim puts it: "I almost went wacko. I was twenty-eight and figured if I wanted to be a musician, it was now or never." He left the Madison Avenue scene and started to pursue his dream of a career in music.

In 1969 he formed the first version of Manhattan Transfer with Gene Pistilli, Marty Nelson, Erin Dickins, and Pat Rosalia. The group had a country/R&B sound. Together they recorded one album in 1971, *Jukin'* (Capitol), which included a version of Stuff Smith's "You'se a Viper" and "Java Jive," which Manhattan Transfer would later record on its self-titled 1975 debut for Atlantic and on 1997's *Swing* for Atlantic. That original Transfer outfit ultimately broke up over differences of direction: Pistilli leaned more toward a country-western/Memphis R&B sound, whereas Hauser was more interested in a jazz/swing sound.

> **"I'm El Dorado Kaddy, the sugar disco daddy."**
> — *Tim Hauser*

After the group disbanded Tim took odd jobs to support himself while still pursuing his musical career. One of his jobs was taxicab driving, where he drove the night line. He can spin innumerable tall tales from those days as a hack, but one of the most incredible stories involves a most serendipitous meeting with someone who is still very much a part of his life today. It was an April night in 1972 and Tim was making the rounds in his cab when suddenly he was flagged down by a tall redhaired waitress who was getting off work. In conversation during the ride Tim discovered that she also happened to be an aspiring singer. Her name was Laurel Masse. At some point Tim mentioned to her that he was also a singer and founder of Manhattan Transfer. Coincidentally (or not) Laurel was hip to their music, having seen them perform at The Fillmore East. She even had a copy of *Jukin'*. Sensing a kindred thing developing in the space of that cab ride, they decided to stop for coffee and pursue it a bit further. They discussed music and arranged to meet again.

Shortly after meeting Laurel, Tim was once more driving his cab when he picked up the conga player for the group Laurel Canyon. Through the course of the conversation the conga player invited Tim to a party, where he met singer Janis Siegel, who was a member of Laurel Canyon at the time. [See Janis Siegel entry in chapter seven.] Tim was impressed with Janis's vocal talents and together with Laurel, they decided to re-form Manhattan Transfer. In search of a fourth partner, a male voice, they sought out Alan

Paul, who was appearing in the Broadway cast of *Grease* at the time. As it turns out Paul had heard Janis perform before. They all met and talked about music and how there was a lack of four-part harmony in the music of the time. They shared their ideas, and the chemistry was there. The four became Manhattan Transfer on October 1, 1972.

In its formative years the group developed a strong cult following while playing such New York clubs as Trudy Heller's, Reno Sweeny's, and Max's Kansas City. In 1975 they cut their eponymously titled Atlantic debut album and landed their own highly experimental television show on CBS. They were particularly successful in Europe, where their next two albums, *Coming Out* and *Pastiche,* brought them a string of Top 10 hits. A live album, *Manhattan Transfer Live,* soon followed.

Masse left the group to pursue a solo career in 1978 and was replaced by a young singer-actress from Mt. Vernon, Washington, named Cheryl Bentyne. The Transfer's next album, 1979's *Extensions,* earned them their first domestic pop hit, "Twilight Zone," penned by Alan Paul and Jay Graydon. The album also featured "Birdland," the piece that has since become Manhattan Transfer's signature tune. Jon Hendricks wrote the lyrics to Joe Zawinul's instrumental homage to New York's landmark nightclub of the 1950s, and Siegel arranged the vocals. The most-played jazz track of 1980, "Birdland" brought Manhattan Transfer its first Grammy Award (Best Jazz Fusion Performance, Vocal or Instrumental) and the award for Best Arrangement for Voices, which Janis took home.

In 1981 Manhattan Transfer made music history by becoming the first group to win Grammy Awards in both pop and jazz categories in the same year. "Boy from New York City," which broke into the Top 10 on the pop charts, garnered them the award for Best Pop Performance by a Duo or Group with Vocal, and "Until I Met You (Corner Pocket)" earned them a Grammy for Best Jazz Performance, Duo or Group. Both of these appeared on the combo's fifth outing for Atlantic, *Mecca for Moderns.*

Over the course of twenty-five years and nearly twenty albums, Manhattan Transfer has made several nods to jive fare, beginning with "Java Jive" from their 1975 self-titled debut for Atlantic and continuing with "Killer Joe" from 1985's *Vocalese,* the group's tribute to vocalese pioneer Jon Hendricks. But perhaps their most jive-laden offering was 1997's acclaimed love letter to the 1930s, *Swing,* which includes spirited renditions of Ella Fitzgerald's monster hit from 1938, "A-Tisket, A-Tasket," backed by Ray Benson and Asleep at the Wheel, vocalese versions of Lionel Hampton's "Air Mail Special" and Bennie Moten's 1932 classic "Moten's Swing," along with a reprise of "Java Jive" and a killer version of Louis Jordan's jump blues anthem, "Choo Choo Ch'Boogie." Manhattan's most recent recording is a tribute to the godfather of jive himself, Louis Armstrong, entitled *Spirit of St. Louis.*

# DAN HICKS

BORN: December 9, 1941, in Little Rock, Arkansas

A MUSICAL ECCENTRIC, Hicks blended in a savvy manner Djangoesque gypsy jazz, country, and swing with jivey call-and-response vocals, jazz phrasing, and a large dose of offbeat humor, helping him to build a unique body of work that earned him a devoted cult following in the early 1970s.

A charter member of the Charlatans, one of the Bay Area's first psychedelic bands, Hicks formed the acoustic group Dan Hicks and His Hot Licks in 1968 as a separate side project. After adding a pair of female backing vocalists— "the Lickettes"—the chemistry clicked and the Hot Licks soon became Hicks's pet project. In 1969 they issued their groundbreaking debut album, *Original Recordings,* and followed up with two tightly swinging acoustic string jazz offerings, 1971's *Where's the Money?* and 1972's *Striking It Rich.* The success of 1973's *Last Train to Hicksville*—which included the jivey tune "'Long Come a Viper," Hicks's homage to '30s viper tunes—

> **"Jesus Christ and God and all them cats, they don't know everything. And besides that, they can't even sing."**
> — *Dan Hicks*

prompted a cover story on Hicks in *Rolling Stone.* But at the peak of the band's popularity—in 1974 (during which time they were making television appearances on the Flip Wilson, Dick Cavett, and Johnny Carson shows)— Hicks broke up the Hot Licks. In 1978 he came out with the solo project *It Happened One Bite,* the soundtrack to an animated feature by Ralph Bakshi. Through the 1980s and 1990s Hicks worked largely behind the scenes as a producer while cutting the occasional jingle for Levi's and McDonalds.

Hicks and his Hot Licks resurfaced in the summer of 2000 with *Beatin' the Heat,* a typically buoyant collection of playful melodies and delightfully wry observations about life, underscored by swing rhythms and jive vocabulary. Special guests on this superb comeback record include longtime fans like Bette Midler on "Strike It While It's Hot!" Tom Waits on the super-jivey "I'll Tell You Why That Is," Rickie Lee Jones on a remake of Hicks's 1969 hit "I Scare Myself," Elvis Costello on the jumped-up "Meet Me on the Corner," and Brian Setzer on "I Don't Want Love." Elsewhere Hicks makes with the rapid, flip patter on "Doin' It," swings out on "Don't Stop the Meter, Mack," and gets giddy on "Hell, I'd Go!" (a wonderfully comic tale about alien abduction with some slick scatting choruses from the aliens themselves, which has shades of Slim Gaillard and Harry "The Hipster" Gibson jamming with Hoagy Carmichael, with vocal support from The Andrews Sisters).

———————————•———————————

## Jivenotes:

A hipster's aura hangs around **Tom Waits,** the enigmatic singer-songwriter-poet who parlayed his eccentric charms into a considerable acting career in the 1980s and 1990s. Born on December 9, 1949, in Ponoma, California, Waits first came to be noticed as a unique solo performer whose free verse and humorous raps set to music suggested a modern-day Lord Buckley. His series of low-life travelogues illuminating the dark world of bars and all-night diners began with 1973's *Closing Time* and continued with 1974's *The Heart of Saturday Night* and 1975's *Nighthawks at the Diner.* His brilliant 1976 album *Small Change*—basically a collection of poetry recitations with jazzy backing provided by a trio consisting of drummer Shelly Manne, saxophonist Lew Tabackin, and bassist Jim Hughart—includes the jivey offerings "Step Right Up" and "Jitterbug Boy." Imagine a cross between Hoagy Carmichael and Captain Beefheart, with a gravelly Satchmo voice.

**Leon Redbone** is another highly eccentric, wholly unique musical personality who emerged on the scene in the 1970s. Influenced by other enigmatic performers like Cliff Edwards and ragtime players of the 1920s, the mysterious Mr. Redbone first came to national attention through a number of performances on the popular *Saturday Night Live* show during its first year on the air. More recently Redbone's gruff vocals and dexterous ragtime guitar work graced a TV commercial for a popular detergent—still invoking bygone eras after all these years.

**Asleep at the Wheel** exhibited an equal fondness for Bob Wills & His Texas Playboys and Louis Jordan on their 1974 self-titled album, which included a rousing rendition of Jordan's "Choo Choo Ch'Boogie." With guitarist-vocalist Ray Benson at the helm, they've been waving the flag for western swing.

# *Recommended Listening*

**THE RHYTHM BOYS**

*Bing Crosby,* Timeless (1926–1932)

*The Bing Crosby Story, Volume 1:*
   *The Early Jazz Years, 1926–1932,*
   Columbia

**CLIFF EDWARDS**

*Ukulele Ike 1922–1944,* Glendale

*The Hottest Man in Town,* ASV/Living
   Era (1922–1924)

*Cliff Edwards and His Hot Combination,*
   Fountain (1922–1928)

*I'm a Bear in a Lady's Boudoir,* Yazoo
   (1924–1928)

*Fascinatin' Rhythm,* Totem (1944)

**EMMETT MILLER**

*The Minstrel Man from Georgia,*
   Columbia/Legacy (1928–1929)

**MEZZ MEZZROW**

*Mezz Mezzrow, 1928–1936,* Classics

*King Jazz Story, Volumes 1–3,* Storyville
   (1945–1947)

**LOUIS PRIMA**

*Louis Prima, Volume 1,* JSP (1934–1935)

*Play Pretty for the People,* Savoy (1940)

*Say It with a Slap,* Buddha (1949–1950)

*The Wildest,* Capitol (1956)

*Louis Prima: Collectors Series,* Capitol
   (1956–1962)

**HARRY "THE HIPSTER" GIBSON**

*Boogie Woogie in Blue,* Musicraft
   (1944–1946)

*Who Put the Benzedrine in Mrs. Murphy's*
   *Ovaltine?* Delmark (1976, 1989)

**JOHNNY OTIS**

*Rhythm & Blues Caravan,* Savoy
   (1949–1951)

*Creepin' with the Cats: The Legendary*
   *Dig Masters,* Ace (1956–1957)

*Live at Monterey,* Epic (1971)

**BOB DOROUGH**

*Devil May Care,* Bethlehem (1956)

*Just about Everything,* Focus (1962)

*Right on My Way Home,* Blue Note (1997)

*Too Much Coffee Man,* Blue Note (2000)

*Who's on First,* Blue Note (2000)

**MOSE ALLISON**

*Back Country Suite,* Prestige (1957)

*Greatest Hits—The Prestige Collection,*
   Prestige (1957–1959)

*Young Man Mose,* Prestige (1958)

*Allison Wonderland: Anthology,*
   Rhino/Atlantic (1959–1989)

*Transfiguration of Hiram Brown,*
   Columbia (1959)

*I Love the Life I Live,* Columbia (1960)

*I Don't Worry about a Thing,*
   Atlantic (1962)

*The Word from Mose,* Atlantic (1964)

*I've Been Doin' Some Thinkin',*
   Atlantic (1968)

*Your Mind Is on Vacation,* Atlantic (1976)

*Middle Class White Boy,* Elektra
   Musicians (1982)

*Ever Since the World Ended,*
   Blue Note (1987)

*My Backyard,* Blue Note (1990)

*The Earth Wants You,* Blue Note (1994)

*Gimcracks and Gewgaws,*
  Blue Note (1998)

## BEN SIDRAN

*Feel Your Groove,* Capitol (1971)
*The Dr. Is In,* Arista (1977)
*The Cat and the Hat,* A&M (1979)
*Old Songs for the New Depression,*
  Antilles (1982)
*Bopcity,* Antilles (1983)
*On the Cool Side,* Magenta (1985)
*Cool Paradise,* Go Jazz (1992)

## TIM HAUSER

**With Manhattan Transfer:**
*Jukin',* Capitol (1971)
*Manhattan Transfer,* Atlantic (1975)
*Coming Out,* Atlantic (1976)
*Pastiche,* Atlantic (1978)
*Extensions,* Atlantic (1979)
*Mecca for Moderns,* Atlantic (1981)
*Bodies and Souls,* Atlantic (1983)
*Vocalese,* Atlantic (1985)
*Bop Doo-Wop,* Atlantic (1990)
*Tonin',* Atlantic (1995)
*Swing,* Atlantic (1997)
*Spirit of St. Louis,* Atlantic (2000)

## DAN HICKS

*Original Recordings,* Epic (1969)
*Where's the Money?* MCA (1971)
*Striking It Rich,* MCA (1972)
*Last Train to Hicksville,* MCA (1973)
*Hey Good Lookin',* Warner Bros. (1975)
*It Happened One Bite,* Warner Bros.
  (1978)
*Beatin' the Heat,* Surfdog (2000)

## TOM WAITS

*The Heart of Saturday Night,*
  Asylum (1974)
*Nighthawks at the Diner,* Aylum (1975)
*Small Change,* Asylum (1976)

## LEON REDBONE

*Across the Track,* Warner Bros. (1975)
*Double Time,* Warner Bros. (1976)
*Champagne Charlie,* Warner Bros. (1977)

## ASLEEP AT THE WHEEL

*Comin' Right at Ya,* United Artists
  (1973)
*Asleep at the Wheel,* Epic (1974)
*Texas Gold,* Capitol (1976)
*Still Swingin',* Liberty (1994)

## CHAPTER 7

# WOMEN JIVESTERS

**Connee Boswell, Ella Fitzgerald, The Andrews Sisters,
Una Mae Carlisle, Ina Ray Hutton, Ella Mae Morse, Nellie Lutcher,
Annie Ross, Janis Siegel, Candye Kane, Lavay Smith,
Katharine Whalen, Ingrid Lucia, Del Rey**

Back in the 1930s *Down Beat* magazine plastered its pages with a plethora of pictures of various "chirps" (as female singers were called at the time) fronting the popular big bands. This pinup concept is at odds with the bold and jazzy innovations made by such spirited jive pioneers as Connee Boswell, Ella Fitzgerald, Ella Mae Morse, and The Andrews Sisters—all major musical stars in their own right.

Of course, the notion of spirited women injecting their songs with insightful observations, biting humor, double entendres, social commentary, and a healthy dose of sass (i.e., jive) goes back to 1920s blues divas like Bessie Smith, Ida Cox, Memphis Minnie, and Alberta Hunter, all of whom inspired the likes of Blue Lu Marker, Ella Mae Morse, Nellie Lutcher, and modern day disciples like Candye Kane, Lavay Smith, and Del Rey . . . all representatives of the distaff branch of jive.

Each of these women made significant contributions as an entertainer and an artist, combining an inherent sense of syncopation and swing with a sly delivery and an all-knowing sense of humor. They are all bold, hep, larger-than-life figures, fully capable of slinging jive alongside their male counterparts.

# CONNEE BOSWELL

BORN: December 3, 1907, in New Orleans, Louisiana
DIED: October 7, 1976, in New York, New York

LEAD SINGER AND ARRANGER of The Boswell Sisters (a hot, swinging vocal jazz group from New Orleans that achieved the peak of its popularity from 1931 to 1935), Connee Boswell was a strong scat singer with a remarkably self-assured sense of rhythm. As John Edward Hasse states in *Jazz: The First Century*, she was one of the first white singers (along with sometime duet partner Bing Crosby, Mildred Bailey, and Jack Teagarden) to absorb and master the African American jazz idiom of the 1920s. In an article by Chris Ellis in *Storyville* magazine Ella Fitzgerald cited Connee as a major influence: "There was only one singer who influenced me. I tried to sing like her all the time because everything she did made sense musically and that singer was Connee Boswell. When I was a girl I listened to all the singers, black and white, and I know that Connee Boswell was doing things that no one else was doing at the time. You don't have to take my word for it. Just check the recordings made at the time and hear for yourself."

**"When that spirit moves you, shout hallelujah. When it hits you, you holler 'Yes indeed.'"**

— *Connee Boswell*

Confined to a wheelchair after contracting polio at the age of three, Connee was the most gifted improviser of the three sisters. Her intuitive scatting ability and blues-drenched vocals were highlighted on a series of early '30s recordings the sisters made for Brunswick, including "Roll on Mississippi, Roll On," "When I Take My Sugar to Tea," "Crazy People," "It's the Girl," and "Everybody Loves My Baby" along with spirited, jivey renditions of Cab Calloway's "Minnie the Moocher's Wedding Day," Clarence Williams's "Shout, Sister, Shout," and Louis Armstrong's seminal scat vehicle "Heebie Jeebies." (Connee made a solo version of this last tune for MCA in the 1950s.)

John Lucas assessed Connee's talents in a 1944 *Down Beat* article: "From the outset she was recognized as a peer by jazzmen such as Benny Goodman, Joe Venuti, Dick McDonough, Artie Bernstein and Chauncey Morehouse. . . . Endowed by nature with rare qualities carefully cultivated from childhood, she developed early a clarity of enunciation and a warmth of tone and an ease of delivery that seem even now incomparable. To the old question, who is truly a jazz singer, she unconsciously supplied the simple answer: the one who swings. Above all, Connee was and is a swinger. Her rhythmic sense is a miracle, enabling her to employ syncopation and introduce tempo changes to remarkable effect."

Throughout their short, hot career The Boswell Sisters conveyed good musical humor, as on delightful three-tongues-in-six-cheeks renditions of "I'm in Training for You," "When the Little Red Roses Get the Blues for You," and "Does My Baby Love?" (in which Connee suggestively declares in a laid-back N'awlins drawl, "Boy, has he got it!").

Billed as the "Syncopating Harmonists from New Orleans," The Boswell Sisters—Martha, Connee (she changed the spelling from Connie during the war years), and Helvetia (or Vet for short)—first recorded in 1925 for Victor ("Nights When I'm Lonely" and "I'm Gonna Cry"). Soon after they began appearing regularly on radio, first in Los Angeles and then in San Francisco. In 1928 they moved to Chicago and held down a regular radio gig for two years, flooding the Windy City airwaves with their Southern brand of syncopated jive. In 1930 they made four recordings for Okeh and the following year they made their New York debut at the Paramount Theater.

Between 1931 and 1935 they cut dozens of sides for Brunswick, many of which featured prominent hot players of the day. Their 1931 rendition of "Heebie Jeebies," a hit for Satchmo five years earlier, features Martha Boswell on piano, Eddie Lang on guitar, Joe Tarto on bass, and Stan King on drums. Their 1932 rendition of "There'll Be Some Changes Made" includes a featured spot by trumpeter Bunny Berigan with accompaniment by the Dorsey brothers.

In a 1944 article for *Down Beat,* Connee explained to writer John Lucas the sisters' modus operandi on those early and influential tracks: "We lil' ole Boswell gals knew best what was best for us. We had no doubt that there were many fine arrangers, but not for the stuff that we were doing. At that time I'm sure that to the average ear we must have sounded like little green people from outer space. . . . We made our name as singers. We revolutionized not only the style of singing, the beat, the placing of voices, the way-out harmony, but also the musical world in general. At an early age we thought that in time we would be doing concert work, but I think the call of the beat got us and we started leaning toward pop music. We had loads of fun with our swinging trio." While Connee worked out the band background,

intros, fill-ins, and special endings, Martha and Vet also contributed to the arrangements. As Connee told *DB:* "Some parts were as free as the breeze, while others were kept right in the saddle. . . . I do want it known, in fairness to my two sisters, that they were very important spokes in the Boswell wheel of success."

The Boswell Sisters appeared in three movies (1932's *The Big Broadcast,* 1933's *Moulin Rouge,* and 1934's *Transatlantic Merry-Go-Round*) and made two European tours, during one of which they received top billing at the London Palladium. By 1936, after recording four sides for Decca, Helvetia dropped out to become a wife and mother, effectively ending the group. Their last record date together was on February 12, 1936. Connee went on to pursue a solo career, highlighted by her many duets with Bing Crosby. Their special, easygoing chemistry was best documented on "Life Is Just a Bowl of Cherries," rousing Dixieland versions of "Basin Street Blues," and "That's a Plenty" from 1937; "Yes Indeed" and "Tea for Two" from a 1940 session backed by Bob Crosby's orchestra featuring trumpeter Mugsy Spanier; as well as a hit recording in 1938 of Johnny Mercer's "Bob White." Check this bit of jivey banter between Connee and Bing on 1940's "Yes Indeed":

> BING: Now has you got it, sister Constance? Tell me, has you got it?
>
> CONNEE: Whoa yeah! I got it, brother Bingstons, now you knows I got it.

In the movies Connee had a cameo appearance in *Swing Parade of 1946,* a zany musical variety film that also featured The Three Stooges and Louis Jordan and His Tympany Five. Through the '40s she continued to record successfully for Decca, turning out hits with "Sand in My Shoes," "Home on the Range," and "Whispers in the Dark," which also appeared in the film *Artists and Models* starring Jack Benny. Other film appearances included *Syncopation* and *Kiss the Boys Goodbye,* in which she sang "Sand in My Shoes" and stole the film.

On radio Connee was in constant demand, co-starring with Bing Crosby and Ralph Burns in NBC's *Kraft Music Hall* and also co-starring with Fanny

Connee Boswell, 1934. Frank Driggs Collection

Brice and Robert Taylor on *Maxwell House Coffee Time* as well as guesting on the shows of Arthur Godfrey and Frank Sinatra while having her own *Connee Boswell Show* on ABC.

On television she made appearances on *The Bell Telephone Hour, The Ed Sullivan Show,* and *The Perry Como Show,* among others. Then in the early 1960s Connee had a recurring role on the television series *Pete Kelly's Blues* (as Savannah Brown, opposite Jack Webb). Her last public appearance was in October of 1975, when she performed at Carnegie Hall to the accompaniment of Benny Goodman's orchestra.

In early 1976 Connee had an operation for stomach cancer, but by the middle of the year it was known that her case was terminal. She asked that no chemotherapy be used to attempt to prolong her life. While in Mount Sinai Hospital in New York, she wrote the following verse on October 7, 1976:

> *My days are numbered and it's just as well.*
> *Just how soon no one can tell.*
> *I hope that it's soon for the pain is vile,*
> *a face filled with frowns instead of a smile.*
> *When the end comes I'll be at rest,*
> *and just remember it's all for the best.*
> *And when I'm gone remember me when*
> *the sun shone brightly.*
> *And now, amen.*

Classically trained, yet hep to the jive, The Boswell Sisters influenced every vocal harmony group from The Andrews Sisters to Lambert, Hendricks & Ross to The Pointer Sisters and The Roches. And Connee was the straw that stirred this highly syncopated drink. A 1944 *Down Beat* article pointed out the contribution that Connee Boswell and her two sisters made to jazz: "Few singers have influenced the development of America's everyday songs more than Connee Boswell. Still fewer have left so deep an impression upon the interpretation of these songs. No singing group, not even the Rhythm Boys, has had such a hand in shaping our popular music as The Boswell Sisters. They sang like nobody else."

And Connee, in her unique blend of rhythmic assuredness and playfulness along with a sly sense of knowing, personified the spirit of jive.

# ELLA FITZGERALD

BORN: April 25, 1917, in Newport News, Virginia
DIED: June 14, 1996, in Beverly Hills, California

THE CELEBRATED "FIRST LADY OF SONG" got her big break at the
age of seventeen in an amateur talent show at the Apollo Theatre in Harlem,
where on a dare she took the stage and sang an impromptu version of "Judy"
in the jivey style of her main influence, Connee Boswell. That not only won
her the $25 prize, but also netted her a gig with Tiny
Bradshaw's band. Jazz saxophonist Benny Carter,
who happened to be in the Apollo audience that
fateful night in 1934, later brought Ella to the
attention of bandleader Chick Webb, who
recruited her to the ranks of his popular
orchestra, a mainstay at the Savoy Ballroom.
Ella started out sharing vocal duties with Taft
Jordan and Louis Jordan before becoming the
featured vocalist with the band. Clear tones, perfect diction, and a girlish voice were the hallmarks of
Ella's straightforward singing style early on. In later years

> "We're singing
> it because you
> asked for it,
> so we're swinging
> it just for you."
> — Ella Fitzgerald

she would develop her improvisational skills to such a degree that she was
widely regarded by male musicians as "one of the cats," capable of swinging
as forcefully and spontaneously as any soloist in the band.

In 1936 the Chick Webb Orchestra scored hits with Fitzgerald fronting
"Sing Me a Swing Song" and "You'll Have to Swing It (Mr. Paganini)" but it
was her 1938 interpretation of a children's nursery rhyme, "A-Tisket,
A-Tasket," that made Ella a household name. During her tenure with Webb
she delivered jive anthems like "Wacky Dust," "Rock It for Me," and "I'm Just
a Jitterbug" along with novelty numbers like "Chew Chew Chew Your Bubble
Gum," "The Dipsy Doodle," "My Wubba Dolly," and "I Want the Waiter with
the Water." While in Webb's employ, she also developed a romance with band
mate Louis Jordan. As John Chilton revealed in his Jordan biography, *Let the
Good Times Roll:* "Ella's close friendship with Louis Jordan was proving
irksome to Chick Webb. Chick, who was happily married to Sally, had no
romantic designs on Ella, but he felt that any romances within his band would

eventually bring heartaches and affect work. He had expressly asked his musicians to bear this in mind when Ella joined the band; most of the sidemen tolerated Ella off-stage but none of them envisaged her as a partner. When Louis joined he soon became openly flirtatious with Ella and she responded to a degree that caused onlookers to realize that a love affair was in the cards."

With the death of Chick Webb in June of 1939 Ella took over the reins of the band at the age of twenty-two, changing the name to Ella Fitzgerald and Her Famous Orchestra and remaining its leader until 1941. The regular staple of tunes she performed with the orchestra during this two-year stint included such giddy, jive-oriented offerings as "Oh Boy I'm in the Groove," "Yodelin' Jive," "Betcha Nickel," "Well Alright! (Tonight's the Night)," "That's All, Brother," and a faithful rendition of Cab Calloway's "Jumpin' Jive" interspersed with sweet ballads and soulfully rendered standards.

The young singer cut her first sides as a soloist for Decca on October 6, 1941. In 1942 she made a cameo appearance in the Abbott & Costello film *Ride 'Em Cowboy,* singing "A-Tisket A-Tasket" while aboard the band bus. In 1943 she teamed with The Ink Spots for a hep version of "Cow Cow Boogie." They reprised their soothing chemistry the following year on "Into Each Life Some Rain Must Fall" and the dreamy "I'm Making Believe." On her tracks with the Delta Rhythm Boys—"It's Only a Paper Moon" and "Cry You out of My Heart," recorded on March 27, 1945—Fitzgerald demonstrated a freer, more mature sense of phrasing while alluding to the remarkably agile Louis Armstrong–influenced scat prowess that would become her trademark in her Jazz at the Philharmonic years. This same freewheeling scat abandon was also apparent on her vocalese showcase of October 4, 1945, a hard-swinging rendition of Lionel Hampton's hit "Flying Home." Four days later she went into the studio with Louis Jordan and His Tympany Five to record two engaging duets with her former Chick Webb band mate and paramour. The calypso-flavored "Stone Cold Dead in the Market" is a humorous conversation between a strong-headed woman and the abusive husband she murdered, sung in West Indian accents. And "Petootie Pie," which features some agile exchanges between Jordan's alto sax and Ella's scat, is rife with sexual innuendo:

> Petootie Pie, Petootie Pie,
> you're such a tasty hunk of pastry, me oh my.

Ella Fitzgerald at the Savoy Ballroom with her Famous Orchestra, 1940. Frank Driggs Collection

*I crave and cram your special jam,*
*you underrated solidated Superman.*

Ella's string of celebrity duets continued in 1946 with the godfather himself, Louis Armstrong. Their nimble, mercurial phrasing and organic chemistry is quite apparent on mellow swinging versions of "You Won't Be Satisfied" and the jivey anthem "The Frim Fram Sauce."

Beginning in 1948, the year she married the great jazz bassist Ray Brown, Ella became a perennial favorite on Norman Granz's Jazz at the Philharmonic circuit, unleashing her formidable scatting chops in the company of such jazz stars as Dizzy Gillespie, Flip Phillips, Roy Eldridge, Herb Ellis, and Oscar Peterson. She hit the charts once again with a high-flying scat-laden version of "Lady Be Good," a song that she would be closely identified with through the rest of her career. As bassist and bandleader Bob Haggart said in Gino Falzarano's liner notes to *Ella Fitzgerald: The War Years* (1941–1947): "Ella would dig all the guys playing solos in the Chick Webb band and could sing along with them. She had a terrific memory and had such a great ear that she could put all those riffs together end to end. She could do 12 choruses if you asked her, and each one would be different!"

Fitzgerald's profile rose in the 1950s through a series of television and concert appearances along with a cameo in the 1955 film *Pete Kelly's Blues.* During this period she also signed with Verve Records and released a string of very popular "songbook" recordings dedicated to the works of Duke Ellington, Cole Porter, Jerome Kern, Irving Berlin, Johnny Mercer, Harold Arlen, and George and Ira Gershwin. One of the most rewarding albums in this series is her 1958 encounter with Louis Armstrong on Gershwin's *Porgy & Bess.* In 1960 she scored another hit with her jivey, upbeat reading of Kurt Weill's "Mack the Knife." After receding a bit from the limelight in the rock-heavy '60s, she re-emerged in the '70s for a series of classy encounters on Norman Granz's Pablo label with the likes of Joe Pass, Oscar Peterson, and Count Basie.

She fell into ill health in the 1980s, was admitted into intensive care for heart trouble in 1986, then made a comeback in 1990, performing in a London concert with the Count Basie Orchestra. By 1994 Ella was in retirement, confined to a wheelchair. She passed away two years later. As one of the most gifted improvisers in vocal jazz, Ella Fitzgerald remains greatly revered by generations of musicians and fans alike—a jazz icon for the ages.

# THE ANDREWS SISTERS

FORMED: 1932 in Minneapolis, Minnesota

INSPIRED BY THE HEP SYNCOPATION and natural swing feel of The Boswell Sisters, The Andrews Sisters became the most popular female act of the boogie-woogie-crazed '40s. The trio's tight harmonies, agile sense of swing, and ebullient stage presence—both in concert and in a string of popular movies through the '40s—earned them the billing of "America's Wartime Sweethearts" as they tirelessly entertained the troops during World War II on USO tours. During their career the amazing trio recorded more than 1,800 songs and sold more than 90 million records.

The Andrews Sisters—LaVerne (Born: July 6, 1911; Died: May 8, 1967), Maxene (Born: January 3, 1916; Died: October 21, 1995), and Patty (Born: February 26, 1918)—were still teenagers when they began performing around the Minneapolis region with the Larry Rich Orchestra. They mounted a vaudeville act by the early '30s and finally made it to New York in the mid-1930s with Leon Belasco's orchestra. They had Patty as the lead soprano, Maxene as the second soprano, and LaVerne completed the sound with a resonant contralto or bass. The sisters were eventually signed to Decca by Dave Kapp and hit big in 1937 with "Bei Mir Bist Du Schoen," a remake of a song from a Yiddish musical with new lyrics which became the first million-selling record for an all-female group.

> **"Beat me daddy, eight to the bar."**
> —*The Andrews Sisters*

In his 1999 biography *Swing It! The Andrews Sisters Story,* author John Sforza recounts the story behind the sisters' first big hit: "Maxene often said in interviews that [Lou] Levy presented the song to her and her sisters, claiming that it was an old Yiddish lullaby that his mother sang to him when he was a child. Sammy Cahn, who, along with Saul Chaplin, would write an English translation to the Yiddish lyrics, claimed in his autobiography, 'I Should Care,' that he gave the sheet music copy of the Yiddish tune to the Andrews Sisters when Patty noticed a copy of it on his piano during a visit to his New York apartment."

The tune had actually been composed several years earlier, in 1932, by Sholom Secunda, who wrote the melody, and by Jacob Jacobs, who penned the Yiddish lyrics. The song was featured in a Yiddish musical, *I Would if I Could,* and the composers sold it to the show's producers for a mere thirty dollars. After learning the Yiddish song phonetically from Levy, the sisters worked out an arrangement with Vic Schoen, their musical arranger and conductor, and soon recorded "Bei Mir Bist Du Schoen (Means that You're Grand)" for Decca.

"Within a matter of days after its release," writes Sforza, "the record that resulted from the trio's history-making session became a smash hit, ousting 'The Music Goes 'Round and 'Round' from its number-one chart position. . . . Disc sales soon amounted to one million copies, making the Andrews Sisters the first female vocal group to achieve a gold record. Total sales of 'Bei Mir' would reach fourteen million by 1950 and the song would gross more than three million dollars by 1960. 'Bei Mir' was such a sensation that the Kapp

**The Andrews Sisters, 1941 (from left to right): LaVerne, Patty, and Maxene.**
**Frank Driggs Collection**

brothers upped the sisters' salary to five hundred dollars a week (they had previously been getting fifty dollars per session)."

"Bei Mir Bist Du Schoen," which unveiled to the public a fresh new vocalized swing sound as danceable as that from any big band, was named Most Popular Song of 1938 by the American Society of Composers, Authors and Publishers. It was also recorded in cover versions by the orchestras of Guy Lombardo, Tommy Dorsey, and Jimmie Lunceford, as well as by Ella Fitzgerald. Judy Garland also recorded the song for MGM's *Love Finds Andy Hardy.* "When Benny Goodman and his orchestra performed their version of the song during Goodman's now-legendary 1938 concert at Carnegie Hall," writes Sforza, "the audience was driven into a hand-clapping, foot-stomping frenzy."

The Andrews Sisters remained popular during the late '30s with "Hold Tight, Hold Tight," "Beer Barrel Polka," "Well All Right (Tonight's the Night)," and their second chart-topper, "Ferryboat Serenade." Their effervescent stage presence, sunny optimism, and all-American looks also made them a natural for Hollywood during wartime, and they cashed in on a few cameo appearances in 1940. The following year they introduced a new hit, "Boogie Woogie Bugle Boy," in the Abbott and Costello war movie *Buck Privates.* By the middle of World War II, they rolled out a string of hits like 1943's "Shoo-Shoo Baby" and "Pistol Packin' Mama" (with Bing Crosby), 1944's "Hot Time in the Town of Berlin" and "Don't Fence Me In" (with Crosby), 1945's "Ac-Cent-Tchu-Ate the Positive" (again with frequent duet partner Crosby), and other catchy ditties like "Don't Sit under the Apple Tree (With Anyone Else but Me)" and "Rum and Coca-Cola." In 1948 they appeared in the fifth of a series of highly successful Bing Crosby–Bob Hope pictures, *Road to Rio.*

Patty made her solo-billed debut in 1949 with "I Can Dream, Can't I?" backed up by sisters LaVerne and Maxene. Both that number and her follow-up, 1950's "I Wanna Be Loved," hit number one, prompting Patty to leave the group in 1953 to pursue a full-time solo career. In 1966 LaVerne had to retire due to poor health. She died of cancer the following year. Patty and Maxene continued to perform with Joyce de Young. In 1970 Patty appeared in a Los Angeles stage musical, *Victory Canteen.* Four years later Patty and Maxene teamed up for a WWII–themed Broadway musical *Over Here,* which ran for 341 performances and also included Marilu Henner, Treat Williams, Ann Reinking, and John Travolta in the cast. Maxene recorded her first solo album in 1985 and made charity appearances several years later before dying in 1995. Patty continued to perform through the '80s and appeared with the Glenn Miller Orchestra.

# UNA MAE CARLISLE

BORN: December 26, 1915, in Xenia, Ohio
DIED: November 7, 1956, in New York, New York

STILL IN HIGH SCHOOL when she was discovered by jive icon Fats Waller, vocalist-pianist Una Mae Carlisle gained national attention in the early 1930s for her regular appearances as Fats's duet partner on broadcasts from radio station WWL in Cincinnati. As Maurice Waller writes in his biography of his father: "In short order, Una Mae became Dad's shadow. Everywhere he was, she was close behind. Pop taught her to drink and to stay up late and party. Their relationship soon went far beyond the protege-master level." Though married, Waller carried on a torrid affair with the young singer, who often expressed her disdain about her role as mistress. Consequently, theirs was a rocky relationship, full of volatile scenes that were played out in public.

Carlisle (or as Fats called her, "Sister Gizzard-hip") made her first appearance on record with Waller at the age of sixteen, cutting a version of "Mean Old Bed Bug Blues" while in New York for summer vacation in July of 1932. They carried on an affair in Cincinnati through the end of 1933. When Waller's contract at WWL expired in 1934, he returned to Harlem on his own. With the romance over, Carlisle went to New York herself and auditioned for and was hired as a dancer at The Cotton Club. She later landed a job with the Blackbirds revue, which traveled to Europe in 1936.

**"I can't give you anything but love . . . baby."**

— *Una Mae Carlisle*

Una Mae spent the next three years in Europe, mostly in London and Paris. In London on May 20, 1938, she recorded some sides for Vocalion (with Leonard Feather producing), including "Don't Try Your Jive on Me" and "Mean to Me." During her time abroad, she also had numerous club dates, did film work in France, operated her own club briefly in Montmartre, and studied harmony at the Sorbonne.

Carlisle returned to New York in 1939 and on November 3 of that year was reunited with Fats Waller on his definitive version of "I Can't Give You Anything but Love," with Fats slinging sly bits of jive and innuendo in between Una Mae's relatively straightforward delivery of that lyrical ballad.

In 1941 she recorded "Blitzkrieg Baby (You Can't Bomb Me)" with tenor sax legend Lester Young and the following year recorded "I See a Million People" with trumpeter Charlie Shavers. In 1944 she recorded "Tain't Yours" with cornetist Ray Nance, a onetime key member of the Duke Ellington Orchestra.

Following Waller's death in 1943, Carlisle continued recording with Fats's former sidemen. Her career picked up in the early 1950s when she began appearing in films, on radio, and in television shows. Her last studio session was on May 8, 1950, for Columbia. Illness forced her to retire in 1954 and she died on November 7, 1956, in New York.

# INA RAY HUTTON

BORN: March 13, 1916, in Chicago, Illinois
DIED: February 19, 1984, in Los Angeles, California

ALTHOUGH SHE NEITHER SANG nor played an instrument, bandleader Ina Ray Hutton was nonetheless pictured on the cover of *Down Beat* magazine in 1940. A stunning blonde who appeared on stage in form-fitting gowns, Hutton wielded a mean baton while emulating the frantic, show-stopping stage presence of Cab Calloway and sporting constant costume changes. (*Down Beat* reported in 1939 that her stage wardrobe included more than four hundred gowns.) At the peak of her popularity she was known as "The Blonde Bombshell of Rhythm."

Born Odessa Cowan, she tap danced in Gus Edwards's revue in 1932 and later the following year worked for impresarios George White and Florenz Ziegfeld. In 1934 she was hired by powerful manager Irving Mills to front an all-female band he was organizing. With help from Mills's publicity machine, Ina Ray Hutton and Her Melodears became hugely popular. She exuded extravagant sex appeal while her eye-catching outfits and onstage antics also helped the band's commercial success.

The Melodears had some fine musicians, notably multi-instrumentalist

Alyse Wills (formerly of the Chicago Women's Symphony), tenor saxophonist Betty Sattley, pianist Betty Roudebush, and drummer Lil Singer. From 1936 the band's repertoire was in the hands of Eddie Durham, who inserted a few jive numbers in each set. Hutton led her band in several Hollywood short films, including *Swing, Hutton, Swing, Club Hutton,* and *Feminine Rhythm.*

When Hutton's all-female band broke up in 1939, she led an all-male band briefly but then drifted from the scene. In 1949 she appeared on local Los Angeles television with an all-female band and in 1955 made the film *Girl Time.* Shortly afterwards she went into married retirement from showbiz. Although by far the best-known of the all-female big bands, Ina Ray Hutton and Her Melodears were outclassed by the International Sweethearts of Rhythm, a seventeen-piece swing group that formed in 1939 and earned acclaim in the mid-1940s through its tightly crafted arrangements and hot soloing. But then—not given to wearing form-fitting dresses and exhibiting the kind of flashy, jivey stage presence that Ina Ray Hutton was noted for—the International Sweethearts of Rhythm never made it to the cover of *Down Beat.*

# ELLA MAE MORSE

BORN: September 12, 1924, in Mansfield, Texas
DIED: October 16, 1999, in Bullhead City, Arizona

A ROMPING RAMBUNCTIOUS boogie-woogie piano player and exceedingly soulful singer, Ella Mae Morse was a hip white chick from Texas who was often mistaken on records for being a black act. Morse was only fourteen when she joined Jimmy Dorsey's band in 1939 (though Dorsey believed at the time that she was actually nineteen). After three years with Dorsey, she was recruited by former Dorsey pianist Freddie Slack, who prominently featured Ella Mae in his band. In 1942 they cut "Cow Cow Boogie," which became Capitol Records's first million-selling single. The following year Morse went solo and produced a string of bawdy jive hits with such titles as "Get

"It was a ditty he learned in the city: comma-ta aya-ay comma-ta yippity-yi-ay."
—*Ella Mae Morse*

off It and Go," "Milkman Keep Those Bottles Quiet," "Fat Meat Is Good Meat," "Mister Five by Five," and "The House of Blue Lights," a '40s precursor to rock 'n' roll that featured some hep jive talk between Morse and Don Raye.

At her peak, in the mid-1940s, Ella Mae recorded with the Nelson Riddle and Billy May orchestras (both of which would later record with Frank Sinatra), and she was also featured in motion pictures such as 1943's *Reveille with Beverly* and 1946's *South of Dixie.*

After laying off the scene for four years, she returned in 1951 with more protorock boogie-woogie material like "Money Honey" and "Oakie Boogie." She even engaged in some rockabilly-styled duets in the early '50s with Tennessee Ernie Ford just as Elvis Presley was beginning to make his big splash. She retired from the scene in 1957 and died of respiratory failure in 1999.

# NELLIE LUTCHER

BORN: October 15, 1915, in Lake Charles, Louisiana

AN OVERNIGHT SENSATION in 1947 on the strength of million-sellers like "Hurry on Down" and the jivey "Real Gone Guy," pianist-singer Nellie Lutcher gained a wide following through her frequent radio and nightclub appearances as well as her hit recordings. That momentum carried into the '50s, '60s, and '70s as she continued to entertain audiences with exuberant flair and an accomplished keyboard style reminiscent of Earl "Fatha" Hines.

Born to musical parents—her father was a professional bass player and her mother an amateur pianist—Nellie began studying the piano at the age of seven and a year later was performing at her local Baptist church. During her school years she also learned mandolin, guitar, and upright bass, but the piano remained her favorite instrument. When Lutcher was fourteen, she played piano behind Ma Rainey at a local booking and the following year quit school to tour through Texas and Louisiana with Clarence Hart's Imperial Orchestra, which included her father on bass and for a time featured the great New Orleans trumpeter Bunk Johnson. She got her baptism in jive with the Southern Rhythm Boys, the first group in which she sang professionally.

In 1935 Lutcher moved to Los Angeles and worked as a single opening act at the Dunbar Lounge. In subsequent years she worked with trumpeter Dootsie Williams and also supplied accompaniment for singers like Lena

Horne and Ivie Anderson. She labored in obscurity for the next several years until 1947, when Capitol Records talent scout Dave Dexter happened to hear Nellie on a March of Dimes benefit radio program in Los Angeles. She performed "The One I Love Belongs to Somebody Else," Dexter was knocked out, and Nellie was quickly signed to Capitol Records. Her first two sessions from 1947 resulted in her two biggest hits, "Hurry on Down" and "He's a Real Gone Guy," both of which have remained signature tunes for Lutcher through the decades. Her other popular recordings were "Fine Brown Frame," "You Had Better Watch Yourself, Bub," "Lake Charles Boogie," her jump blues number "The Song Is Ended," and the risqué "Come and Get It, Honey." At the peak of her popularity she recorded duets with Nat "King" Cole and Louis Jordan.

> **"You had better watch yourself, Bub."**
> — *Nellie Lutcher*

Lutcher's vibrant swing-styled piano worked well with her eccentric scatting and exaggerated pronunciation of words. However, no other hits followed her string of good fortune in the late '40s and by 1952 she was dropped by Capitol. There were isolated recordings for Epic (1952–1953), Liberty (1956), and Imperial (1957), but the singer-pianist made very few records after 1957, working instead at the local Musicians Union and gigging locally. Nellie Lutcher re-emerged in 1980, playing a long engagement at The Cookery in New York. She continued working on a part-time basis into the 1990s, but was still most famous for her recordings of 1947.

# ANNIE ROSS

BORN: July 25, 1930, in Surrey, England

IF ANNIE ROSS had done nothing more in her career than "Twisted," her 1952 vocalese version of saxophonist Wardell Gray's famous solo, she would still merit mention in the Jive Hall of Fame. But this hip, boppish singer-trumpeter would go on to break new ground with Lambert, Hendricks &

**Nellie Lutcher, 1947. Courtesy the Institute of Jazz Studies at Rutgers University**

Ross, a pioneering group in vocal jazz. Their debut album, 1957's *Sing a Song of Basie* (Impulse!), was something of an experiment in the art of overdubbing in which the trio overlaid tracks to recreate the full, punchy effect of Count Basie's big-band arrangements on signature tunes like "One O'clock Jump," "Little Pony," "Down for the Count," "Blues Backstage," and the jivey "Avenue C."

> "My analyst told me that I was right out of my head, but I said 'Dear doctor, I think that it's you instead.'"
>
> — *Annie Ross*

Annie provided the trumpet section parts for much of that landmark album, which caused a sensation and led to a string of successful recordings, including *The Swingers, The Hottest New Group in Jazz,* and *Lambert, Hendricks & Ross Sing Ellington.* At the time, critic Leonard Feather wrote of Ross: "Technically she is the most remarkable female vocalist since Ella Fitzgerald."

Born Annabelle Macauley Allan Short in Surrey, England, Annie Ross moved to Los Angeles with an aunt at the age of three. By the age of five she had begun studying drama and landed roles in the popular *Our Gang* series. She later studied acting in New York, then moved back to England where she began singing in nightclubs. Her recording debut came in Paris with a quartet including James Moody. By 1952 she was back in New York and recording with most of the Modern Jazz Quartet for her first album, *Singin' and Swingin'*. Later that year, she recorded an album with vocalese pioneer King Pleasure, *King Pleasure Sings/Annie Ross Sings,* which included her "Twisted" vocalese landmark.

After a 1953 tour of Europe with Lionel Hampton's band, she remained in the UK for four years, working with bands led by Jack Parnell and Tony Crombie. She returned to the States in 1957 and that year was recruited as a vocal coach by Dave Lambert and Jon Hendricks, who had assembled a group of singers to rehearse vocalese arrangements of Count Basie standards. That original idea was scrapped when it was decided by the artists and producer Creed Taylor to multitrack the arrangements using Lambert, Hendricks and Ross with a rhythm section of Nat Pierce, Freddie Green, Eddie Jones, and Sonny Payne. Their chemistry immediately clicked and an act was born. The trio revolutionized vocal music with their nimble, high-speed scatting and bop-oriented phrasing.

Ross left the group in 1962 and returned to England to pursue a solo career in music and films. She freelanced in the UK from 1962 to 1966, singing on TV shows while running her own nightclub, Annie's Room. She also appeared regularly at Ronnie Scott's nightclub in London and at festivals throughout Europe. Through the 1970s she performed in various theater productions throughout the UK. In 1985 she moved back to Los Angeles and became active as a singer and actress, appearing in such high-profile movies as *Superman III, Pump up the Volume,* and Robert Altman's *Short Cuts.* For the latter film, she recorded several numbers for the soundtrack. She reemerged with a new recording in 1995, *Music Is Forever,* and a 1996 follow-up, *Skylark,* both on the DRG label. In 1999 Annie reunited with former vocalese partner Jon Hendricks for a week-long engagement at the Blue Note in New York. It was their first nightclub gig together since the Kennedy administration.

# JANIS SIEGEL

BORN: July 23, 1952, in Brooklyn, New York

JANIS SIEGEL'S UNMISTAKABLE VOICE and elastic range have become one of Manhattan Transfer's most recognizable trademarks. A gifted arranger, she has brought an added zest to the group's overall sound in her inventive charts. She wrote the vocal arrangement for the group's big radio-play hit of 1980, "Birdland," from the *Extensions* album, and was awarded a Best Arrangement for Voices Grammy for her efforts. She arranged many of the songs on *Swing,* having mastered the art of working over Fletcher Henderson's charts into wonderful, "singable" songs. As she told *Jazziz* magazine at the time of the album's release: "I don't find swing to be terrifically intellectual. Instead, it is really dance music that has incredible energy and spirit. Swing has long been the backbone of the group's repertoire since the inception. It was tremendous fun making the album because we would just sit and play all of this music for each other and have a ball. I found it very interesting to analyze Fletcher Henderson's arrangements and find out exactly what makes them tick and swing, learn the way that he wrote for dancers—including the rhythmic figures behind the leads, which really push the songs along. After studying the arrangements, I think Fletcher Henderson was the real King of Swing."

Janis recently contributed vocal arrangements to Manhattan Transfer's latest project, a tribute to the great godfather of scat and jive, Louis Armstrong. "Rather than do a literal tribute kind of album, we were really just trying to capture the spirit of Satchmo as a vocalist," Janis said. "His spirit was so strong. I mean, he just had so much fun with the music. So we listened extensively to everything and picked a bunch of songs that we thought would best capture that quality. And we did some very interpretive renditions of some songs associated with Armstrong like 'What a Wonderful World,' 'Sugar,' 'Blue Again,' 'Old Man Mose,' 'Do You Know What It Means to Miss New Orleans,' and 'A Kiss to Build a Dream On.' And we also did two vocalese numbers, 'Mahogany Hall Stomp' and 'Hotter Than That.' And the producer, Craig Street, steered the album in a direction that was totally unlike what we would've thought of ourselves. There's only one trumpet to be found on the album and Jon Hassel is playing it. So it's really very interpretive."

Siegel's first experience as a professional singer came at the age of twelve. While still in eighth grade, she founded an all-girl trio, The Young Generation, with her friends Dori Miles and Rona Rothenberg. They soon hired a manager, Richard Perry, and the group was groomed to become the next Shangri-La's. The Young Generation recorded one single for the Red Bird label and sang together throughout high school, changing their name to The Loved Ones and recording another single on Kapp Records. That group later mutated into an all-female acoustic folk band called Laurel Canyon. "We took the name Laurel Canyon from a Joni Mitchell song, and did the kind of folk and pop that she was known for," Janis recalled. "We all played guitar, I was writing quite a bit, and we became regulars in Manhattan coffeehouses."

Soon after she quit college to pursue her musical career full-time with Laurel Canyon, Siegel met Tim Hauser at a party. Impressed by her vocal abilities, he asked her to sing on some demo recordings he was making. "Tim wanted singers to do demos, and I liked the material—early jazz stuff like [Cab Calloway's] 'Minnie the Moocher' and 'Blue Champagne' along with some folk stuff. So we collaborated."

At that point Janis abandoned her guitar and concentrated on straight singing. Tim also expressed interest in forming a four-part singing group. And on October 1, 1972, Janis joined with Tim, Laurel Massie, and Alan Paul to become Manhattan Transfer. The band has persevered and prospered during the past twenty-eight years and fifteen albums, racking up critical accolades and a couple of Grammy Awards along the way.

A longtime student of scat singing and vocalese, Janis says she got hip to the jive pioneers gradually. "The way I found out about Leo 'Scat' Watson was because I had a radio show in Los Angeles on the public station KCRW. I played a lot of jazz on that show and came across Leo through his recordings with Gene Krupa. But also, Jon Hendricks hipped me to Leo Watson. He said, 'That's where I got it from.' He was the first one to use this stream of consciousness, very surrealistic kind of scat singing, but it was also incredibly musical and, of course, very entertaining and very humorous. But not light and campy. It was all very musical stuff."

> "Down the stairs, lose your cares. Where? Down at Birdland."
> — Janis Siegel

The next jive pioneer that she got hep to was Slim Gaillard, whose surreal 'vout' language underscored his sly, syncopated sense of humor. "I actually used to go see him a lot in Los Angeles when he was playing a couple of little clubs regularly. I was way into his recordings, I think, because of the sense of humor. I was very attracted to that. I just responded to the insanity and surrealism in the music, whether it was Leo Watson, Slim Gaillard, or Bam Brown. But at the same time I found it very musical."

Siegel was waitressing in New York at the very earliest stages of Manhattan Transfer when she encountered another jive icon. "I was working at this horrible place in Times Square called Le Joint, where I had to dress like a French sailor," she recalled. "So one day, in walks Babs Gonzales. He was wearing a cape, of course. He used to come in once in a while and I struck up a little friendship with him and he gave me an autographed copy of his book, *I Paid My Dues*. What a character."

After the success of the Transfer's self-titled debut album of 1975, they landed a short-lived CBS television variety show. "We actually did a Slim Gaillard tune on that show," Janis recalled. "We did 'Ya Ha Ya,'" which is a typically crazy, hilarious Slim tune. That's probably why we never got picked up."

Janis released her first solo album, *Experiment in White,* in July 1982. Her second solo album, 1987's *At Home,* earned her a Grammy nomination for Best Female Jazz Vocal. Her third and fourth solo releases are collaborations with pianist Fred Hersch—1990's *Short Stories* and 1995's *Slow Hot Wind.* Her most recent solo outing is a Sinatra tribute, 1999's *The Tender Trap.*

# CANDYE KANE

———•———

BORN: in Los Angeles, California

SHE'S A LITTLE BIT OF MAE WEST, a little bit Big Mama Thornton, with a touch of Bette Midler and Patsy Cline mixed in. A voluptuous R&B/blues diva with a cartoon figure (54-38-48, size 20) and a self-assured sense of swing, Candye Kane is literally both *Diva la Grande* (the title of her 1997 Antone's album) and *The Toughest Girl Alive* (the title of her 2000 Bullseye Blues release).

A former teenage mother on welfare who turned to topless modeling and hardcore porn to make a living for herself and her child, Kane reinvented herself as a hefty blues belter with her debut release in 1994 of *Home Cookin'* on Antone's. While that album revealed a fondness for Patsy Cline–styled country music, she stepped into more bluesy terrain with her 1995 follow-up, *Knockout,* which featured guest appearances by Cesar Rosas of Los Lobos, The Blasters's Dave Alvin, and The Fabulous Thunderbirds's Kim Wilson.

*Diva la Grande* showcased Candye flexing her songwriting muscles with some originals that carried outspoken political and social commentary ("The Lord Was a Woman," "You Need a Great Big Woman," and the raucous X-rated boogie showstopper "All You Can Eat and You Can Eat It All Night Long"). That provocative album, with Candye depicted as a multiarmed Hindu goddess on the cover, landed her in the pages of *People* magazine and on CNN. Her fourth CD, 1998's *Swango* (Sire), caught the attention of the burgeoning neo-swing community with its infectious big-band–styled arrangements and won her live television appearances on *Roseanne, The Donny and Marie Show,* and *Penn & Teller's Sin City Spectacular.* As Penn Jillette wrote of her performance on his wacky variety show in the liner notes to *The Toughest Girl Alive:* "One day our cutest producer, Adam, came to me really excited. 'Candye Kane has a swing band and plays piano with her breasts. She has quite a rack.' 'Book her,' I said. I mean, that would be enough, right? I mean, what more do you want? I mean, let's not be greedy. Well, it turns out in Candye's case, I lacked the imagination to want as much as she was going to deliver. There she was with a real swing band and they were swinging. About the hottest band we had on the show. The music had a vintage feel to it but there as nothing old fashioned about it. It had the swing beat but it was brand new. The lyrics killed me. She killed on our show.

Killed. The crowd was jumping. Teller and I were dancing. The taping turned into a party of pure joy. Oh yeah, she did play the piano with her breasts, throwing some ample 20th century classical tone clusters into the swing. Goddamn, she's sexy. Goddamn!"

More accolades came in from Michael Heaton of the *Cleveland Plain Dealer:* "I wish I could say I knew Candye Kane from way back to *Home Cookin',* her first ass-kicking album in '94. Or better yet from high school chemistry class. Because she's got chemistry, my friend. Like China's got chopsticks. But I can't say that. I'm relatively new to this party that's getting bigger all the time. In fact, I only picked up the last album, *Swango,* because I was amused by the dead-on '50s rumpus-room decor on the cover and amazed by the girl with the cleavage like the San Andreas fault. Something good was going on there, I just wasn't sure what it was. After I got home and gave the steel wheel some serious rotation I was flat-out, drop-jaw knocked out. Forget the San Andreas fault. The songs on that album were without fault . . . it swing, swang, swung, man. It rocked not only the house but the entire street. Ms. Kane combined the blues of Bessie Smith with the jump of Etta James. And she frosted and flavored that big old groove-cake with the sass and brass of Bette Midler. Her music lifted me up, laid me out and sent me home smiling. When's the last time that happened to you?"

Candye's fifth and most playful offering, *The Toughest Girl Alive,* blends bits of Cab Calloway (a "Minnie the Moocher"–styled "For Your Love" and a "Jumpin' Jive" number in "Who Walks in When I Walk Out") with raucous jump blues tunes ("Who Do You Love?" "[Hey Mister!] She Was My Baby Last Night"), a taste of rockabilly ("I Can't Go on without My Cadillac"), a pinch of Jimmie Lunceford–styled big-band swing ("Get Happy"), and a touch of Patsy Cline ("To See a Grown Man Cry"). Backed by her band, The Swinging Armadillos, Candye Kane has a live show that is part campy, part swinging and has been described as "a revival meeting in the parking lot of an X-rated bookstore" in which she encourages her audiences to shatter stereotypes, celebrate their sexuality, and live their dreams. Both in concert and on record, she lives up to her randy anthem, "200 Lbs. of Fun."

> **"I'm the baddest girl in town, don't mess with sister or you'll go down."**
> — *Candye Kane*

# LAVAY SMITH

BORN: November 7, 1969, in Long Beach, California

MORE THAN JUST A NOVELTY BAND with a vivacious "chirp," Lavay Smith & Her Red Hot Skillet Lickers is a percolating Basie-styled swing/jump blues unit with a cast of seasoned jazz players backing a sultry, impossibly charismatic lead singer with a direct line to jive. But it's their collective sense of groove along with their sophisticated arrangements and superb soloing that separates this band from the pack of retro-swingers.

Formed in 1989 in San Francisco—several years before the neo-swing movement kicked in—the band took its name from an obscure band of the 1920s and 1930s that recorded on the Smithsonian label. Starting out at The Blue Lamp, a dive in the Tenderloin district of San Francisco, they instantly struck a chord with listeners young and old, touching off a wave of enthusiasm that continues to build momentum as the band branches out. Their 1997 debut recording, *One Hour Mama* (named after a tune written by 1930s blues diva Ida Cox), sold a respectable forty thousand units and sparked interest among the neo-swing set with its varied influences of Count Basie, Fats Waller, Bessie Smith, Billie Holiday, Louis Armstrong, and Louis Jordan. Their 2000 follow-up, *Everybody's Talkin' 'bout Miss Thing* (Fat Note), peaked at number ten in the *Billboard* jazz polls and received a four-and-one-half-star rating from *Down Beat* magazine. The album features seven songs arranged by David Berger, best known for his masterful transcriptions of Duke Ellington's music, that form a large part of the repertoire performed regularly by Wynton Marsalis and the Lincoln Center Jazz Orchestra.

Today the Red Hot Skillet Lickers have become a San Francisco landmark. And Lavay Smith—named one of L.A.'s sexiest people by *Los Angeles* magazine—is being touted as the crown jewel of the retro-swing revival. "I've been singing since I was a little kid," she said. "I'm not one of those Star Search types but I have been singing, just in our own homemade talents shows on the block. I started in school plays and then I started playing guitar and singing and writing tunes."

An avid record collector, Lavay has amassed an impressive collection of great vocalists from Dinah Washington and Billie Holiday to Helen Humes and Little Esther Phillips. "In my late teens I bought a Bessie Smith record. That was a pivotal moment for me. And then I started listening to all the blues queens of the 1920s—Ida Cox, Sippie Wallace, Victory Spivey, Alberta Hunter. They were all compiled on these records called *Mean Mothers* and *Super Sisters* that were put out by a real profeminist record company in New York called Rosetta Records. I loved these records. And now some of the tunes that I'm singing have lyrics that are straight out of the '20s, like "The Busy Woman's Blues," but with a Basie kind of rhythm feel to it. So it's really a continuation of the *Mean Mothers/Super Sisters* lyrics with a modern twist."

Aside from her vocal appeal, Smith rarely looks anything less than stunning on stage. And whether it's a body-fitting '50s Marilyn Monroe–styled gown or a '30s bias-cut dress with a low back and sparkling rhinestone jewelry, she wears it well.

"I love dressing up," says the raven-haired bombshell who oozes sexiness with each syllable. "It's part of celebrating the music and the performance. I think that's a really important part of my show. And it's a tradition that comes from people like Ethel Waters, Bessie Smith, Billie Holiday. Those women dressed up when they performed. All my favorite singers showed amazing style on stage. It's really important to just catch people. I mean, I really like to have people won over when I just walk out on stage. That's half the battle right there."

The other half is delivering music that feels real and swings hard. And on that end, the Red Hot Skillet Lickers do not falter. Thoroughly schooled in the nuances of swing, bebop, and jumpin' jive, they provide Lavay with suitably groovy backing. As pianist-bandleader Chris Siebert told the *San Jose Mercury News:* "We perform classic jazz and blues from the '30s through the '50s. A lot of the bands on the swing scene today took the horns and put it on a rock groove. Those are the ones who got signed to a major label and are now getting dropped. Other bands got into the loungey, Las Vegasy kitsch sound. It was never really a jazz thing. We are a real jazz and blues band."

**"You know I got to be the boss but Daddy you can wear the pants."**
— *Lavay Smith*

A noted authority on swing, jazz, and blues music, Siebert has spent time as a professional consultant for MCA Records working on reissues of the classic Decca recordings of Count Basie, Lionel Hampton, and Ella Fitzgerald. Other notables in the Red Hot Skillet Lickers include seventy-five-year-old alto saxophonist Bill

Stewart, who began his career in the mid-1940s at the end of the swing era; tenor saxophonist Hal Stein, who apprenticed in New York with the likes of Don Byas, Erroll Garner, and Charlie Parker; saxophonist Jules Broussard, who worked with Ray Charles and Big Mama Thornton; and trumpeter Allen Smith, who toured with Johnny Otis in 1947 and has recorded with both Duke Ellington and Benny Goodman. "We're so lucky to play with these musicians," says Smith. "The older guys have so much experience. I'm always learning from them."

Together on *Everybody's Talkin' 'bout Miss Thing* they turn in tastefully swinging renditions of "Gee Baby, Ain't I Good to You?" Billie Holiday's jump blues number "Now or Never," Jay McShann's "Hootie Blues," Jimmy Rushing's 1937 signature number "Sent for You Yesterday," and Dizzy Gillespie's humorous "He Beeped When He Should Have Bopped." Their originals—like the Pete Johnson–Big Joe Turner homage "Roll the Boogie," the hard-driving jump blues "Blow Me a Fat Note," or the Louis Jordan–flavored "Honey Pie"—are solidly in the jive tradition.

And Lavay carries on in that good-timey, celebratory spirit every time she hits the stage. "I tend to relate more to the playful aspects of entertaining audiences," she says. "Dizzy Gillespie was a good example of that. He had this amazing band but he was also a real showman who loved to have a good time. Fats Waller was a virtuoso piano player but he also liked to clown. I mean, you can't help it if you're funny. So I think it really depends on the person's personality. You can't change that. Miles Davis had a very serious personality, Dizzy was more playful with it. I like to be playful with it, and that kind of attitude helps to bring jazz to a lot of people who normally would not listen to it."

Today, in this climate of corporate labels cloning pop stars for superprofit, Smith regards jazz as a healthy alternative. "It's just a way of opening up people's ears to noncorporate rock. To me, most jazz is real alternative music, and that's why I got into it. . . . I was looking for a real alternative and I found it in people like Billie Holiday and Lester Young and Dizzy Gillespie. And when I fell in love with this music I knew that other people would like this music, too, that there were a lot of other people like myself. . . . I don't even look at it as 'old music' at all . . . and I never try and make it sound dated when I perform it. It stays fresh as long as it's being performed with a fresh attitude." She adds, "The bottom line is, people need to be entertained. That

---

**Lavay Smith, 1999. Courtesy Lavay Smith**

was true in the time of Louis Jordan and Fats Waller and it's true now."

Proving once again that the real deal is a timeless thing indeed.

# KATHARINE WHALEN

BORN: 1968 in Chapel Hill, North Carolina

FRONTING A MEGASUCCESSFUL BAND does have its rewards. As lead singer of the fabulously eccentric and wildly popular Squirrel Nut Zippers, Katharine Whalen was immediately thrust into the limelight in the wake of the band's platinum-selling breakthrough CD of 1997 *Hot* (spurred on by the catchy, frequently repeated MTV video clip for "Hell") and its eagerly anticipated follow-up in 1998, *Perennial Favorites*. Whalen's sultry voice and alluring delivery drew immediate comparisons to jazz divas Julie London, Chris Connors, Connee Boswell, Lena Horne, and Billie Holiday. And there was more than a small bit of jive in her playfully swinging rendition of "Fat Cat Keeps Getting Fatter" from *Perennial Favorites* or her Mae West–styled reading of "Danny Diamond" from 1995's *The Inevitable*.

**"What are my arms for? Use your imagination."**

—*Katharine Whalen*

In 1999 Whalen stepped out to test the solo waters with her *Jazz Squad*. A collection of classy, swinging tunes from the '20s and '30s, it showcased a more poised and refined side of the North Carolina chanteuse in the company of some accomplished jazz musicians, including fellow Zipper and husband Jimbo Mathus.

On emotive, bittersweet renditions of vintage jazz standards like "My Old Flame," "Yesterdays," "There Is No Greater Love," and "Just You, Just Me," she conjured up an intimate, affecting vibe that went down as easy as late night cognac. Nimbly shifting moods from jaunty ("My Baby Just Cares for Me") to melancholy ("Yesterdays"), from coquettish ("Greater Love") to sassy ("Now or Never"), from fragile ("My Old Flame") to lithely swinging ("That Old Feeling"), Whalen cast a spell on listeners with her abundant vocal charms.

From the very beginning of her career Katharine had alluded to this jazzy chanteuse side. (Check out "Wished for You" and "You're Driving Me

Crazy" from the Zipper's 1995 debut, *The Inevitable*.) With the release of *Jazz Squad,* she took a giant step forward into that jazzier realm. The vintage material on *Jazz Squad,* she explained, was culled mainly from her own personal record collection. "They're the songs I was listening to and practicing along with when I first started trying to learn how to sing," she said. "A lot of this music, though it is old, really rings true for me. My father used to sing this stuff to me. So I kind of grew up with these songs, in a way. There's a lot of romance attached to them for me."

Whalen's sultry delivery and burnished pipes seem especially well suited to this material from yesteryear. "Those tunes cover my main influences up 'til now," she says. "The versions that I learned the songs from are mostly by Billie Holiday or Chet Baker." She concedes that *Jazz Squad*'s opener, an effervescent, breathy rendition of the mid-1920s hit "Deed I Do," is a direct homage to another important vocal influence, New York cabaret singer Blossom Dearie. "She's kind of obscure," says Katharine. "You have to look a little harder to find her records. Someone actually turned me on to her and I'm so glad they did."

Growing up in North Carolina, Katharine found herself drawn to records from bygone eras that she dug up in local thrift shops. "I didn't grow up with television," she confesses, "so I sort of missed this whole chunk of popular music that most people experienced. I didn't really ever listen to radio either, except for a lot of '50s oldies stuff. So all the '70s, '80s, and '90s really have been pretty much untouched by me."

Mention iconic pop names from her own youth—everyone from Joni Mitchell and Grace Slick to Patti Smith and Pat Benatar, Stevie Nicks and Chrissie Hynde right up to Annie Lennox and Madonna—and Whalen will draw a blank. "Yeah, I know they're there," she admits. "I'm just not sure what it is they do."

Some of Katharine's earliest musical memories are of attending bluegrass fiddler's conventions with her parents and listening to their Beatles records. "So to my parents, this kind of music that I'm now doing was really more their parents' music. And they were sort of rebelling against it by listening to the Beatles."

While she delved into an eclectic wellspring of music after joining the Squirrel Nut Zippers (at Jimbo Mathus's urging) back in 1993, Whalen narrowed her focus considerably on *Jazz Squad.* "The Zippers is my first band I've ever been in and my first musical experience of any kind," she explained.

"And it's a job as well, so we have a certain amount of material we're responsible for from night to night. But by the same token, I really felt like I was needing some extracurricular stimulus apart from the Zippers. I needed to get better faster than I could get better with them. I felt like I needed to sing with a piano player and sing with some other horn players and tackle some real jazz . . . more standard stuff."

She is in fast company on *Jazz Squad*. Pianist Robert Griffin brings a tasty sensibility and jazzy sophistication to the proceedings and guitarist Jimbo Mathus swings like Tiny Grimes (check out his own instrumental offering "Badisma") while tenor saxophonist Cecil Johnson recalls Lester Young's vocal quality throughout (particularly on "All My Life"). But Katharine is more than up to the challenge, singing with verve and swinging with self-assured style on eleven jazz chestnuts.

"It ended up sounding so good going to tape that we were all excited," she recalled. "We thought, 'This sounds really clean, just like all these recordings we love so much. Let's see if some other folks will like it.'"

Die-hard Zipper fans naturally dug what Whalen was putting down on her solo debut. "There's certainly tons for me to learn," she humbly offered at the time of its release. "But I think I'm getting pretty close to the way I probably will sound when my voice fully matures. I may need more strength and improvisational skills, but I think I'm gettin' there."

# INGRID LUCIA

BORN: in New Orleans, Louisiana

HER SEDUCTIVE, SOULFUL VOICE conjures up comparisons to singing stars of the '30s and '40s—Ethel Waters, Mildred Bailey, Connee Boswell, Billie Holiday. But stunning vocalist Ingrid Lucia and The Flying Neutrinos are enlivening that old-school charm with their own affecting brand of "Americana pop."

"The roots of our music has elements of blues and second-line rhythms and some swing and jive stuff from the 1930s with a little bit of country aspect thrown in," said Ingrid. "But in writing our own material we're incorporating those qualities into original tunes with stories that apply more to modern times and people today. The songwriting style from back in the '30s, for instance, was really pretty innocent. So we're dealing with roots music but we're changing the stories a little bit to make them more contemporary."

On the band's 2000 release, *The Hotel Child* (Artists Only), Ingrid and the Flying Neutrinos apply their easy-swinging aesthetic to blues and jazz chestnuts like Willie Dixon's "Violent Love," Louis Armstrong's "Someday You'll Be Sorry," and the Dixieland classic "Some of These Days." The album's closer is a striking, retro-fied cover of the Velvet Underground's "After Hours."

A follow-up to *I'd Rather Be in New Orleans,* the band's self-produced debut, *The Hotel Child* was a major leap forward in the history of this singular group that traces its saga back to the nomadic family band that sang and danced for dimes on the streets of New Orleans eighteen years ago.

> **"Open the door, light her cigarette, say she looks nice, and see what you get."**
> — *Ingrid Lucia*

It's been an incredible musical odyssey since 1982, when family patriarch Papa Neutrino formed The Flying Neutrinos with his ragtag bunch of spirited young entertainers. "It's pretty odd how it all came about," says Ingrid. "Dad thought it would be a good way to promote our creativity by doing the band, so he asked all of us what instruments we wanted to play and we went to the pawn shop and thrift store and got them secondhand. Then we started learning from the street performers in New Orleans. There were eight of us in the band and we'd play on Jackson Square and Royal Street. We'd make money by passing the hat. Meanwhile, we were living off peanut butter sandwiches and eggs. It was pretty lean times."

Quintessential troupers, they added vaudevillian touches to further entice crowds to their daily street performances. Ingrid would dance out in front of the band with tap-dancing cousin Todd Londagin, the seven-year-old trombone player of the group, while little sister Jessica added cutesy appeal to the act.

By 1986 Papa Neutrino decided to test the waters up North. As Ingrid recalls, "The economy was really bad down there in New Orleans and the heat was unbearable, so we loaded up the station wagon and came up to New York. On the first day we got here it was raining and our car broke down and we didn't have any money. Instead of playing in the streets we played in the subways."

The family's genuine chemistry and folksy appeal was an immediate hit with jaded New Yorkers. "We played at the Times Square subway station every day for four hours and made about $400 to $500 every time." says Ingrid. "We stayed at the penthouse suite of the Carter Hotel on Forty-third Street and spent the whole summer just having a great time in New York."

By winter the family headed back down South, splitting their time between New Orleans and Mexico. "In Mexico, we played in plazas and eventually hooked up with a traveling circus, where we sang and learned to do various circus acts," says Ingrid.

In 1990 Papa Neutrino decided to leave the band in order to devote more time to his ongoing interest in raft building. (At different times during their career, The Flying Neutrinos actually lived on houseboats that he constructed.) Ingrid took the helm and quickly relocated with cousin Todd back to New York City, playing in the subways and on the streets. "And bit by bit we started adding musicians. We got a drummer so I could focus on my singing and we found a guitar player. And eventually we started getting into the clubs."

Their first experience with the club scene was a seven-month run at Fanny's Oyster Bar, followed by a regular Sunday slot at the Rodeo Bar and sporadic gigs at other clubs like Nell's, the Supper Club, Brownies, and Coney Island High. On a tip from a friend, they went hunting for gigs in Atlantic City, ultimately landing a lucrative six-week stint at The Showboat Casino. The money that Ingrid earned there that summer of 1995 helped finance the group's first CD, *I'd Rather Be in New Orleans,* which includes Ingrid's seductive reading of the Andrews Sisters's 1937 hit "Bei Mir Bist Du Schoen" and also features a guest appearance from legendary New Orleans trumpeter Doc Cheatham. As Ingrid explained, "At the time, Doc had a regular weekend brunch gig at Sweet Basil's and I'd go and sit in with him there every Sunday. And when it came time to do our record I asked him if he would like to do the title track. He agreed. So he came down to the studio and just kept playing. He ended up doing three other songs as well."

Since the release of that ebullient debut, The Flying Neutrinos have successfully toured the States, the UK, and Europe, opening for rock bands like Porno for Pyros and Fun Loving Criminals as well as other big-name acts like Tony Bennett, Brian Setzer, and Susan Tedeschi. Their song "Mr. Zoot Suit," the opening track from *The Hotel Child,* has appeared in two movies— *Blast from the Past* starring Brendan Frasier and Alicia Silverstone and *Three to Tango* starring Neve Campbell. They also have two songs in the Jonathan Demme film *The Opportunist,* starring Christopher Walken.

The musical odyssey continues with *The Hotel Child,* the title of which is a testament to Ingrid Lucia's amazing, nomadic life as an itinerant street musician and charismatic front woman of The Flying Neutrinos. "When I took over the band from my father," said Ingrid, "it was my goal to bring the roots of New Orleans music to a younger generation." She's doing that with style and sass, and a wondrously alluring warble.

# DEL REY

BORN: December 22, 1959, in Los Angles, California

FROM HER WACKY ATTIRE—trademark two-tone sunglasses, thrift shop straw hat, and outrageous dresses—to her parlor-sized galvanized metal resonator guitar with a dramatic cutaway, Seattle's resident guitar queen Del Rey cuts a wholly unique figure on stage. But beneath the kitschy veneer is a country blues scholar, impressive fingerstyle player, and jive connoisseur, as evidenced by the inclusion of the obscure Louis Jordan nugget "(She Dyed Her Hair) Chartreuse" on her fifth self-produced release, *X-Rey Guitar* (Hobemian Records).

Highly proficient in both Piedmont and Delta styles, the enigmatic Miss Rey feels a particular kinship with the more eccentric players from the 1920s and 1930s. "I tend to favor the oddballs in all styles," she said. "I love all of the unpredictable players. I get a little bored with Robert Johnson. Everybody's been so hyped on him for so long but I want to hear the people who are not so well known. I'm fascinated by people like Henry Spaulding and Henry Townshend, both St. Louis guys. I love the few recordings we have of Mattie Delaney, who is a Delta bluesman but certainly nowhere near as well known as Robert Johnson or Charlie Patton. And I like listening to guys like Dusty Thomas and Little Hat Jones, a Piedmont-styled player who hardly anybody knows about. They are both great guitar players and such unique characters."

> **"You went too far in the beauty booth when you dyed your hair chartreuse."**
> — *Del Rey*

Rey's most important role model to date has been the legendary Memphis Minnie, a pioneering woman guitarist from the '30s whose fingerstyle chops were so formidable that she once bested both Big Bill Broonzy and Tampa Red in a fabled guitar showdown.

"I had been playing classical guitar since I was four," she recalled, "but when I was thirteen I wandered into this tiny record store in San Diego called Folk Art and the owner gave me a tape of early Memphis Minnie stuff to listen to. I hadn't really run into many women guitar players at that point so I was really excited to find out about her. She was so great and so inspiring. That was really the beginning for me."

Rey demonstrates her own fingerstyle prowess on Memphis Minnie's "Let's Go to Town" and on "Memphis Minnie," an unaccompanied ode to her guitar idol. Elsewhere on *X-Rey Guitar,* she reflects the influence of two-fisted pianists like Little Brother Montgomery, Van "Piano Man" Walls, and Roosevelt Sykes, along with the great New Orleans ivory-ticklers and jivesters James Booker and Professor Longhair, creator of the rhumba-boogie, and pounding-piano mamas like Dorothy Donegan and Camille Howard. "I think one of the reasons my guitar-playing sounds a little different than the mainstream is that for years I mostly listened to piano players, not guitar players," she said. "That kind of keeps your ears fresh so you're not subconsciously absorbing your colleagues' stuff."

Rey's appreciation of Louis Jordan and all things jive goes way back. "When I was a teenager, reading that Mezz Mezzrow book [*Really the Blues*] was a pretty defining moment for me. Of course, he was more of a hanger-on of the 1930s jive scene. I guess that book was the first documented case of a wanna-be, but I found it totally fascinating." Other jive-oriented material in her repertoire over the years has included Wynonie Harris's "Down Boy Down," Hot Lips Page's "I Got an Uncle in Harlem," and Louis Jordan's "A Dollar Down and a Dollar When I Can."

"I've been at this for a while now," she said. "I've been playing guitar for what . . . thirty-five years. That's a helluva long time. And I've been into this specific kind of music since 1974, at least. So I mean, after a few missteps I think that I'm starting to have it so it's integrated into an identifiable voice. I'm trying to add something to it, maybe just a tiny little thing. But I don't want it to be imitative, because you can't. I didn't grow up in the South. I didn't grow up in the '30s. I'm not black. So I'm never going to be an imitation of Memphis Minnie or Louis Jordan or whoever. I can only take inspiration from that music and try to give something back to it."

# Jivenotes:

Cab's older sister, **Blanche Calloway,** was a well-known singer and performer in the theaters and nightclubs of the 1920s. Established nearly ten years before anybody had ever heard of her brother, she fronted a band led by Charlie Gaines in 1931 and later fronted the Andy Kirk band before forming her own group, Blanche Calloway and Her Joy Boys, which included tenor saxophonist Ben Webster, trombonist Vic Dickerson, and drummer Cozy Cole. A pioneering jivestress, she left performing by the late 1940s to manage the career of R&B singer Ruth Brown and later became a disc jockey. **Cleo Patra Brown** was another popular entertainer of the 1930s and 1940s whose boogie-woogie piano style and sly, risqué vocals were often compared to Nellie Lutcher's. In Chicago in the 1930s she recorded "It's a Heavenly Thing," which established her infectious signature.

Pop star and actress **Bette Midler** deserves honorary mention in jive annals for her faithful recreation of The Andrew Sisters's 1941 hit "Boogie Woogie Bugle Boy" on her 1973 debut album, *The Divine Miss 'M.'* Another popular singer and Hollywood star of a different era, comedienne **Martha Raye** was renowned for her formidable scatting ability and would often engage in scintillating after-hours scat duels with fellow musical comedienne Ella Logan in 1934 at Adrian's Tap Room, a popular musicians' hangout in Manhattan run by musician Adrian Rollini. Raye also revealed a fondness for jive and syncopation in the 1936 Bing Crosby movie *Rhythm on the Range.* During this period, she adopted "You'll Have to Swing It (Mr. Paganini)," a tune previously recorded by Ella Fitzgerald with the Chick Webb Orchestra, as her theme song. Born Margaret Teresa Yvonne O'Reed in Butte, Montana, Raye was influenced by her parents, a pair of struggling vaudevillians, and at the age of three became part of their act. At the age of thirteen, she was a singer with a band and by the age of nineteen she began an acting career. Raye began entertaining troops all over the world in 1942. Known as "Colonel Maggie," she would dress in fatigues (including combat boots, a tie, and a green beret) and raise morale with her singing and comedic talents. She traveled to and from Vietnam for nine years, sometimes performing services as a nurse as well as on stage. In 1955 she hosted a TV variety show, in 1967 she replaced Ginger Rogers in a Broadway production of *Hello Dolly,* and in 1972 was the lead in *No, No Nanette.* Her solo recordings include 1951's *Martha Raye Sings* (Discovery) and 1954's *Here's Martha Raye* (Columbia). All the highs and lows of her journey are documented in Jean Maddern Pitrone's biography *Take It from the Big Mouth.*

In the early '70s **The Pointer Sisters** perpetuated a slick image and nostalgic sound that recalled the close harmony vocal jazz of The Andrews Sisters while also blending in elements of R&B, gospel, and disco. Their self-titled debut of 1973 included a ripping vocalese rendition of Dizzy Gillespie's bop anthem "Salt Peanuts" while the title track of their 1974 follow-up was the old Swing Era standby "That's a Plenty." In subsequent albums they drew from more contemporary sources like Bruce Springsteen, Graham Parker, Loggins and Messina, Steely Dan, Ian Hunter, and Bob Seger while maintaining a glamorous, vivacious veneer. Kudos to pop star **Joni Mitchell** for reviving Annie Ross's vocalese anthem "Twisted" on her 1974 *Court and Spark* album and then engaging in similarly acrobatic verbal jive on "Dry Cleaner from Des Moines" from her 1979 *Mingus* album. Austin-based singer-songwriter **Natalie Zoe** revealed her love of jive in her 1998 CD, *Never Too Old to Swing* (Mozo). The title track is a Tiny Grimes original first recorded in 1941 with The Cats & The Fiddle. Also worthy of mention here are **The Early Sisters,** a late '70s Milwaukee-based vocal harmony group in vintage threads who patterned their act after The Andrews Sisters, and **Robyn Pluer**, the Milwaukee-based jivestress who fronted The R&B Cadets in the '70s and The Milwaukeeans through the '80s and into the '90s.

And a final word about **Helen Kane,** the original boop-boop-a-doop girl from the late 1920s. A popular screen and recording star of the Roaring Twenties, the Bronx native got her first big break in a 1927 musical production of *A Night in Spain.* But it was at a 1928 appearance at the Paramount in New York that she first uttered the novelty catchphrase "boop-boop-a-doop" during a performance of the risqué tune "That's My Weakness Now." Audiences were charmed and fascinated by this seemingly nonsensical phrase inserted in between the lyrics, and Kane began singing that same catchphrase in her baby-doll voice on other signature tunes like "I Wanna Be Loved By You" and "Button up Your Overcoat." Her popularity as a singer led to numerous screen appearances in 1929 and 1930. By then she was a big star, pulling in $8,000 a week. Around that same time cartoonists Max and Dave Fleischer had patterned their vampish Betty Boop character after Kane (with voiceover by Mae Questal, who would later supply the voice for the Fleischers' Olive Oyl character in the *Popeye the Sailorman* series). Kane sued the Fleischers and Paramount studios for stealing her act, but in court it was revealed that she herself had lifted the "boop-boop-a-doop" catchphrase from an obscure black singer named Baby Esther. Betty Boop would go on to jam with the likes of Cab Calloway, Louis Armstrong, and Don Redman in various animated shorts. After attempting a comeback in the late 1940s and early 1950s, Kane faded from the limelight. But her unique vocal style had a profound impact on such stars as Marilyn Monroe and Cyndi Lauper.

# Recommended Listening

**CONNEE BOSWELL**

*It's the Girls,* ASV (1925–1931)

*The Boswell Sisters,* Collector's Classics (1931–1932)

*That's How Rhythm Was Born,* Sony (1931–1935)

**ELLA FITZGERALD**

*Chick Webb and His Orchestra Featuring Ella Fitzgerald,* Folkways (1935–1939)

*In the Groove,* Buddah (1939)

*75th Birthday Celebration,* Decca (1939–1955)

*The War Years,* Decca (1941–1947)

*The Complete Ella Fitzgerald Songbooks,* Verve (1956–1964)

*Mack the Knife: The Complete Ella in Berlin Concert,* Verve (1960)

**THE ANDREWS SISTERS**

*The Best of The Andrews Sisters (Millennium Collection),* MCA (1938–1944)

*Their Greatest All-Time Hits,* Decca/MCA (1938–1947)

*Greatest Hits: The 60th Anniversary Collection,* MCA (1938–1950)

*50th Anniversary Collection, Volumes 1 & 2,* MCA (1938–1956)

*Beat Me Daddy, Eight to the Bar,* MCA (1940–1943)

*Sing, Sing, Sing,* Decca/MCA (1940–1945)

*Boogie Woogie Bugle Girls,* MCA (1941–1945)

*Swingin' Harmony,* Starline (1946–1956)

**UNA MAE CARLISLE**

*Fats Waller,* Bluebird (1934–1939)

*Lester Young, 1939–1942, Volume 2* Masters of Jive

*The Complete Una Mae Carlisle,* RCA (1940–1942)

**INA RAY HUTTON**

*Girls' Night Out,* Sony (1936–1939)

*1943–1944 Spotlight Band Broadcast,* Soundcraft

**ELLA MAE MORSE**

*The Very Best of Ella Mae Morse,* Collectables (1942–1948)

*Barrelhouse Boogie and the Blues,* Bear Family (1942–1957)

**NELLIE LUTCHER**

*The Best of Nellie Lutcher,* Capitol (1947)

*Nellie Lutcher & Her Rhythm,* Bear Family (1947–1957)

*Ditto from Me to You,* Juke Box Lil (1947–1957)

*Real Gone,* Pausa (1951)

**With Nat "King" Cole:**

*Jazz Encounters,* Capitol (1949)

**With Louis Jordan:**

*Rock 'n' Roll Call,* RCA/Bluebird (1955)

**ANNIE ROSS**

*Singin' and Swingin',* Savoy (1952)

*King Pleasure Sings/Annie Ross Sings,* Original Jazz (1952)

*Sings a Song with Mulligan,* EMI (1957)

*A Gasser!* World Pacific (1959)

*Music Is Forever,* DRG (1995)

*Skylark,* DRG (1996)

**With Lambert, Hendricks & Ross:**

*Sing a Song of Basie,* Impulse! (1957)

*Everybody's Boppin',* Sony/Columbia (1959)

*The Hottest New Group in Jazz,*
 Sony/Columbia (1959)

## JANIS SIEGEL
*At Home,* Atlantic (1987)
*Short Stories,* Atlantic (1990)
*The Tender Trap,* Monarch (1999)
**With Manhattan Transfer:**
*Manhattan Transfer,* Atlantic (1975)
*Coming Out,* Atlantic (1976)
*Pastiche,* Atlantic (1978)
*Extensions,* Atlantic (1979)
*Mecca for Moderns,* Atlantic (1981)
*Bodies and Souls,* Atlantic (1983)
*Vocalese,* Atlantic (1985)
*Bop Doo-Wop,* Atlantic (1990)
*Tonin',* Atlantic (1995)
*Swing,* Atlantic (1997)
*Spirit of St. Louis,* Atlantic (2000)

## CANDYE KANE
*Home Cookin',* Antone's (1994)
*Knockout,* Antone's (1995)
*Diva la Grande,* Antone's/Discovery
 (1997)
*Swango,* Sire (1998)
*The Toughest Girl Alive,* Bullseye Blues
 (2000)

## LAVAY SMITH
*One Hour Mama,* Fat Note (1997)
*Everybody's Talkin' 'bout Miss Thing,*
 Fat Note (2000)

## KATHARINE WHALEN
*Jazz Squad,* Mammoth (1999)
**With the Squirrel Nut Zippers:**
*The Inevitable,* Mammoth (1995)
*Sold Out,* Mammoth (1997)
*Hot,* Mammoth (1997)

*Perennial Favorites,* Mammoth (1998)
*Christmas Caravan,* Mammoth (1998)
*Bedlam Ballroom,* Mammoth (2000)

## INGRID LUCIA
*I'd Rather Be in New Orleans,*
 Artists Only (1995)
*The Hotel Child,* Artists Only (2000)

## DEL REY
*Cafe Society,* Kicking Music (1985)
*Chartreuse,* Hobemian (1991)
*Boogie Mysterioso,* Hobemian (1993)
*Hot Sauces,* Hobemian (1995)
*X-Rey Guitar,* Hobemian (2000)

## BETTE MIDLER
*The Divine Miss 'M,'* Atlantic (1973)

## MARTHA RAYE
*Here's Martha Raye,* Columbia (1954)

## THE POINTER SISTERS
*The Pointer Sisters,* ABC/Blue Thumb
 (1973)
*That's a Plenty,* ABC/Blue Thumb (1974)
*Having a Party,* ABC/Blue Thumb
 (1977)
*Energy,* Planet (1978)
*Priority,* Planet (1979)

## JONI MITCHELL
*Court and Spark,* Elektra (1974)
*Mingus,* Elektra (1979)

## NATALIE ZOE
*Never Too Old to Swing,* Mozo (1998)

## HELEN KANE
*The Original Boop-Boop-A-Doop Girl,*
 Louisiana Red Hot (1928–1930)

## CHAPTER 8

# RETRO JIVESTERS

Royal Crown Revue, Big Bad Voodoo Daddy,

Brian Setzer Orchestra, Cherry Poppin' Daddies,

Squirrel Nut Zippers, Roomful of Blues,

Ray Gelato & His Giants of Jive, Colin James and The Little Big Band,

Paul Cebar, Jet Set Six, The Yalloppin' Hounds

Contrary to myth, the retro-swing or neo–jumpin' jive or whatever-you-wanna-call-it movement was not hatched with a single ad on TV. Certainly, that infamous sixty-second spot for The Gap back in 1998—the one featuring khaki-clad Lindyhoppers writhing athletically to Louis Prima's "Jump, Jive an' Wail"—did galvanize public attention around something that had already been fermenting silently underground for the previous ten years. In retrospect, that infectious commercial did help launch the bandwagon. And many bands did jump on at that time, copping vintage threads and hastily piecing together a swing repertoire in hopes of cashing in on the latest lucrative trend.

But there were also those who connected, simply and purely, with the ebullient spirit of Louis Jordan, Louis Prima, Cab Calloway, Fats Waller, Slim Gaillard, and other jive icons. Like countless others before them, they were swept away by this timeless, swinging music and their interest in it predated any trend. Their motive behind playing it was genuine—more about paying homage than paying the rent. These torchbearers for jive have come in waves through the '70s and '80s, subsisting like monks in cultish cliques until the floodgates finally burst wide open in 1988, the year that The Gap brought swing to mainstream consciousness. But the roots of this retro movement go back further than that.

As early as the mid-1970s, bands like Asleep at the Wheel, Roomful of Blues, and Dan Hicks and His Hot Licks began waving the flag for jump blues, Texas swing, and jive. On its 1976 self-titled debut for RCA, Dr. Buzzard's Original Savannah Band brought big-band sheen and Cab Calloway–styled showmanship to the disco era before mutating into the more Latin-tinged Kid Creole & The Coconuts by the early '80s. In 1980 antic comedians Dan Aykroyd and John Belushi from TV's popular *Saturday Night Live* succeeded in bringing Cab Calloway out of semiretirement for a cameo appearance in their film *The Blues Brothers,* rekindling a second career for the jive icon in the process. Then in 1981 British pop star Joe Jackson surprised jive purists with his A&M release *Jumpin' Jive.* As the popmeister (who had hit big in 1976 with "Is She Really Going out with Him") put it in the brief notes on the back cover of that retro jive opus: "When my Dad was my age, jazz was not respectable. It played in whorehouses not Carnegie Hall. These classics of jump, jive, and swing are all from the 1940s. 'Jumpin' Jive,' 'We the Cats' and 'San Francisco Fan' from Cab Calloway; 'Symphony Sid,' a Lester Young tune with words by King Pleasure; 'Tuxedo Junction,' our tribute to Glenn Miller; and the rest, all performed at one time or other by our main inspiration, Louis Jordan, the 'King of Jukeboxes,' who influenced so many but is acknowledged by so few. Like us, he didn't aim at purists, or even jazz fans—just anyone who wanted to listen and enjoy. Reap this righteous riff."

The second and more commercial wave began washing up on stateside shores in the early '90s. Bands like Big Bad Voodoo Daddy, Cherry Poppin' Daddies, Brian Setzer Orchestra, and Royal Crown Revue spearheaded this grassroots movement, which culminated in the big splash of 1998 and triggered a rash of bandwagon jumpers that followed in their wake. Jumpin' jive fever also spread north across the border to Canada via Colin James and The Little Big Band and to Europe through the constant touring and recording of Ray Gelato & His Giants of Jive. Newer bands like Jet Set Six, The Love Dogs, The Atomic Fireballs, Steve Lucky & The Rhumba Bums, and The Yalloppin' Hounds continue pumping life into the neojive scene.

# ROYAL CROWN REVUE

FORMED: 1989 in Los Angeles, California

A KEY PLAYER in the swing revival, Royal Crown Revue was one of the first modern swing bands to land a major label recording contract (with Warner Bros. in the spring of 1995). Fronted by charismatic vocalist Eddie Nichols and fueled by the Big Jay McNeely–inspired honking tenor work of raucous saxophonist Mando Dorame, the seven-piece band has a manic appeal that draws on punk energy while dressing it up in retro threads and disciplined arrangements.

In its earliest incarnation, RCR was invariably placed on heavy-metal bills—opening for the likes of Foghat, Night Ranger, and Kiss—mainly because there was no retro-swing audience to speak of at the time. In 1991 the group released its first self-produced album, *Kings of Gangster Bop,* on which they revived the 1943 number "Stormy Weather," and began converting audiences across America and Europe, playing hundreds of shows and preaching the gospel of swing. These grassroots missionaries would help trigger a full-scale movement by decade's end.

> **"Mugzy's in the mood for losing cat. He's gonna beat it downtown to where it's at."**
>
> — *Royal Crown Revue*

In 1993 Royal Crown Revue began a two-year residency at The Derby, a fabulous art deco club in Hollywood built in the 1920s by Cecil B. DeMille. Within months RCR was playing to packed houses, creating a huge buzz in L.A. and beyond, and drawing influential Hollywood players interested in seeing how the old could be made new again. One such observer was Chuck Russell, who asked the band to re-create their turbocharged stage show for his film *The Mask,* which starred Jim Carrey and Cameron Diaz. RCR's cameo in the 1994 film—playing their tom-tom beating mambo original "Hey Pachuco" while a zoot-suited Carrey and Diaz cut a rug on the dance floor—helped boost the band's profile overnight. That song's infectious jungle groove and shout chorus went on to grace countless film scores, Las Vegas revues, an Acura ad campaign, and gymnastic and skating routines at the 1996 Olympics. It even made an appearance on the Miss America Pageant. RCR also served as inspiration for the hit movie

*Swingers,* which brought the new music, dance, and fashion groundswell to a larger public. Writer and star John Favreau originally scripted the film's dance sequence around his experiences as a Derby regular at RCR's now legendary Wednesday night shows.

In 1995 producer/A&R man Ted Templeman witnessed the Crown's magic at the Derby and signed them to Warner Bros. The resulting album, *Mugzy's Move,* formally established the band's "hard-boiled" style while registering with the record-buying public. They had similar success with 1997's *Caught in the Act* (an independent live recording that captures the blistering energy of their show) and their second studio effort on Warner Bros., 1998's *The Contender,* which features the musical homage "Walkin' like Brando" and the Dizzy Gillespie romp "Salt Peanuts." The band's 1999 offering, *Walk on Fire,* was recorded using vintage instruments and recording gear, including original RCA "44" ribbon microphones, in an attempt to faithfully re-create the sound of the '40s.

The *New York Times* weighed in on the merits of RCR in this 1998 review of a live show: "The new swing movement has its charlatans and its trend hoppers, but Royal Crown Revue, formed 10 years ago in Los Angeles, is in it for the long haul, emanating a deep knowledge of mid-century American macho in clothes, manner, and music . . . their show is a larger picture of American music than most books can give, encompassing not just swing, but bebop, East Los Angeles r&b, and calypso."

Their quick-tempoed dance music, delivered with gangster-punk elan, has kept Royal Crown Revue at the top of the retro-swing heap.

## BIG BAD VOODOO DADDY

FORMED: 1992 in Ventura, California

THIS HORN-POWERED OCTET got its initial buzz from a pair of home-made albums (1993's self-titled debut and 1995's *Watchu' Want for Chistmas?* both for Hep Cat Records) that earned them a rep on L.A.'s lounge revival scene of the early 1990s. National attention came after their featured appearance in the low-budget 1996 cult film *Swingers,* which brought out hordes of hepcats and chicks in vintage clothing to their gigs. The soundtrack album to that film includes their jumpin' "Go Daddy-O" along with a jivey take on the Louis

Prima–Phil Harris duet from Disney's *The Jungle Book,* "I Wanna Be like You," and their signature number "You & Me & the Bottle Makes 3 Tonight (Baby)," which became a smash hit single and popular MTV video clip in 1998. The band's visibility peaked the following year with a performance during the halftime extravaganza at the 1999 Super Bowl and subsequent appearances on the popular television shows *Ally McBeal* and *Melrose Place.*

> **"You and me and the bottle makes three tonight, baby."**
> — *Big Bad Voodoo Daddy*

Fronted by vocalist-guitarist Scotty Morris, a former punk rocker turned born-again swingster, BBVD's exuberant brand of jumpin' jive reveals a fondness for Cab Calloway (they covered "Minnie the Moocher" on 1998's self-titled major label debut for Coolsville/EMI/Capitol) and Louis Jordan while also appealing to the modern rock camp with a pumped-up energy level.

"I grew up listening to this music," Morris told *Guitar Player,* "and I always knew that this was what I wanted to do." The band's moniker, he explains, came from a rare encounter with one of his boyhood guitar idols, bluesman Albert Collins. "I was a big Collins fan," he recalled, "and I saw him play one night—I had to sneak in with my older brother's ID—and he absolutely tore the place down. He was such a great showman. He had a long cable, so he was able to walk into the crowd and stand on tables. Had the audience on their feet the whole time. After the show, I asked him for his autograph, and he wrote, 'To Scotty—the Big Bad Voodoo Daddy.' I immediately thought it was a great name for a band, and it was given to me on such a special night. It was almost like Albert was giving me the ticket to ride. I'm really superstitious, so when things like that happen, I follow my gut."

And Morris has followed his gut to retro-swing stardom with his high-octane, nitro-jive ensemble.

# BRIAN SETZER ORCHESTRA

FORMED: 1993 in Los Angeles, California

A ONE-TIME PUNK ROCKER turned rockabilly guitarist and devotee of Eddie Cochran, Brian Setzer (Born: April 10, 1959, in the Greenwich Village neighborhood of New York City) fronted the Long Island–based Bloodless Pharoahs in the mid-1970s and the more successful Stray Cats in the late '70s. With Slim Jim Phantom on a stand-up drum kit and Lee Rocker vigorously slapping and simultaneously spinning his painted upright bass behind Setzer's passionate front man work, the Stray Cats drew a small but fervent following on the Long Island–Manhattan bar band circuit. Frustrated by the American scene, the Stray Cats traveled to London in 1980 and took the UK by storm with their raw energy and uncompromising style.

The group was eventually signed to Arista Records and released a series of albums that sold well on the strength of rockabilly rave-ups like "Rock This Town," "Stray Cat Strut," and "She's Sexy and 17," all of which garnered heavy rotation on MTV. Setzer later played in Robert Plant's retro-blues group The Honeydrippers and released two solo albums—1986's *Knife Feels like Justice* and 1988's *Live Nude Guitars*—before forming his own raucous, kick-ass seventeen-piece big band in the late summer of 1992. And the way the big band came together was purely through an act of serendipity. Apparently, a group of horn players were holding an impromptu jam session at the home of Brian's neighbor, Michael Acosta. Brian and Michael had never met before this date when, to Michael's embarrassment, one of the other musicians noticed Brian outside and called out, "Hey Brian, go get your guitar and come over!" Brian went back to his house and walked over with one of his classic Gretsch guitars and a small practice amp. They all had such a good time that by the end of the night, Brian and Michael decided to start working on charts and putting the big band together in hopes of doing a few shows around Southern California.

"The big-band thing makes total sense to me," Setzer told *Guitar Player* at the time, "because it's an extension of the roots and the vibe of the rockabilly sound. The original rockabilly guys were influenced by big-band jazz and blues, and that music has always been a big influence on me, so it feels completely natural."

The Brian Setzer Orchestra made its debut at the Coach House in San Juan Capistrano, California, in December of 1992. A reviewer from *The Orange County Register* praised that first performance: "By the end of the third song, 'Lovin' Machine,' the audience jumped to its feet in abandon . . . the crowd was delirious after just three songs . . . in heaven before the 17

Brian Setzer with his orchestra, 1998.

musicians on stage pulled out 'Stray Cat Strut.'"

Enthusiasm about the band quickly spread and by the time they played their second gig, at the Roxy in Los Angeles in January of 1993, the club was filled with record company executives. The independent Hollywood Records signed the Brian Setzer Orchestra in August of 1993 and hosted the band's New York debut at the Supper Club shortly before the release of 1994's *The Brian Setzer Orchestra.* "This is a new concept to a lot of people," Setzer said at the time, "but when they hear us rockin', they love it. There's so much going on musically and it's as loud as any rock band I've ever heard. I like to think that we're taking the best of American music, throwing it in a pot and stirring it up. I also like the fact that it's got a real city vibe to it; this is the first time I've ever felt comfortable singing in a New York accent."

**"That's the kind of sugar Papa likes."**
— *Brian Setzer*

After jumping to Interscope Records in 1996, Setzer came out with *Guitar Slinger,* which was produced by the legendary Phil Ramone. The timing of his third big-band album couldn't have been better. *The Dirty Boogie* (Interscope) not only came out in 1998, right around the same time as the aforementioned Gap ad, but it also contained a cover of the same Louis Prima anthem, "Jump, Jive an' Wail," that appeared in that popular TV commercial and grabbed the public's fancy. The result was predictable. Setzer struck pay dirt with *The Dirty Boogie* (which had platinum-plus sales) while also earning two Grammy Awards for that breakthrough offering, which includes quality covers of Bobby Darin's "As Long as I'm Singin'," Leiber & Stoller's "You're the Boss," Louis Prima's "Jump, Jive an' Wail" as well a big-band rendition of his own Stray Cats hit, "Rock This Town."

In effect Setzer not only helped resurrect a genre, he injected new life into the swing thing with his pent-up, in-your-face rock 'n' roll energy. As he put it in a *Guitar Player* interview: "If you just copy what they did in 1947, it's not going to be a real band but it's just doing it the same. To make music viable you have to make it new and you have to make it your own."

Setzer's latest, 2000's *Vavoom!* (Interscope), includes jumped-up covers of Duke Ellington's "Caravan," Glenn Miller's "Pennsylvania 6-5000," Kurt Weill's "Mack the Knife," along with two jivey originals in "That's the Kind of Sugar Papa Likes" and "Gettin' in the Mood."

# CHERRY POPPIN' DADDIES

FORMED: 1989 in Eugene, Oregon

OTHER MAJOR PLAYERS in the neoswing revival of 1998, these jump blues hounds have been methodically touring small clubs and theaters for years, mixing their vibrant swing appeal with harsher overtones. The focal point of their show is hypertheatrical front man (and former punk rocker) Steve Perry, who maintains, "We're on more of a tradition-less trip. The idea was to fuse the energy of punk rock, the rhythmic feel of swing, and the lyric sensibilities of the modern period into one unified sound. But what we do is really just dance music."

> "He's a friend to all the stars, made his fortune sellin' cars."
> — *Cherry Poppin' Daddies*

Through the first half of the 1990s the Daddies performed an eclectic and highly irreverent blend of power-punk, swing, and ska (as heard on 1990's *Ferociously Stoned,* 1994's *Rapid City Muscle Car,* and 1995's *Kids on the Street,* all on Space Age Bachelor Pad). Then in March of 1997 in a clever bit of marketing, they decided to package up all the rockin' swing tunes from their previous three CDs and release them as the compilation *Zoot Suit Riot: The Swingin' Hits of the Cherry Poppin' Daddies* (Universal). Predictably, in the heat of swing revival fever, the album was well received by a jumpin' jive-hungry public. It quickly went platinum, selling more than one million units, and climbed into the *Billboard* Top 20. And the Cherry Poppin' Daddies have been dressing in vintage threads and laying down jumpin' jive ever since—albeit with tongue planted firmly in cheek. And like many bands in the swing revival, the Daddies's allegiance to Cab Calloway and Louis Jordan is palpable.

# SQUIRREL NUT ZIPPERS

FORMED: November of 1993 in Efland, North Carolina

MORE FASCINATED WITH PROHIBITION-VINTAGE hot jazz from the '20s and '30s than Frank Sinatra and Dean Martin's Rat Pack of the '50s, the

Squirrel Nut Zippers emerged as an anomaly in the retro-swing movement with their breakthrough novelty hit of 1996, the calypso shout-along song "Hell" from *Hot* (Mammoth Records).

The core of this idiosyncratically swinging group is the couple Jimbo Mathus (vocals, guitar, trombone) and Katharine Whalen (vocals, banjo), who decided to form a band in 1993 as a lark after meeting Don Raleigh (bass) and Ken Mosher (guitar, saxophone, vocals), both of whom shared an interest in hot jazz. Before long Chris Phillips (drums, percussion), Tom Maxwell (vocals, guitar, baritone saxophone, clarinet), and Je Windenhouse (trumpet) were added to the group, which was later named after an old-fashioned chewy, peanut-based candy, Squirrel Nut Zippers. (The candy's motto, like the band's, is "If it's good enough for Granddad, it's good enough for me.")

> **"If it's good enough for Granddad, it's good enough for me."**
> — *Squirrel Nut Zippers*

The group made its live debut in a Chapel Hill basement bistro, decked out in their favorite vintage threads, and within months had developed a large fan base throughout the South. By the end of 1994 the Zippers had signed with Mammoth Records and released their debut album, *The Inevitable,* in the spring of 1995. The album didn't make much of an impact but the group continued to tour. For their second album, *Hot,* the Zippers made a pilgrimage to New Orleans and recorded there the way their heroes had—live to tape in single takes with very few microphones. By the fall of 1996 the single from that record—Maxwell's calypso-flavored ditty, "Hell"—broke loose and became a hit on such influential radio stations as Los Angeles's KROQ. MTV soon made the video into a buzz clip. By the spring "Hell" was a staple on modern rock radio stations across the country. The album went gold and a second single, "Put a Lid on It," was released in the summer of 1997. *Sold Out,* a follow-up EP released around Christmastime of 1997, contains the hilarious viper number "Santa Claus Is Smoking Reefer."

The Zippers continued their momentum in 1998 with their third full-length CD, *Perennial Favorites,* which contained the zesty Dixieland single

**Cherry Poppin' Daddies, 1998, frontman-vocalist Steve Perry, bassist Dan Schmid.**

"Suits Are Picking up the Bill," a snide commentary on the so-called pleasures of success (the video clip for this tune depicts the band members being offered up as a cannibalistic sacrifice). Recorded in an 1870s house in tiny, rural Pittsboro, North Carolina, *Favorites* plumbs hot jazz, klezmer, jump blues, Western swing, and New Orleans brass and calypso. As Don Heckman of the *Los Angeles Times* wrote of this third release: "The Zippers can play, and their focus clearly seems to be on making their own creative variations rather than simply offering rehashed dance rhythms." Or as Jay Walljasper wrote in the *Utne Reader:* "I can't think of a recent record whose lyrics have engaged my mind so thoroughly even as the music delighted my soul and set my feet to tapping. A real gem."

In 1999 Katharine Whalen put her sultry, Billie Holiday–styled vocals to good use on her solo outing, *Jazz Squad* (Mammoth). And she reunited with her Zippers bandmates the following year for *Bedlam Ballroom,* which continued their string of charmingly idiosyncratic retro-swing.

Throughout their history, the Zippers have been adamant about distancing themselves from the whole swing revival, even though they are invariably lumped in by critics and writers as leading lights of that retro movement. "To call it swing music or even hot jazz is to miss the point," Maxwell, who discounts the entire swing revival as nothing more than a savvy marketing tool, told *USA Today.* "We're not concerned with nostalgia or sentimentality or revivals. Our goal is to make music that endures and has a timeless quality."

# ROOMFUL OF BLUES

FORMED: 1968 in Providence, Rhode Island

LONG BEFORE BRIAN SETZER stepped in front of a horn section, years prior to the advent of all the retro-swing Daddies, be they Big Bad Voodoo or Cherry Poppin', Roomful of Blues was knee-deep in swing, captivating audiences with its exuberant, good-time blend of blues, R&B, rock 'n' roll, and jumpin' jive.

Long hailed as "the best little big band in America," this nine-piece jump blues outfit can trace its roots back to 1968 when pianist Al Copley and guitarist Duke Robillard got together to play Chicago-style blues in coffee houses. In 1970 the band added Greg Piccolo on tenor sax and Rich Lataille on alto sax. The following year baritone sax ace Doug James filled out the horn section and by 1973 Roomful of Blues was playing dates with jump blues legends like Syl Austin, Red Prysock, and Eddie "Cleanhead" Vinson while establishing longstanding residencies at the Knickerbocker Cafe in Westerly, Rhode Island, and Brandy's in Boston.

In 1974 Roomful began playing dates with Count Basie, who called them "the hottest blues band I've ever heard." By 1977 legendary songwriter Doc Pomus helped secure their first self-titled record date for Island. They followed that up in 1979 with the rousing *Let's Have a Party* and in 1981 with *Hot Little Mama* while further establishing their jump blues credentials with a number of dates backing legendary blues shouter Roy Brown. Two landmark recordings followed for Muse—a 1982 collaboration with Eddie "Cleanhead" Vinson and a 1983 project with Big Joe Turner featuring special guest Dr. John (both albums were recently repackaged and reissued as a two-CD set on 32 Blues). Following a 1984 appearance at Carnegie Hall backing up Stevie Ray Vaughan, the band was signed to a two-album deal with Rounder Records, debuting with the jumpin' jivey *Dressed up to Get Messed Up*. There followed a string of lively horn-based jump blues recordings for the label,

**Roomful of Blues, circa mid-1980s.**

including 1994's *Dance All Night,* 1995's *Turn It On! Turn It Up!* 1997's *Roomful of Christmas,* and 1998's *There Goes the Neighborhood.*

Various charismatic, swaggering front men have gone through the Roomful ranks through the years, including soulful vocalists Curtis Salgado and Mac Odom, blues diva Lou Ann Barton, and harmonica ace Sugar Ray Norcia. Founding member Duke Robillard left the band in 1979 to pursue a solo career and subsequently put out gems like 1987's *Swing* (Rounder) and 1992's follow-up, *After Hours Swing Session* (Rounder). Both jazzy, blues-drenched offerings were inspired by the likes of T-Bone Walker, Tiny Grimes, and Nat "King" Cole.

**"Let's get dressed up to get messed up."**

—*Roomful of Blues*

# RAY GELATO & HIS GIANTS OF JIVE

FORMED: 1988 in London, England

SAXOPHONIST-SINGER RAY GELATO helped kick off a swing revival in the UK some fifteen years ago with his energized renditions of Louis Prima and Louis Jordan numbers. And judging from a 1999 appearance at the Montreal Jazz Festival (in which Gelato and His Giants had a crowd of some thirty thousand jumping in the streets all night long), it's safe to say the man has not lost his touch.

It was Ray's father, an Italian-American GI stationed in Britain, who played the music at home that first got Ray interested in the saxophone. The records that Ray heard in his childhood were predominantly those of the great American jazz and swing artists, including such luminaries as Count Basie, Frank Sinatra, Louis Prima, Benny Goodman, Louis Jordan. Ray also listened to the raw rock 'n' roll of Bill Haley and Little Richard, both favorites of Ray's parents.

It was these early influences that inspired Ray to take up the saxophone, although at the relatively late age of seventeen. Starting out largely self-taught he soon moved on to study with private teachers and also to enroll in various jazz courses at the City Lit College in London.

Ray's first paid gigs were with a rock 'n' roll band called Dynamite around 1980 to 1981, but he soon felt a need to expand his musical horizons to develop more as a player. He teamed up with a French guitar player living in London named Patrice Serapiglia but who was calling himself Maurice Chevalier. This was the start of what was to become The Chevalier Brothers, a seminal jump blues 'n' jive group in London. Maurice encouraged Ray to sing as well as play tenor sax, and was even responsible for giving Ray the stage name Gelato.

By early 1983 the band had expanded from a duo into a five-piece and was gigging extensively in the London clubs, delighting audiences with their energetic stage show and their eclectic mix of Louis Jordan jump tunes, Django Reinhardt–style gypsy jazz, frantic swing instrumentals, and madcap original songs. The visual style was the '40s zoot suit gangster look, several years before Royal Crown Revue would adopt the same look. The band's popularity soon spread beyond the London clubs such as Dingwalls, The Dublin Castle, The Fridge, and The Half Moon as they began appearing on TV shows and touring abroad to places like the Montreux Jazz Festival, the North Sea Jazz Festival, and one memorable visit to Japan in 1986.

After Maurice departed, Ray formed his seven-piece band, Ray Gelato & His Giants of Jive, and began focusing on scaled down big-band arrangements of '40s era jump and swing tunes. Success on the festival, club, and college circuit continued, with new markets also opening up for the band, particularly in Italy, where the band started to tour frequently. From 1988 to 1994 this lineup recorded three hard-hitting albums of jumpin' jive—
*Giants of Jive, A Taste of Gelato,* and *Gelato Espresso.*

In 1994 Ray headed down a different musical path with his new band, The Ray Gelato Giants. This band emphasized Ray's big-toned swinging tenor and his exuberant Louis Prima–styled vocal delivery while also incorporating the influences of Nat "King" Cole, Frank Sinatra, Duke Ellington, and even Dean Martin. The results of this shakeup can be heard on 1995's *The Full Flavor.*

**"Josephine please no lean on the bell."**
— *Ray Gelato*

Gelato's Giants continue to play numerous major jazz festivals around the world, including the San Sebastian Festival in Spain, the Molde festival in Norway, the Burghausen festival in Germany, the Marciac festival in France, and the Montreal Jazz Festival in Canada, although they have yet to make a significant hit on the States.

# COLIN JAMES AND
# THE LITTLE BIG BAND

FORMED: 1993 in Vancouver, Canada

VIRTUALLY OVERLOOKED IN THE SWING REVIVAL is the accomplished Canadian blues guitar hero Colin James, who went from being an impassioned Stevie Ray Vaughan disciple in the late '80s to fronting a thirteen-piece orchestra with the release of his 1993 swing album *Colin James and The Little Big Band*. That album, released a full year before rockabilly guitarist Brian Setzer's similar big-band experiment, achieved double platinum status in Canada, triggering a jump blues 'n' jive revival north of the border.

Growing up in Regina, Saskatchewan, Colin first experimented musically with the pennywhistle and mandolin. He began playing guitar at the age of eight and by the time he was sixteen he quit school and left home, playing on street corners in Vancourver, Toronto, and Montreal. He later worked with a succession of bands, including the Hoo Doo Men and Night Shades, before performing under his own name. By the age of twenty, he had hooked up with the legendary Stevie Ray Vaughan, who took Colin on the road to open shows for him in Canada and the United States. A self-financed twelve-inch single featuring the songs "Five Long Years" and "Why'd You Lie" was hand-delivered to radio stations across Canada, garnering Colin his first radio exposure and helping to build a national reputation that led to his first major label record deal with Virgin. His self-titled 1988 debut for that label was the fastest-selling album in Canadian music history. He followed that up in 1990 with another urgent and highly popular blues rocker, *Sudden Stop,* while continuing to tour as an opening act for Bonnie Raitt, Stevie Ray Vaughan, and The Rolling Stones.

In 1993, five years before the swing revival was in full force, James unveiled his Little Big Band. Their self-titled album for Virgin was a collection of jump blues and swing standards from the 1940s, including a killer rendition of Tiny Bradshaw's "The Train Kept A-Rollin'." Their follow-up five years later included spirited finger-snappin', jumpin' jive fare like

> "She was jumpin'
> from six to six,
> got herself
> in a heckuva fix."
> — Colin James

"Jumpin' from Six to Six," Cab Calloway's frantic "C'mon with the C'mon," Jimmy McCracklin's "Think" (recorded by The Five Royales and James Brown), raucous organ-powered shuffles like "Let's Shout (Baby Work Out)" and "I'll See It Through," and a rousing rendition of Louis Prima's "Oh Babe." There are several allusions to Louis Jordan and His Tympany Five along the way, with strong contributions from former Stevie Ray Vaughan organist Reese Wynans and studio horn aces Kaz Kazanoff on baritone sax and Greg Piccolo on tenor sax.

Says James, "I've always found the whole amazing legacy of this music fascinating. I have been playing some of these songs since I was eighteen. There was a great period between when the big-band days were waning and rock 'n' roll was just emerging, from about 1949 to 1955, when bands were scaling down their horn sections and infusing it with rock, which wasn't even called rock then. It was a magical era that I have always had a fondness for."

This Little Big Band definitely gives the Brian Setzer Orchestra a run for its money, though its records aren't as widely distributed through the States and the band rarely tours outside of Canada. But for infectious swing factor and killer guitar riffs, Colin & Company are right up there at the top of the retro-swing heap. Summing up the late '90s swing revival, James said, "I think its recent popularity may be a reaction to some of the early '90s nihilism. Music got real introspective for a while, and this is a way to get out of your skin a little bit."

# PAUL CEBAR

BORN: December 4, 1956, in Milwaukee, Wisconsin

THE IDIOSYNCRATIC, ALWAYS ECLECTIC, and endlessly appealing Paul Cebar was a lone troubadour with a guitar back in the mid-1970s, playing and singing tunes by Louis Jordan ("Dyed Your Hair Chartreuse," "Early in the Morning"), Jimmie Lunceford ("Easy Street"), Percy Mayfield ("Baby You're Rich"), Smokey Robinson ("Ain't That Peculiar"), Charlie Rich ("Mohair Sam"), and King Pleasure ("Do You Know What I Heard?") on the Milwaukee circuit before forming his powerhouse jump blues 'n' jive outfit, The R&B Cadets, in 1979. This six-piece groove orchestra toured relentlessly around the Midwest through the early '80s, spreading the gospel of joy through the music of New Orleans jivesters like Eddie Bo, Huey "Piano" Smith, and Lee Dorsey along with well-chosen covers of more obscure artists such as The Five Royales, Clarence Garlow, and Bettye Swan. As John Morthland wrote in *The Village Voice* (when reviewing the band's first New York gig in 1983): "Milwaukee's R&B Cadets don't play rhythm and blues so much as they synthesize styles from '40s jump to '60s soul. . . . Paul Cebar looks like a philosophy grad student gone funky and sings like the cat that just swallowed the canary . . . his cheery phrasing and cool demeanor makes their eclectic set all of a piece. . . . The groove springs eternal."

Touted by other critics as "the best unsigned band in the country," the Cadets soon drew the attention of British pop star and rockabilly revivalist Nick Lowe, who became a vocal booster and said of the group: "Nobody back home plays that old-time rhythm and blues so well."

Boasting a showstopping female vocalist-accordionist in Robyn Pluer and a secret weapon in female bari sax player Juli Wood, who also could belt out a soul song with the gospel holler intensity of young Aretha Franklin, The R&B Cadets continued their assault on groove hounds with their exhilarating

Photo credit: Frank Ford

**Paul Cebar with The Milwaukeeans, circa 1992 (back row, left to right): Tony Jarvis, Peter Roller, Juli Wood, Randy Baugher, Al Anderson; (front row): Paul Cebar, Robyn Pluer.**

live show. As Cebar noted at the time: "Our mission is to nurture the next generation of dancing thinkers." In 1986 they released *Top Happy* on the Minneapolis-based Twin/Tone label before eventually dissolving The R&B Cadets and mutating into The Milwaukeeans by 1987.

A prolific writer and audacious lyricist with a gift for thoughtful, witty verse, Cebar prospered at the helm of The Milwaukeeans, churning out such poetic gems as "I Will Keep," "'Round Every Corner," "You Make Me Feel So," and "Slither Awhile," all of which appeared on the band's 1993 Shanachie Records debut, *That Unhinged Thing*. Cebar continued his golden touch with songwriting on 1995's funkified *Upstroke for the Downfolk* and 1997's *The Get Go,* both for Don't.

> **"Your tree is where I want to be and your limbs I'd linger on."**
> — *Paul Cebar*

The Milwaukeeans's mission was eloquently stated in a band bio that carried the blaring tabloid headline: *Milwaukeeans Issue Dance Imperative, Thousands Fall Sway, Give It Up.* "Paul Cebar and the Milwaukeeans featuring Robyn Pluer are a seven-piece neo-provincial dance music combine flipping like a flag on a pole for you. With a pronounced bent toward letting the proverbial all hang out, these inveterate groovehounds draw upon New Orleans R&B, soukous, Stax/Volt, Hi, Kwela, Motown, Yotown, rhumba and any other damn thing worth shaking a stick or hip at in a hellbent effort to spread the live dance music of the Midwestern fertility cults from whence they've sprung."

A perpetual favorite in Chicago, Milwaukee, Minneapolis, and New Orleans, these irrepressible hipsters continue to pump out infectious music that draws heavily on American roots music while taking in elements from way beyond. As Cebar puts it: "Not roots, not bark . . . the whole tree, baby, the whole tree."

# JET SET SIX

FORMED: 1994 in New York, New York

THE DIRECT DESCENDANT of the late '80s experimental lounge trio Beat Positive, Jet Set Six manages to bridge the punk aesthetic of the Sex Pistols's

Johnny Rotten and The Sands's Dean Martin. Named after a Tony Bennett album from the early '60s, Jet Set Six is dedicated to the prospect of living it up. As lead singer John Ceparano told *Swing Time* magazine: "When the band first started back in the late '80s, the 'Beat' was for a beatnik kind of thing and 'Positive' was forward moving. We started as a trio and stayed a trio for many years. We were always doing a swing kind of thing, but early on it was way more experimental. As time went on the sound evolved into something that had nothing to do with that trio any more, so I felt as though I wanted to wipe the slate clean. Now I feel we have a name that actually reflects that the band is the late '50s and early '60s. At that time jet-setting was synonymous with the swinging, and Tony Bennett actually had an album called *Songs for the Jet Set*. It was all in the spirit of living it up and that kind of swingin' thing."

**"What we do is all in the spirit of living it up."**

— *Jet Set Six*

Hence, the following lyrics from his opus, "Livin' It Up":

> *It's always been a dog-eat-dog world*
> *Ever since I was a little pup.*
> *Now I'm out of the dog house*
> *And I'm livin' it up.*

Add three horns to a swank sharkskin-suit-wearing trio and you have Jet Set Six, one of the hippest bands on the burgeoning New York retro-swing scene.

## THE YALLOPPIN' HOUNDS

FORMED: 1998 in New York, New York

ANOTHER BUSY BAND on the New York scene is also the first to successfully combine swing with hip-hop styles. The Yalloppin' Hounds derive their name from a running gag among the musicians of the Illinois Jacquet Big Band. One day at a French concert, Jacquet poked fun at another well-known swing band from New York by referring to them as a bunch of "yallopping hounds," so when founding members Joey "G-Clef" Cavaseno, Lord Sledge, and Eli Yamin (all Jacquet alumni) got together to think up a name for their new swing band, the choice was obvious. "We knew enough about each other already to hear a sound in our heads . . . and the sound was that of a bunch of barking dogs," explains bandleader and alto saxophonist Cavaseno, whose credits include work with such authentic swing bands as Panama Francis and the Savoy Sultans, Arvell Shaw's Louis Armstrong Legacy, and Lionel Hampton.

> **"Jacquet, stop da racket. Jacquet, here's ya jacket."**
> — *The Yalloppin' Hounds*

Trumpeter-vocalist Sledge, a former member of the ska band The Toasters, is also a born entertainer who conjures up images of the three Louises—Prima, Jordan, and Armstrong. A recent addition to the group is house-rockin' vocalist Georgia Jones, who delivers classic swing tunes with wit and verve. But the strength of this hybrid swing band is its original material, which can be heard on the aptly titled *Ghetto Swing* (Yalloppin' Entertainment).

---

### Jivenotes:

Montreal-born, Bronx-bred jivester August Darnell (born Thomas Browder) joined forces in 1974 with his brother Stony Browder to form **Dr. Buzzard's Original Savannah Band,** which successfully combined Cab Calloway's jive appeal and aspects of '30s dance band music with a disco beat. After three successful records, including their gold-selling self-titled debut in 1976, the brothers split up. Stony kept the original band together while August went on to form the Latin-tinged modernist disco band **Kid Creole & The Coconuts** with former Savannah Band–singer Andy Hernandez. Adapting Kid Creole as his alter ego, Darnell performed in Cab-styled white zoot suit and broad-brimmed hat while singing risqué comic numbers like "Mister Softee" (about impotence), "I'm a Wonderful Thing, Baby," and "Annie, I'm Not Your Daddy." The band flourished in the early '80s on the strength of dance hits like "Me No Pop I," "Stool Pigeon," and "Dear Addy." The original lineup disbanded in 1985 but Darnell regrouped the following year and continued recording and touring through the '80s. He took time off in 1989 to write *In a Pig's Valise,* an Off-Broadway show that ran for twelve weeks. Kid Creole & The Coconuts resurfaced in 1990 and continued recording and touring through the '90s. The band still performs in Germany, England, and Japan while playing the casino circuit of Las Vegas and Atlantic City in the States.

The New England–based **Bellevue Cadillac** mix elements of Louis Jordan, Cab Calloway, Glenn Miller, and T-Bone Walker in their appealing jump blues 'n' jive stew, as heard on their 1998 album *Prozac Nation* (Hep Cat). They also boast tight horn arrangements, wailing guitar work from Doug "The Professor" Bell and real deal soul from singer "Gentleman Joe" Cooper. **The Love Dogs,** a revved-up group of Boston-based jump blues hounds led by frantic front man E. Duato Scheer blend West Coast–, Kansas City–, and New Orleans–flavored jive in their high-powered act. Their third CD for Tone-Cool, *New Tricks,* includes a bristling cover of Tiny Bradshaw's jump blues classic "Well Oh Well."

Washington, D.C.–based drummer-singer Big Joe Maher has demonstrated a knack for jump blues 'n' jive for the past thirteen years with his band **Big Joe & The Dynaflows.** Their 1989 Powerhouse album *Good Rockin' Daddy* is solidly in the groove as is Joe's 1998 outing for Severn, *I'm Still Swingin'.* New Jersey's **Crescent City Maulers** formed in 1993 and have since been entertaining East Coast jump blues/jive fans with their spirited renditions of Louis Jordan, Cab Calloway, and Louis Prima material, which can be heard on their 1997 Slimstyle release, *Screamin'.* Detroit's **Atomic Fireballs** deal in Louis Jordan–style jump blues on their 1998 release *Birth of the Swerve* as well as their 1999 major label debut for Atlantic, *Torch This Place.* In Oakland **Steve Lucky & The Rhumba Bums** are lighting up crowds with their faithful covers of T-Bone Walker, Hadda Brooks, Tiny Grimes, and Professor Longhair material. Singer and rhythm guitarist Carmen Getit radiates star quality along with a solid command of sophisticated chordal voicings. The group's 1998 release on Rumpus, *Come out Swingin',* is a good Bums primer and features a killer rendition of T-Bone's "Bye Baby Bye."

Formed in 1985 in Texas by the accomplished boogie-woogie pianist Red Young, **Red & The Red Hots** have turned in jivey renditions of Louis Jordan's "Ain't Nobody Here but Us Chickens" and "Choo Choo Ch'Boogie," along with spirited jump blues 'n' boogie originals. The Bronx-based **The Blues Jumpers** are a vital East Coast sextet with vibrant vocalist Elridge Taylor summoning up the spirit of Big Joe Turner. New Orleans–based, Armstrong-influenced trumpeter **Duke Heitger,** who played on the Squirrel Nut Zippers's megahit "Hot," formed his own purist, '20s/'30s–style swing band in 1999 after a lengthy stint with hot jazz diva Banu Gibson. Their Fantasy Records debut, *Rhythm Is Our Business,* swings forcefully and in the ebullient spirit of Jimmie Lunceford (title track), Duke Ellington ("Stevedore Stomp"), Gene Krupa ("Swing Is Here"), and vintage Louis Armstrong ("Hear Me

Talkin' to You," "I Hope Gabriel Likes My Music"), with no concessions to rock 'n' roll whatsoever.

Guitarist **Nick Palumbo & His Flipped Fedoras** have been heating up the dance floor with their weekly hits at the Supper Club in Manhattan. The classy fifteen-piece **Bill Elliott Swing Orchestra,** modeled after the Tommy Dorsey and Jimmie Lunceford orchestras, has become a modern swing icon on the West Coast. San Francisco–based **Indigo Swing** covered Louis Jordan's "Choo Choo Ch'Boogie" on their eponymous disc of 1995. Before joining the cast of the Broadway musical *Swing!* scat singer–ukulele player Casey MacGill drew a strong local following around Seattle with his jive outfit **Casey MacGill & The Spirits of Rhythm,** named after the '30s band featuring vocal pioneer Leo "Scat" Watson. And lastly, Milwaukee's longest-running, hardest-working rhythm 'n' blues show band and revue, the **Booze Brothers,** have been pledging allegiance to jump blues and jive since 1979. Originally formed as a tribute band in the wake of Dan Aykroyd–John Belushi's highly successful Blues Brothers act, this powerhouse horn band has branched off to include several jumped-up originals and scintillating jive anthems, including "Minnie the Moocher" and Johnny Otis's "Willie and the Hand Jive."

## *Recommended Listening*

### ROYAL CROWN REVUE

*Kings of Gangster Bop,* Big Daddy (1991)

*Mugzy's Move,* Warner Bros. (1996)

*Caught in the Act,* Surfdog (1997)

*The Contender,* Warner Bros. (1998)

*Walk on Fire,* Warner Bros. (1999)

### BIG BAD VOODOO DADDY

*Big Bad Voodoo Daddy,* Hep Cat (1993)

*Whatchu' Want for Christmas?* Hep Cat (1995)

*Big Bad Voodoo Daddy,*
   Coolsville/EMI/Capitol (1998)

### BRIAN SETZER

*The Brian Setzer Orchestra,*
   Hollywood (1994)

*Guitar Slinger,* Interscope (1996)

*The Dirty Boogie,* Interscope (1998)

*Vavoom!* Interscope (2000)

### CHERRY POPPIN' DADDIES

*Rapid City Muscle Car,* Space Age
   Bachelor Pad (1994)

*Kids on the Street,* Space Age Bachelor
   Pad (1995)

*Zoot Suit Riot: The Swingin'
   Hits of the Cherry Poppin' Daddies,*
   Universal (1997)

*Soul Caddy,* Universal (2000)

### SQUIRREL NUT ZIPPERS

*The Inevitable,* Mammoth (1995)

*Hot,* Mammoth (1996)

*Sold Out,* Mammoth (1997)

*Perennial Favorites,* Mammoth
   (1998)

*Bedlam Ballroom,* Mammoth
   (2000)

**ROOMFUL OF BLUES**

*Let's Have a Party,* Antilles (1979)

*Hot Little Mama,* Blue Flame/Varrick (1981)

*Roomful of Blues with Joe Turner/Eddie "Cleanhead" Vinson,* 32 Blues (1982–1983)

*Dressed up to Get Messed Up,* Rounder (1984)

*Dance All Night,* Bullseye/Rounder (1994)

*Turn It On! Turn It Up!* Bullseye/Rounder (1995)

*There Goes the Neighborhood,* Bullseye/Rounder (1998)

**RAY GELATO & HIS GIANTS OF JIVE**

*Giants of Jive,* Blue Horizon (1989)

*A Taste of Gelato,* High Five (1992)

*Gelato Espresso,* Durium (1993)

*The Full Flavor,* Linn (1995)

*The Men from Uncle,* Double Scoop (1998)

**COLIN JAMES AND THE LITTLE BIG BAND**

*Colin James and The Little Big Band,* Virgin (1993)

*Colin James and The Little Big Band II,* Elektra (1998)

**PAUL CEBAR**

**With The R&B Cadets:**

*Top Happy,* Twin/Tone (1986)

**With The Milwaukeeans:**

*That Unhinged Thing,* Shanachie (1993)

*Upstroke for the Downfolk,* Don't (1995)

*The Get Go,* Don't (1997)

**JET SET SIX**

*Livin' It Up,* Mutiny (1998)

**THE YALLOPPIN' HOUNDS**

*Ghetto Swing,* Yalloppin' Entertainment (1999)

**DR. BUZZARD'S ORIGINAL SAVANNAH BAND**

*Dr. Buzzard's Original Savannah Band,* RCA (1976)

*Meets King Pennett,* RCA (1978)

*Goes to Washington,* Elektra (1979)

**KID CREOLE & THE COCONUTS**

*Off the Coast of Me,* Ze (1980)

*Fresh Fruit in Foreign Places,* Ze (1982)

**BELLEVUE CADILLAC**

*Black & White,* Ardeon (1996)

*Prozac Nation,* Hep Cat (1998)

**THE LOVE DOGS**

*New Tricks,* Tone-Cool (2000)

**BIG JOE & THE DYNAFLOWS**

*Good Rockin' Daddy,* Powerhouse (1989)

*I'm Still Swingin',* Severn (1998)

**THE ATOMIC FIREBALLS**

*Birth of the Swerve,* Orbital (1998)

*Torch This Place,* Atlantic (1999)

**STEVE LUCKY & THE RHUMBA BUMS**

*Come out Swingin',* Rumpus (1998)

**RED & THE RED HOTS**

*Red & The Red Hots,* Red Young
Productions (1995)

*The Boogie Man,* Red Young
Productions (1998)

**THE BLUES JUMPERS**

*Wheels Start Turning,* Ridge (1998)

**DUKE HEITGER**

*Rhythm Is Our Business,* Fantasy (2000)

**BILL ELLIOTT SWING ORCHESTRA**

*Callin All Jitterbugs!* Wayland (1997)

**INDIGO SWING**

*Indigo Swing,* Welt & Placket (1995)

*All Aboard!* Time Bomb (1998)

**CASEY MACGILL &
THE SPIRITS OF RHYTHM**

*Jump,* SR (1999)

**BOOZE BROTHERS**

*Rockin' Rhythm 'n Blues,*
Spectacular (1980)

# THE LANGUAGE OF JIVE

The material in the following two entries—the A–Z Jive Dictionary and Jive Expressions—were culled primarily from Cab Calloway's *Hepster's Dictionary*, Dan Burley's *Original Handbook of Harlem Jive*, and Babs Gonzales's *Be-Bop Dictionary*. However, there are selected Lester Young-isms, some Mezz Mezzrow-ese, and a few Harry "The Hipster" Gibson-isms sprinkled throughout.

## A–Z JIVE DICTIONARY

### A

**Ace**   A dollar bill, close friend, companion

**Ace-deuce**   Three

**Ace lane**   A husband

**Air bags**   Lungs

**A hummer**   Exceptionally good

**Alligator**   A swing fan, a musician

**Anxious**   Wonderful, excellent

**Apple**   New York City

**Apron**   A bartender, a barkeeper

**Armstrongs**   Trumpet notes in the extreme high register

**Attic**   The head

**Avenue tank**   A Fifth Avenue bus

**Axe**   An instrument

### B

**Baby kisser**   A politician

**Bad**   Good

**Bag**   A particular style or way of doing things, as in "That's not my bag."

**Bagpipe**   A vacuum cleaner

**Bank**   A toilet

**Banter**   An attractive young girl

**Barbecue**   An attractive young girl

**Barkers**   Shoes

**Barrelhouse**   Free and easy

**Basket**   A stomach

**Battle**   An unattractive woman

**Bean**   The sun

**Bear**   A poor, depressed condition

**Beat**   Lacking something, as in "I'm beat for cash."

**Beat up**   Sad, uncomplimentary, tired

**Beef**   To state or inform, as in "He beefed me to that."

**Benny**   An overcoat

**Bible**   The gospel truth

**Big Apple**   Harlem, New York City

**Birdwood**   Something to smoke

**Biscuit**   A pillow, the head

**Black**   Night

**Blinkers**   Eyes

**Blip**   Something cool or groovy, as in "That's a blip."

**Blow**   To smoke marijuana

**Blue Broadway**   Heaven, the Milky Way, a way to heaven

**Bondage**   Debt

**Boo**   Gage, Mary Jane, pot, tea, marijuana

**Boot**   To inform or educate, as in "Let me boot you to the situation."

**Boulevard cowboy**   A taxicab driver

**Box**   A piano

**Boxed**   Juiced, high, stoned, intoxicated

**Bread**   Loot, currency, money, dough

**Bree**   A girl

**Bright**   Day

**Brightnin'**   Daybreak

**Bring-down**   A drag, an upsetting circumstance

**Broom**   To walk, to leave, to run, to stroll

**Buddy ghee**   A fellow

**Bug**   To annoy someone

### C

**Canary**   A female vocalist

**Capped**   Outdone, surpassed

**Cat**   A musician in a swing band, a jive fan

**Chick**   A girl

**Chime**   The hour of the day, as in "I went to bed at ten chimes."

**Chirp**   A female singer

**Choker**   A tie

**Chops**   Lips, jaw, technique

**Clambake**   An ad-lib session, jam session

**Clipster**   A confidence man

**Cogs**   Sunglasses

**Cold-meat party**   A funeral

**Collar**   To understand, as in "Do you collar this jive?"

**Cool on**   To ignore, as in "I'm coolin' on her."

**Cooling**   Unemployed

**Cop**   To get something, to obtain

**Corny**   Old-fashioned, stale

**Crib**   A dwelling, a house, a shop, an apartment

**Crumb crushers**   Teeth

**Crumb-snatcher**   A baby

**Cubby**   A room, a flat, a home

**Cut out**   To leave, to depart

**Cutrate**   Low-class

## D

**Dead presidents**   Paper currency of any denomination

**Deep six**   A grave

**Deep sugar**   A persuasive line of talk

**Desk piano**   A typewriter

**Deuce**   Two dollars, a pair

**Dicty**   High-class, nifty, smart

**Dig**   (1) To meet, as in "I'll dig you later." (2) To notice, as in "Dig that chick!" (3) To comprehend, as in "Do you dig this jive?"

**Dil-ya-bla**   A phone call

**Dim**   Evening

**Dime note**   A ten-dollar bill

**Dip**   A hat

**Do the Vonce**   To make love

**Doghouse**   A bass fiddle

**Dome**   The head

**Domi**   A home

**Doss**   Sleep, as in "I'm beat for doss."

**Drag**   (1) A bring-down or disappointment (2) A boring, joyless person

**Drape**   Suit of clothes, dress, a costume

**Draped down**   Dressed up

**Dreambox**   The head

**Dreamers**   Bed covers, blankets

**Dribble**   To stutter

**Dried barker**   Fur

**Drifter**   A floater

**Drink**   An ocean, a sea, a river, water, a stream

**Dry goods**   Suit of clothes, dress, costume

**Ducks**   Tickets

**Duck uncle**   To avoid the military draft

**Duke**   A hand, mitt

**Dust**   To leave

**Dustbin**   A grave

**Dutchess**   A girl

## E

**Early black**   Evening

**Early bright**   Morning

**Eighty-eights**   A piano

**Enamel**   Skin

**Expense**   A newborn baby

**Expubidence**   Inherent talents, charm, personal charisma

## F

**Face**   A white man

**Fall out**   To be overcome with surprise and delight, as in "The cats fell out over that solo."

**Feeler**   Finger

**Fell**   To be incarcerated

**Fillmill**   A tavern

**Final**   To exit, as in "I finaled that scene."

**Finale**   Death, a last out

**Fine dinner**   An attractive woman

**Fine Fryer**   An attractive young girl

**Fizzical culturist**   A bartender

**Flag spot**   A bus stop

**Flaps**   Ears

**Flicker**   A moving picture

**Flychick**   A young girl about eighteen

**Flip**   To go wild, to go insane

**Foxy**   Shrewd

**Frail**   A woman

**Frame**   The body

**Frantic**   Great, wonderful

**Fraughty issue**   A sad state of affairs

**Freakish high**   A state of extreme inebriation

**Freebie**   No charge, gratis

**Frolic pad**   A place of entertainment, a theater, a nightclub

**Front**   A suit of clothes

**Fry**   To straighten out kinky hair

## G

**Gabriel**   Trumpet player

**Gage**   A marijuana cigarette

**Gal officer**   A lesbian

**Gams**   Legs

**Gaper**   A mirror

**Gas**   To converse

**Gasser**   A high compliment, as in "When it comes to dancing, he's a gasser."

**Gate**   A male person

**Gazer**   A window

**Geets**   Money

**Gestapo**   Out-of-town union delegates

**Get straight**   To work it out, to make a deal

**Gig**   A job for one night

**Glims**   The eyes

**God box**   An organ

**Goof**   One whose mind goes astray for awhile

**Goola**   A piano

**Grape-chick**   A female devotee of wine

**Gravy**   A profit

**Grease**   To take in food, as in "To grease one's chops."

**Groan box**   A bass fiddle

**Groovy**   Fine

**Ground Grippers**   New shoes

**Growl**   Raspy tones from a trumpet

**Gut-bucket**   Low-down, bluesy music

## H

**Hat**   A chick, a wife

**Hard**   Sharp, stylish, as in "That's a hard tie you're wearing."

**Hard spiel**   An engaging line of talk

**Harlem toothpick**   A pocketknife, a switchblade

**Have eyes**   To like someone or something

**Hawk**   Cold weather

**Hawkins**   The wind

**Have a ball**   To let loose, to live it up

**Head Knock**   God

**Headlight**   A diamond

**Hep cat**   A savvy guy who is in the know and understands jive

**Hideaways**   Pockets

**Hide-beater**   A drummer

**Hincty**   Conceited, snooty

**Hip**   Aware, enlightened

**Hipster**   A character who likes hot jazz

**Hit**   A draw on a marijuana cigarette

**Hit on**   To pester, to annoy, to flirt

**Hollywood eyes**   A pretty girl

**Home-cooking**   Something very nice

**Homey**   (1) A person from one's hometown (2) One who isn't hip

**Hot**   Musically torrid

**Hung up**   Mixed up, confused, misled, addicted

**Hush hush**   A pistol, a revolver

**Husk**   To undress

**Hype**   Persuasive talk, hard sell, build up

## I

**Ice palace**   A jewelry store

**Icky**   One who is not hip, a square

**Idea pot**   The head

**Igg**   To ignore, as in "Don't igg me!"

## J

**Jack**   A name for close male associates

**Jam**   To improvise on swinging themes

**Jeff**   A pest, a bore, an icky

**Jelly**   A freebie, on the house

**Jitterbug**   A swing fan

**Jive**   Coded speech of the jitterbug scene

**Joy root**   A marijuana cigarette

**Jug**   A bottle of liquor

**Juices**   Liquor

**Jump**   To dance vigorously

## K

**Kick**   A pocket, as in "I've got five bucks in my kick."

**Kill**   To thrill, to fascinate, to enthrall

**Kill joy**   A policeman

**Kite**   An air-mail letter

**Knobs**   Knees

**Knock**   To give, as in "Knock me a kiss."

**Knothole**   A doughnut

**Knowledge-box**   The brain, the head

**Kong**   Whiskey, moonshine liquor

## L

**Lamb**   One who is easy prey for con men

**Lamp**   To see, to look at

**Lamps**   Eyes

**Land o' darkness**   Harlem

**Lane**   A working-class male, a regular Joe

**Latch on**   To grab, to take hold, to get wise to

**Lay dead**   To stay in one place, to not move

**Lead sheet**   A topcoat
**Left raise**   Left side
**Lid**   A hat, headgear, a cap
**Light up**   To smoke reefer
**Licks**   A musician's stock phrases on his chosen instrument
**Lily whites**   Bed sheets
**Line**   The cost of an object, as in "What is the line on this drape?"
**Lock up**   To lay exclusive claim to something as in "I've got the chick locked up."
**Lung-duster**   A cigarette

## M

**Mad**   Fine, capable
**Main drag**   Seventh Avenue
**Main kick**   The stage
**Main on the hitch**   A husband
**Main queen**   A favorite girlfriend, a sweetheart
**Main stem**   (1) Bustling avenue (2) Street-corner hangout
**Man in gray**   A postman
**Map**   The face
**Marble town**   A cemetery
**Mellow roof**   A head
**Melted out**   Broke
**Mess**   Something extremely good, as in "That last solo was a mess."
**Meter**   A quarter, twenty-five cents
**Mezz**   Anything supreme, genuine, as in "This is really the mezz."
**Mister speaker**   A gun, a revolver
**Mitt pounding**   Applause
**Moo juice**   Milk
**Mootah**   Marijuana
**Mop**   The finale
**Mop-shi-lu**   To be disappointed
**Mouse**   A pocket, as in "I've got two bucks in the mouse."
**Muggin'**   Clownin', making 'em laugh

## N

**Nab**   Office of the Law
**Napolean**   An insane man, as in "That cat is strictly a Napolean."
**Nasty**   Excellent
**Nicklette**   A jukebox
**Nickel note**   A five-dollar bill
**Nix out**   To cancel, to eliminate

## O

**Ofay**   A white person
**Office piano**   A typewriter
**Oiler**   One who will fight
**Old Man Mose**   Father Time, death
**Orchestration**   An overcoat
**Oxford**   Black, Negro

## P

**Pad**   A bed
**Paddles**   The hands
**Pail**   The stomach
**Pan**   The face
**Pay dues**   To spend money on a chick or fellow
**Pecking**   A dance introduced at the Cotton Club in 1937
**Peekers**   The eyes
**Pegs**   Trousers
**Peola**   A light, almost white person
**Piccolo**   A juke box
**Pies**   Eyes
**Pigeon**   A young girl
**Pink**   A white girl
**Pins**   The legs
**Plates**   The feet
**Play**   A scheme, a plan, as in "Let me boot you to my play."
**Poke**   A purse, one's money
**Pops**   A nickname for all male friends
**Pounder**   A detective, a policeman
**Pour man**   A bartender
**The president**   Lester Young
**Props**   Legs
**Pumpkin**   The moon
**Put down**   To say, to perform, to describe, to do

## Q

**Queen**   A beautiful girl
**Quit the scene**   To split, to leave, to cut out

## R

**Rag out**   To dress up
**Rank**   To lower or degrade
**Rat hole**   A pocket
**Reefer**   A marijuana cigarette
**Reefer man**   A dope peddler
**Reet**   Excellent
**Ride**   To maintain an even tempo while playing or singing

**Riff**   A hot lick, a musical phrase

**Righteous**   Splendid, most enjoyable, as in "Reap this righteous riff."

**Rind**   The skin

**Rock me**   To inspire one to move with rhythm

**Rope**   A marijuana cigarette

**Ruff**   A quarter, twenty-five cents

**Rug cutter**   An expert jitterbug dancer

### S

**Sad**   Very bad, as in "That was the saddest trumpeter I ever heard."

**Salty**   Angry, ill-tempered

**Saw**   A landlady

**Scarf**   Food, dinner, a meal

**Scoff**   To eat

**Screaming-gasser**   A patrol wagon, a police squad car

**Send**   To joyfully arouse the senses, as in "That song really sends me!"

**Sender**   A superb musician, as in "He's a solid sender."

**Sharp**   Neat, smart, distinctive,  as in "That hat is sharp as a tack."

**Shutters**   Eyes

**Signify**   To declare yourself, to brag, to boast

**Sing**   To play with one's best feelings

**Skate**   To get by without paying

**Skins**   Drums

**Skin-beater**   A drummer

**Sky piece**   A hat

**Slave**   A gig

**Snatcher**   A detective

**Sniffer**   A nose

**Soft-top**   A stool

**Solid sender**   An inspired musician capable of transporting listeners

**Solid stud**   An influential man in the entertainment field

**Sound off**   To speak, to declare

**Spiel**   To talk, to discuss, or to make a speech

**Square**   An unhep person, not hip

**Squat**   To sit down

**Stache/stash**   To file, to hide away

**Stand one up**   To act with little regard for someone else

**Stick**   A reefer

**Stir**   A jail

**Stomps**   Shoes

**Straps**   Suspenders

**Stud**   A male

**Stumble**   To hit a streak of misfortune

**Susie-Q**   A dance introduced at the Cotton Club in 1936

**The Sweatshop**   A working musician's reference to the Apollo Theatre

### T

**Tab action**   To borrow, to request a loan

**Tab issue**   To ask, to beg, to borrow

**Take off**   To play a solo

**Tea**   Marijuana

**The man**   The law

**Thinkpad**   A head, a brain

**Thin one**   A dime, ten cents

**Threads**   A suit, dress, or costume

**Three-pointer**   A corner

**Tick**   A minute, as in "I'll dig you in a few ticks."

**Timber**   A toothpick

**Tog**   To dress

**Tom-o-reeni**   A person who thinks he's inferior

**Top sergeant**   A lesbian

**Torture eyes**   A southern tour

**The track**   The Savoy Ballroom

**Trap**   A draft board

**Treaders**   Shoes

**Tree-suit**   A coffin

**Trilly**   To leave, to depart, as in "Well, I guess I'll trilly."

**Truck**   To walk somewhere, as in "I think I'll truck on down to the bar."

**Trucking**   A dance introduced at the Cotton Club in 1933

**Tubs**   A set of drums

**Turkey**   A fool, a square

**Turn on**   To smoke cigarettes, generally of the marijuana variety

**Twig**   A tree

**Twister**   A key

**Two cents**   Two dollars

### U

**Uncle**   A pawnshop operator

**Unhep**   Not wise to the jive, square, uncool

**Unhipped**   State of being unaware, uncool

**Upstairs**   Heaven, the sky

## V

**V-8**   A chick who is snooty and spurns company
**Vacuum Cleaner**   Lungs
**Vine**   A suit of clothes

## W

**Waders**   Boots
**Washer**   A saloon, a tavern
**Weed**   Marijuana
**Weepers**   Funeral attire
**Whipped up**   Worn out, exhausted
**White one**   A shirt
**Wig**   Head, mind, as in "That solo blew my wig."
**Wolf**   A male who chases women

**Wolverine**   A woman who chases men
**Wren**   A chick, a queen
**Wrong riff**   The wrong thing said or done, as in "You're coming up on the wrong riff."

## Y

**Yarddog**   Uncouth, badly attired, unattractive male or female
**Yellow eye**   An egg
**Yoke**   A jitterbug collar
**Young bantam**   A little girl

## Z

**Zoo**   A sad-looking chick or stud
**Zoom**   To get in free, to sponge
**Zoot suit**   Overexaggerated jitterbug clothes

# JIVE EXPRESSIONS

## A

**Ain't coming on that tab**   Won't accept the proposition
**All reet**   All right

## B

**Backbeat of the trey thirty**   The third day of the month
**Ball all night**   To party all night
**Ballin' the jack**   Moving down the road rapidly
**Balloon room**   A private room at a party where pot smoking is permitted
**Balloon without a parachute**   The same room as mentioned above, minus the reefer
**Banter play built on a coke frame**   A young woman with a seductive shape on the order of a Coca-Cola bottle
**Be really in there**   To know the answers
**Beat for the yolk**   Without or short of gold or money
**Beat it out**   To play one's instrument in a rhythmically exuberant fashion
**Beat up the chops/Beat up the gums**   To talk, to converse, to be loquacious
**Bells**   An expression of approval, similar to "Awesome!" or "Cool!"
**Big red with the long green stem**   New York City on Seventh Avenue
**Blow their wigs**   To thrill them to no end

**Blindfolded lady with the scales**   Justice, court
**Blow the top**   To be overcome with emotion and delight, as in "That sax solo really blew my top."
**Bluff cuffs with the solid sender**   Ballooning trousers with size thirteen cuffs
**Bouncy in one's deuce of benders**   Scrape and bow in Uncle Tom fashion
**Brace of horned corns**   Aching feet with corns
**Break it up**   To score heavily, to stop the show with applause
**Bring him**   To embarrass him
**Broom to the slammer that fronts the drape crib**   To walk to the door of the closet where your clothes are kept
**Brown Abes and buffalo heads**   Pennies and nickels
**Bust your conk**   To try very hard at accomplishing something

## C

**Call off all bets**   To die
**Cats who long ago trilled**   Those who are dead
**Catting**   Pursuing women
**Clip side of the big moist**   Other side of ocean where shooting is going on
**Collars a broom with a solid zoom**   To leave in a hurry
**Come again**   An expression of confusion, similar to "Would you repeat that?"

**Come on like gangbusters** To wow onlookers with prodigious talent

**Cop a drill** To leave quickly, to disappear

**Cop a nod/Cop z's** To sleep, to take a nap

**Cop a squat** To be seated, to sit down

**Creep out like the shadow** To make an impact in a very suave manner

**Cut on down/Cut out** To leave

**Cute suit with the loop droop** Suit whose coat is similar in length to a frock or cut-away jacket

## D

**Dagger-pointed goldies** Sharp-toed yellow shoes

**Davy Crocketts** Draft board officials

**Deuce o' dims and darks on the cutback** Two nights and days ago

**Deuce of benders** Knees

**Deuce of demons** Two dimes, twenty cents

**Deuce of haircuts** Two weeks

**Deuce of nods on the backbeat** Two nights before

**Deuce of ruffs** Twenty cents

**Deuce of ticks** Two minutes

**Dig the dip on the four and two** To take a bath every six days

**Dig those mellow kicks** To know how to live

**Dims and brights unhipped on the black and whites** Days ahead seem dark and dreary both night and day

**Dip and dive on this mess o' jive** To have some fun

**Down with it** To understand, to know, to be ready for action

**Drilling** Walking

## F

**Fall in on that mess** To play that thing

**Fess and two** Money or cash in small quantity

**Fews and twos** A small quantity of money

**Flyer with the roof slightly higher** A hat similar to a modified ten-gallon Stetson

**Fresh water trout** A pretty girl

**Frisk the whiskers** To play a few bars before a jam session

**From front** An expression meaning to start again, similar to "From the beginning."

**Fruiting** Fooling around promiscuously

## G

**Gammin'** Being showy or flirtatious

**Get evil** To develop a dark, despondent mood

**Get in there** To go to work, to get busy, to give it all you've got

**Get your business straight** To attend to something

**Gimme some skin** An exclamation indicating an invitation to shake hands

**Good for nothin' mop** A no-good woman

**Got your boots on** To know what it is all about, to be a hep cat, to be wise

**Got your glasses on** To be snooty, to fail to recognize your friends

**Gotta catch some cups** Must go to sleep

**Gray issue on the cornpone is of the black and white split** Situation with the white folks down South across the Mason-Dixon line

**Gray wouldn't play the game like it should be played** A white person who doesn't act right

**Great-er-ee-de** An expression of agreement

**Groovy little stash** A cozy spot

**Guzzlin' foam** Drinking beer

## H

**Half a stretch away** Half a block away

**Half past a colored man** 12:30 A.M.

**Have big eyes** To have great desire, as in "I have big eyes for that gig."

**Have no eyes** To have an aversion, to be disinclined

**Heavy heat stretch** Summer

**His story is great** He is a successful man about town

**Hold back the dawn** To go on this way forever

**Hop a twig** To die

**House of countless drops** A bar and grill, a tavern

**Hype you for your gold** To take you for the bankroll

## I

**I've got a mellow banter, a real enchanter** I have a pretty girlfriend

**In the groove**  Perfect, no deviation

**In there**  A superb situation, a thrill, a top-flight performance

**I'm hippin' you, man**  I'm putting you wise

## J

**Jack the bear**  Nowhere

**Jersey side of snatch play**  To be over thirty-eight years old

**The joint is jumping**  The place is lively, the club is leaping with fun

**Jump in port**  To arrived in town

## K

**Keyhole a round tripper**  To look at something really beautiful

**Killer-diller**  An expression of affirmation in response to something that is a great thrill

**King Cole Trio**  Harlem's three most-famous police

**King of the Be-Bop**  Dizzy Gillespie

**Kite with no string**  An air-mail letter

**Knock a nod**  To go to sleep

**Knock a scoff**  To eat a meal

**Knock me down to her**  Introduce me to her

**Knock off hen tracks on a rolltop piano**  To write letters on a typewriter

## L

**Land of many squints**  The Orient

**Lay an Apollo play on me**  To pretend

**Lay it on (you) straight**  To tell (you) the truth

**Lay some iron**  To dance with tape shoes

**Lay your racket**  To promote your proposition

**Layout across the drink**  The continent of Europe

**Let him down for his chimer**  To steal his watch

**Lick the chops**  (See frisk the whiskers)

**Like a motherless child**  Sedate

**Long ones with many links**  Key chain

**Lop-pow**  An expression of conciliation, similar to "Everything is okay."

**Lu cu pu**  A gesture said when departing at the end of the evening, similar to "Goodnight."

**Lu-E-Pa**  An inquisitive greeting, similar to "What's your story?"

**Lush yourself to all ends**  To get very drunk

## M

**Mash me a fin**  A demand for five dollars, similar to "Give me five bucks."

**Mellow**  An affirmation of alright-ness, as in "Everything is mellow."

**Mow the lawn**  To comb the hair

**Murder**  An exclamation of something terrific, as in "This is murder!"

## N

**Neighbo, Pops**  An expression of dismissal, similar to "No way, pal."

## O

**Off the cob**  Corny, out of date

**Off-time jive**  A sorry excuse

**Oop-pop-a-da**  A greeting, similar to "Hello."

**Out of the world mellow stage**  Ecstatically drunk

**Out of this world**  A perfect rendition, as in "That sax chorus was out of this world."

**Ow!**  An exclamation made by a lane when a beautiful chick passes by

## P

**Peel a fine green banana**  To make love to a pretty mulatto girl

**Peeps dig the range**  Eyes take in the scene

**Pick up on**  To understand, to appreciate

**Pitch a ball**  To have a good time

**Play the dozens with one's uncle's cousins**  To do everything wrong

**Put the issue on someone**  To give someone a uniform, a gun, and the military training to go with it

## R

**Rah-rah drapes**  Collegiate-styled clothing

**Really in there solid chick**  An attractive young girl

## S

**Sadder than a map**  Terrible

**Sam got you**  You've been drafted into the army

**Same beat groove**  Bored

**Scarf-ring trilly 'round the chimer**  To dine three times a day

**The scene is clean**  I have a job

**Scoff fishheads and scramble for the gills** To have a hard time of it

**Set of seven brights** One week

**A shape in a drape** A woman who looks good in clothes

**Slide your jib** To talk freely

**Slops and slugs** Coffee and doughnuts

**Snap a snapper** To light a match

**Snip a dolly** To cut out, to leave, to become absent

**So help me** It's the truth, that's a fact

**Solid** An expression of high approval

**Solid blow my top** To go crazy

**Solid give me my kicks** To have lots of fun

**Spin a hen/spin a wren** To dance with a woman

**Spoutin'** Talking too much

**Suffering with the shorts** Broke, down and out

### T

**Tag the play with the slammer issue** To solve the problem by putting the culprit in jail

**Take a powder** To leave, to disappear

**Take it slow** To be careful

**Togged to the bricks** Dressed in splendid fashion, from head to toe

**Too much** An expression of highest praise, as in "You are too much!"

**Trig the wig** To think quickly

**Trump the hump** To climb the hill

**Twister to the slammer** The key to the door

### W

**Weed a holler note, until his mudder comes in** To loan him a $100 bill until his horse comes in

**What's your story?** An inquisitive greeting, similar to "What do you want?" "What have you got to say for yourself?" "How are tricks?" or "What excuse can you offer?"

**Wringling and twisting** Discrimination and segregation

### Y

**Yeah, man** An exclamation of assent

**You're stickin'** You're flush, you're carrying a bankroll

# JIVE RESOURCES

## BOOKS

*All Music Guide to Jazz.* Edited by Michael Erlewine with Vladimir Bogdanov, Chris Woodstra, and Scott Yanow. San Francisco: Miller Freeman Books, 1996.

*All Music Guide to the Blues.* Edited by Michael Erlewine, Vladimir Bogdanov, Chris Woodstra, and Cub Koda. San Francisco: Miller Freeman Books, 1996.

Balliett, Whitney. *Night Creature: A Journal of Jazz, 1975–1980.* New York: Oxford University Press, 1981.

Barker, Danny. *A Life in Jazz.* Edited by Alyn Shipton. New York: Oxford University Press, 1986.

Berendt, Joachim E. *The Jazz Book: From Ragtime to Fusion and Beyond.* Translated by H. and B. Bredigkeit. Westport, CT: Lawrence Hill Books, 1992.

Berry, Jason, Jonathan Foose, and Tad Jones. *Up from the Cradle of Jazz: New Orleans Music Since World War II.* New York: Da Capo Press, 1992.

Boulware, Marcus Hanna. *Jive and Slang of Students in Negro Colleges.* Hampton, VA: Purchase from M.H. Boulware, 1947.

Burley, Dan. *Dan Burley's Original Handbook of Harlem Jive.* Illustrations by Melvin Tapley. New York: [self-published], 1944.

Calloway, Cab, and Bryant Rollins. *Of Minnie the Moocher and Me.* With illustrations selected and edited by John Shearer. New York: Crowell, 1976.

Calloway, Cab. *Hepster's Dictionary.* New York: [self-published], 1944.

Carr, Ian, Digby Fairweather, and Brian Priestley. *Jazz: The Rough Guide.* With contributions from Chris Parker;

photographs by Jak Kilby. London:
The Rough Guides, 1995.

Carr, Roy, Brian Case, and Fred Dellar.
*The Hip: Hipsters, Jazz & The Beat
Generation.* London: Faber and Faber, 1986.

Chilton, John. *Let the Good Times Roll:
The Story of Louis Jordan & His Music.*
Ann Arbor: The University of Michigan
Press, 1997.

Chilton, John. *Who's Who of Jazz:
Storyville to Swing Street.* London:
MacMillan, 1976.

Collier, James Lincoln. *The Making of Jazz:
A Comprehensive History.* Boston:
Houghton Mifflin Company, 1978.

Dahl, Linda. *Stormy Weather: The Music
and Lives of a Century of Jazzwomen.*
New York: Pantheon Books, 1984.

*The Encyclopedia of Popular Music.* Edited
by Colin Larkin. New York:
MacMillan, 1977.

Giddins, Gary. *Satchmo.* New York:
Anchor Books, 1988.

Gillespie, Dizzy, with Al Fraser. *To Be,
or Not . . . to Bop.* Garden City, NY:
Doubleday, 1979.

Gillett, Charlie. *The Sound of the City:
The Rise of Rock & Roll.* New York:
Da Capo, 1996.

Giovanni, Nikki. *Black Feeling, Black Talk.*
New York: Afro Arts, 1968.

Gitler, Ira. *Jazz Masters of the Forties.*
New York: Collier Books, 1966.

Gold, Robert S. *A Jazz Lexicon.* New York:
Alfred A. Knopf, 1964.

Gonzales, Babs. *Be-Bop Dictionary.*
New York: Arlain Publishing, 1948.

Gonzales, Babs. *I Paid My Dues: Good
Times . . . No Bread, A Story of Jazz . . .
And Some of Its Followers, Shyster Agents,
Hustlers, Pimps and Prostitutes.* East
Orange, NJ: Expubidence, 1967.

Gonzales, Babs. *Moving on Down de Line.*
East Orange, NJ: Expubidence, 1975.

Gridley, Mark C. *Jazz Styles: History
and Analysis.* Upper Saddle River, NJ:
Prentice Hall, 2000.

Hannusch, Jeff. *I Hear You Knockin':
The Sound of New Orleans Rhythm
and Blues.* Ville Platte, LA: Swallow
Publications, 1985.

Hentoff, Nat, and Nat Shapiro. *Hear Me
Talkin' to Ya.* New York: Peter Davies, 1955.

Holiday, Billie, and William Dufty.
*Lady Sings the Blues.* New York:
Avon Books, 1956.

Horne, Elliott. *The Hiptionary: A Hipster's
View of the World Scene.* New York:
Simon & Schuster, 1963.

*The Illustrated Encyclopedia of Black Music.*
New York: Harmony Books, 1982.

*The Illustrated Encyclopedia of Rock.*
New York: Harmony Books, 1982.

James, Michael. *Kings of Jazz: Dizzy
Gillespie.* New York: A. S. Barnes, 1961.

*Jazz: The First Century.* Edited by John
Edward Hasse. Forewords by Quincy
Jones and Tony Bennett; with contribu-
tions by Larry Appelbaum. New York:
William Morrow, 1999.

John, Dr., with Jack Rummel. *Under a Hoodoo
Moon: The Life of Dr. John the Night
Tripper.* New York: St. Martin's Press, 1994.

Kerouac, Jack. *On the Road.* New York:
Viking, 1957.

Mailer, Norman. *The White Negro.*
San Francisco: City Lights, 1957.

Major, Clarence. *Juba to Jive:
A Dictionary of African-American Slang.*
New York: Viking, 1994.

Mezzrow, Mezz. *Really the Blues.*
New York: Random House, 1946.

Murray, Albert. *Stomping the Blues.*
Produced and art directed
by Harris Lewine. New York:
McGraw-Hill, 1976.

*MusicHound Swing! The Essential Album
Guide.* Edited by Steve Knopper.
Detroit: Visible Ink Press, 1999.

*New Grove Dictionary of Jazz.* Edited by Barry
Kernfeld. London: Macmillan, 1988.

Otis, Johnny. *Listen to the Lambs.* New York:
W. W. Norton, 1968.

Palmer, Tony. *All You Need Is Love:
The Story of Popular Music.* New York:
Penguin Books, 1977.

Pener, Degen. *The Swing Book.* Boston:
Back Bay Books, 1999.

Pitrone, Jean Madden. *Take It from the Big Mouth: The Life of Martha Raye.* Lexington: University Press of Kentucky, 1999.

Sallis, James. *The Guitar Player.* Lincoln: University of Nebraska Press, 1982.

Sforza, John. *Swing It! The Andrews Sisters Story.* Lexington: University Press of Kentucky, 1999.

Shaw, Arnold. *Honkers and Shouters: The Golden Years of Rhythm and Blues.* New York: Macmillan, 1978.

Shaw, Arnold. *The Street That Never Slept.* New York: Coward, McCann & Geoghegan, 1971.

Sidran, Ben. *Black Talk.* New York: Da Capo Press, 1981.

Skowronski, JoAnn. *Black Music in America: A Bibliography.* Metuchen, NJ: Scarecrow, 1981.

Smith, Stuff. *Pure at Heart.* Edited by Anthony Barnett and Eva Løgager. Lewes: Allardyce, Barnett, 1991.

Southern, Eileen. *The Music of Black Americans: A History.* New York: W.W. Norton & Company, 1965.

Stearns, Marshall Winslow. *The Story of Jazz.* New York: Oxford University Press, 1956.

Tosches, Nick. *Unsung Heroes of Rock 'n' Roll: The Birth of Rock in the Wild Years before Elvis.* New York: Da Capo, 1999.

Waller, Maurice, and Anthony Calabrese. *Fats Waller.* New York: Schirmer Books, 1977.

Williams, Martin. *The Jazz Tradition.* New York: Oxford University Press, 1983.

Wilmer, Valerie. *Jazz People.* London: Allison and Busby, 1977.

## ARTICLES

### Chapter One: The Godfathers of Jive

"Back Comes the King of Hi-De-Ho." *Melody Maker* (August 11, 1951).

Burley, Dan. "What Ever Became of Cab Calloway?" *Sepia* (May, 1959).

Crouch, Stanley. "Laughin' Louis." *Village Voice* (August 14, 1978).

Feather, Leonard. "Pops Pops Top on Sloppy Bop." *Metronome* (October 1949).

"Fetch Me My Liquid Ham and Eggs." *Melody Maker* (September 17, 1949).

"The Greatest of All Is Gone." *Life* (July 16, 1971).

"Harlem's Sultan of Stride." *Time* (June 5, 1978).

"If Youse a Viper." *Crawdaddy* (December, 1977).

Levin, Michael. "Wolff's Article Is Garbage." *Down Beat* (July 1, 1949).

"Louis Speaks out on Racial Injustice." *Down Beat* (April 22, 1965).

"Louis, Babe Ruth Go Hand in Hand." *Down Beat* (July 14, 1950).

Lowe, Wilfred. "The Jazz Jester?" *Jazz Journal* (September, 1954).

"Mezz on Satch." *Melody Maker* (May 5, 1956).

"Mezzrow Talks about Jim Crow." *Melody Maker* (November 17, 1951).

"My Idol None but Bunk Johnson." *Down Beat* (July 14, 1950).

"Reverend Satchelmouth." *Time* (April 29, 1946).

"Satchmo Blitzes Governor Faubus." *Melody Maker* (September 28, 1957).

"Satchmo Loved Pot." *Jet* (October 21, 1971).

"Satchmo Still the Greatest Entertainer." *Melody Maker* (June 22, 1968).

"Swinging Again with the King of Corn." *Melody Maker* (April 23, 1966).

Wolff, D. Leon. "Bop/Armstrong Are Nowhere." *Down Beat* (June 17, 1949).

### Chapter Two: The Golden Era of Jive

Burley, Dan. "King of Vout." Slim Gaillard feature. *Ebony* (August, 1950).

Crouch, Stanley. Slim Gaillard review. *Village Voice* (October 22, 1983).

Feather, Leonard. "Louis Jordan: The Good Times Still Roll." *Down Beat* (May 29, 1969).

Feather, Leonard. "The James Joyce of Jazz." Leo "Scat" Watson profile. *Down Beat* (June, 1945).

"Freed Breaks Record: Jive Big in Harlem," *Billboard* (April 23, 1955).

Gayer, Dixon. "Hot Jazz." Stuff Smith feature. *Disc* (November, 1946).

Harris, Pat. "I'm No Musician: Gaillard." *Down Beat* (October 21, 1949).

"Hepcats to Hipsters." *New Republic* (April 21, 1958).

Horne, Bob. "Found: Slim Gaillard." *Down Beat* (June 27, 1968).

"Louis Doesn't Swing." *Melody Maker* (October 12, 1957).

"Louis Is Not an Uncle Tom." *Melody Maker* (October 12, 1957).

Louis Jordan review. *Billboard* (September 16, 1950).

"Louis Jordan and Fame Took Separate Roads." *Melody Maker* (January, 1943).

"Louis Jordan: The Missing Link Between Swing and Rock." *Pulse!* (June, 1985).

Shane, Ted. "Song of the Cuckoo." Slim Gaillard profile. *Collier's* (October 5, 1946).

Slim Gaillard feature. *Metronome* (September, 1951).

Slim Gaillard profile. *Time* (March 31, 1947).

"Slim Gaillard." *Life* (May 5, 1947).

Stuff Smith obituary. *Down Beat* (November 16, 1967).

Tosches, Nick. "The Hep Cosmogony: Louis Jordan, Forefather of Rock 'n' Roll." *Village Voice* (August 18, 1992).

"Vout-Talk Is Sweeping the States." *Melody Maker* (June 28, 1947).

"What's a Floogee?" Slim Gaillard feature. *Melody Maker* (July 9, 1938).

### Chapter Three: Jump Blues 'n' Jive

"King of the Blues in '52." Feature on Lloyd Price. *Color* (March, 1953).

### Chapter Four: Bebop 'n' Jive

"Babs Gonzales." *Metronome* (April, 1949)

Balliet, Whitney. Dizzy Gillespie profile. *The New Yorker* (September, 1953).

Balliet, Whitney. "Pres." Lester Young profile. *The New Yorker* (February 23, 1981).

Buddy Stewart obituary. *Metronome* (March, 1950).

Coss, Bill. "Your Pleasure." King Pleasure profile. *Metronome* (July, 1954).

Crawford, Carol. "Eddie Jefferson, Vocalese Giant." *Jazz Magazine* (Fall, 1978).

Crouch, Stanley. "From Spirituals to Swing." Jon Hendricks profile. *Village Voice* (December 4, 1984).

Deffaa, Chip. Dizzy Gillespie obituary. *The New York Daily News* (January 7, 1993).

Edmonds, Ben. "Voice of Wisdom." Jon Hendricks feature. *The Detroit News* (September 2, 1994).

"Everything's Crazy to Babs Gonzales." *Melody Maker* (May 21, 1951).

Feather, Leonard. "Dizzy—21st Century Gabriel." *Esquire* (October, 1945).

Feather, Leonard. "Dizzy Is Crazy like a Fox." *Metronome* (September, 1944).

Feather, Leonard. "Prez." Lester Young feature. *Playboy* (1959).

Giddins, Gary. Eddie Jefferson obituary. *Village Voice* (May 21, 1979).

Gillespie, Dizzy. "Jazz Is Too Good for Americans." *Esquire* (June, 1957).

Gleason, Ralph J. "Humor in Jazz." *Philadelpia Bulletin* (June 14, 1959).

Gleason, Ralph J. "Jazz Vocalese Expert Shoots for Big Time." King Pleasure profile. *Cleveland Plain Dealer* (May 6, 1961).

Goodman, George W. "Jon Hendricks Singing Tongue-Twisting Tunes." *The New York Times* (November 30, 1984).

Joe Carroll obituary. *The New York Times* (February 2, 1981).

Lees, Gene. "Dizzy Gillespie: Problems of Life on a Pedestal." *Down Beat* (June 23, 1960).

McKean, Gilbert S. "The Diz and the Bebop." *Esquire* (October, 1947).

Schillinger, Mort. "Dizzy Gillespie's Style, Its Meaning Analyzed." *Down Beat* (February 11, 1946).

Seymour, Gene. "Scat Coming on Home from the '60s." *Newsday* (January 27, 1999).

Simon, Bill. "Dizzy Attacks Louis." *Melody Maker* (May 18, 1957).

Stein, Ruth. "Buddy Stewart: From Ballads to Scat Singing." *Down Beat* (November 5, 1947).

Watrous, Peter. Dizzy Gillespie obituary. *The New York Times* (January 7, 1993).

West, Hollie I. "The Master of Scat Comes Back." Jon Hendricks profile. *The Washington Post* (July 26, 1980).

Wilson, John S. "Jon Hendricks Brings Back Style of Big-Band Era." *The New York Times* (April 2, 1982).

### Chapter Five: N'awlins Jive

Crouse, Timothy. "Resurrecting New Orleans: The Gulf Coast Originals Never

Left Home." *Rolling Stone* (May 11, 1972).

Giddins, Gary. "Dr. John Without Voodoo." *Village Voice* (January 10, 1989).

Giddins, Gary. "Professor Longhair Woogies." *Village Voice* (June 4, 1979).

Goldman, Albert. "Rock's Raunchy Grandpappy." *Life* (October 27, 1972).

Goldman, Albert. "Satchel Paige of the Piano." Professor Longhair feature. *Esquire* (March 28, 1978).

Goodwin, Michael. "James Booker Goes to Heaven." *Village Voice* (January 10, 1989).

"King of the Blues in '52." *Color* (March, 1953).

Mathews, Bunny. "Professor Longhair: The Man Who Taught New Orleans Music." *Figaro* (June 29, 1977).

Palmer, Robert. "Blue Professor Gives a Lesson." *The New York Times* (December 2, 1977).

Palmer, Robert. "Professor Longhair Is Swinging at the Gate." *The New York Times* (May 18, 1979).

"Professor Longhair Talks to Max Jones." *Melody Maker* (April 1, 1978).

## Chapter Six: The White Connection

Ben Sidran feature. *Illinois Entertainer* (January, 1980).

Erikson, Chris. "Frantic: Harry The Hipster." *New York Daily News* (October 13, 1999).

Hentoff, Nat. Manhattan Transfer feature. *New York Sunday News.* (August, 1975).

Scott, Allen. "Country and Eastern Jazz Pianist." *Metronome* (March, 1959).

Siegel, Joel E. "Spreading Joy: Bob Dorough." *Jazz Times* (December, 1997).

Silsbee, Kirk. "The Hipster's Crazy Shit." Harry "The Hipster" Gibson feature. *Los Angeles Reader* (November 13, 1992).

"Skiffle Artificial." *Jazz Journal* (April 11, 1956).

"Ripping off Black Music: From Thomas 'Daddy' Rice to Jimi Hendrix." *Harpers* (January, 1973).

Troup, Stuart. "Bob Dorough, a Twangy Charmer." *Newsday* (October 24, 1986).

## Chapter Seven: Women Jivesters

Amstrong, Alicia. "Nellie Lutcher Is Still an Individualist." *Down Beat* (February 9, 1951).

Balliet, Whitney. Nellie Lutcher profile. *The New Yorker* (April 7, 1980).

Connee Boswell feature. *Down Beat* (August, 1938).

Connee Boswell obituary. *The New York Times* (October 12, 1976).

Ellis, Chris. Connee Boswell feature. *Storyville* (October, 1976).

Giddins, Gary. "It Sisters." Boswell Sisters feature. *Village Voice* (March 17, 1999).

Lucas, John. "Cats Hepped by Connee's Chirping." Connee Boswell feature. *Down Beat* (October 15, 1944).

Lucas, John. "Visionary Scoring Put Boswells Over." *Down Beat* (November 1, 1944).

Morrissey, Judi. "Well-Sung Hooks, Pinup Looks Define Skiller Lickers' Smith." *San Jose Mercury News* (December 19, 1999).

Shewey, Don. "Sibling Harmony." Boswell Sisters feature. *SoHo News* (June 17, 1981).

Tanner, Peter. "Real Gone Gal: The History of Nellie Lutcher." *Jazz Journal* (August, 1948).

Yanow, Scott. "Back on Track." Manhattan Transfer feature. *Jazziz* (August, 1998).

## Chapter Eight: Retro Jivesters

Edgers, Geoff. "Sometimes They Feel like Nuts." Squirrel Nut Zippers feature. *Details* (September, 1988).

Forman, Bill. "Rites of Swing!" *Pulse!* (September, 1998).

Gill, Chris. "Brian Setzer's Big Band Boom." *Guitar Player* (June, 1994).

Gundersen, Edna. "Squirrel Nut Zippers 'Perennial' Swingers." *USA Today* (August 7, 1998).

Haden, Mark. "The Zipper Factor." Squirrel Nut Zippers feature. *Denver Post* (August 2, 1998).

Heckman, Don. "Separating the Faddies from the Real Swingin' Daddies." *Los Angeles Times* (August 2, 1998).

Isola, Gregory. "Swing Bass." *Bass Player* (December, 1998).

Komp, John. "The Religion of Dance." Paul Cebar & The Milwaukeeans feature. *WAM* (June, 1987).

Stephenson, William. "Swing! Rebirth of a Revolution." *Jazziz* (August, 1998).

Walljasper, Jay. Squirrel Nut Zippers review. *Utne Reader* (November, 1998).

## LINER NOTES

### Chapter One: The Godfathers of Jive
**Louis Armstrong**
Avakian, George. *Ambassador Satch* (Columbia/Legacy, 1956).
Avakian, George. *Satch Plays Fats* (Columbia/Legacy, 1955).
O'Meally, Robert G. *The Complete Hot Five and Hot Seven* (Columbia/Legacy, 2000).
**Cab Calloway**
Quaglieri, Al. *Are You Hep to the Jive?* (Columbia/Legacy, 1994).
**Fats Waller**
Thompson, Butch. *A Good Man Is Hard to Find* (Bluebird, 1995).

### Chapter Two: The Golden Era of Jive
**The Cats & The Fiddle**
Cohn, Lawrence. *I Miss You So* (Bluebird, 1976).
Goldberg, Marv. *Killin' Jive* (Dee-Jay, 1999).
Goldberg, Marv. *Hep Cats Swing* (Dee-Jay, 1999).
**The Four Blazes**
Grendysa, Peter. *Mary Joe* (Delmark, 1997).
**Nat "King" Cole**
Goldberg, Joe. *Hit That Jive, Jack* (Decca/MCA, 1990).
**Slim Gaillard**
Morgan, Alun. *And His Friends at Birdland, 1951* (Hep, 1979).
Priestly, Brian. *Laughing in Rhythm* (Verve, 1994).
Robertson, Alastair. *The Legendary McVouty* (Hep, 1989).
Schenker, Anatol. *1939–1940* (Classics, 1993).
Schenker, Anatol. *1940–1942* (Classics, 1994).
Schenker, Anatol. *1945* (Classics, 1995).
**Louis Jordan**
Bouchard, Fred. *I Believe In Music* (Black & Blue/Evidence, 1980).
Fein, Art. *Five Guys Named Moe* (Decca/MCA, 1992).
Grendysa, Peter. *At the Swing Cat's Ball* (MCA, 1999).
Grendysa, Peter. *Just Say Moe!* (Rhino, 1992).
Grendysa, Peter. *Let the Good Times Roll* (Decca/MCA, 1999).

Laredo, Joseph F. *The Best of Louis Jordan* (Decca/MCA, 1999).
White, Cliff. *Look Out!* (Charly, 1983).
**Slim & Slam**
Gorodetsky, Eddie. *The Groove Juice Special* (Columbia/Legacy, 1996).
**Stuff Smith and His Onyx Club Boys**
Schenker, Anatol. *1936–1939* (Classics, 1993).
**Various Artists**
Katz, Dick. *52nd Street Swing: New York in the '30s* (Decca/GRP, 1994).
Morgenstern, Dan. *The Changing Face of Harlem* (Savoy, 1977).
Porter, Bob. *Black California, Volume 2: Anthology* (Savoy, 1995).
Porter, Bob. *The Savoy Story, Volume 1: Jazz* (Savoy, 1999).
Willard, Patricia. *Black California, Volume 1* (Savoy, 1976).
**Leo Watson**
Visser, Joop. *The Original Scat Man* (Indigo, 1999).

### Chapter Three: Jump Blues 'n' Jive
**Blues Masters**
Grendysa, Peter. *Volume 5: Jump Blues Classics* (Rhino, 1992).
Grendysa, Peter. *Volume 14: More Jump Blues* (Rhino, 1993).
**Clarence "Gatemouth" Brown**
Dahl, Bill. *Just Got Lucky* (Evidence, 1993).
**Floyd Dixon**
Vera, Billy. *His Complete Aladdin Recordings* (Capitol, 1995).
**Tiny Grimes**
Burke, Tony. *And His Rocking Highlanders, Volumes 1 & 2* (Gotham, 1986/1987).
Penny, Dave. *And Friends* (Gotham, 1988).
**Amos Milburn**
Humphrey, Mark. *Blues, Barrelhouse & Boogie Woogie: 1946–1955* (Capitol, 1996).
**Roy Milton**
Porter, Bob. *Instant Groove* (Classic Jazz, 1981).
Vera, Billy. *Groovy Blues* (Specialty, 1992).
**Big Joe Turner**
Balliet, Whitney. *Have No Fear, Big Joe Turner Is Here* (Savoy, 1945–1947).
Keepnews, Peter. *I've Been to Kansas City* (Decca/MCA, 1990).

**T-Bone Walker**
Gleason, Ralph J. *T-Bone Blues* (Atlantic, 1972).
Vera, Billy. *The Very Best of T-Bone Walker* (Rhino, 2000).
Welding, Pete. *The Complete Imperial Recordings, 1950–1954* (EMI, 1991).
**Various Artists**
Driggs, Frank. *West Coast Jive* (Apollo, 1992).
Vera, Billy. *Legends of Jump Blues, Volume 1* (Specialty, 1994).

## Chapter Four: Bebop 'n' Jive
**Babs Gonzales**
Gitler, Ira. *Weird Lullaby* (Blue Note, 1992).
**Eddie Jefferson**
Feather, Leonard. *The Jazz Singer* (Evidence, 1976).
Steingroot, Ira. *There I Go Again* (Prestige, 1980).
**Lambert, Hendricks & Ross**
Dance, Stanley. *Sing a Song of Basie* (Impulse! 1965).
**Various Artists**
Koester, Bob. *East Coast Jive* (Apollo, 1994).
Vera, Billy. *Jumpin' & Jivin'* (Specialty, 1997).

## Chapter Five: N'awlins Jive
**James Booker**
Boyd, Joe. *Junco Partner* (Hannibal, 1992).
Mathews, Bunny. *Classified* (Rounder, 1983).
**Dr. John**
Hannusch, Jeff. *Mos' Scocious: The Dr. John Anthology* (Rhino, 1993).
Rebennack, Mac. *Goin' Back to New Orleans* (Warner Bros., 1992).
**Professor Longhair**
Snowden, Don. *The Professor Longhair Anthology* (Rhino, 1993).
**Lloyd Price**
Vera, Billy. *Lawdy!* (Specialty, 1990).
**Various Artists**
Hannusch, Jeff. *New Orleans Party Classics* (Rhino, 1992).
Snowden, Don. *Chess New Orleans* (Chess/MCA, 1995).
Vera, Billy. *Creole Kings of New Orleans, Volume 2* (Specialty, 1992).
Warner, Alan. *Crescent City Soul* (EMI, 1996).

Wexler, Jerry. *Creole Kings of New Orleans, Volume 1* (Specialty, 1989).

## Chapter Six: The White Connection
**Mose Allison**
Hentoff, Nat. *I Don't Worry about a Thing* (Prestige, 1962).
**Bing Crosby**
Carr, Larry. *The Bing Crosby Story* (Columbia, 1967).
Simon, George T. *A Legendary Performer* (RCA, 1977).
**Harry "The Hipster" Gibson**
Magee, Thomas. *Who Put the Benzedrine in Mrs. Murphy's Ovaltine?* (Delmark, 1996).
*Boogie Woogie in Blue* (Musicraft, 1986)
**Emmett Miller**
Wolfe, Charles. *The Mintrel Man from Georgia* (Columbia/Legacy, 1995).
**Louis Prima**
Shea, Scott. *Collectors Series* (Capitol, 1991).

## Chapter Seven: Women Jivesters
**The Boswell Sisters**
Bamberger, Rob. *Syncopating Harmonists from New Orleans* (Take Two, 1992).
**Ella Fitzgerald**
Falzarano, Gino. *The War Years* (Decca/GRP, 1994).
Friedwald, Will. *In the Groove* (Buddha, 2000).
**Candye Kane**
Gillette, Penn. *The Toughest Girl Alive* (Bullseye Blues, 2000).
Heaton, Michael. *The Toughest Girl Alive* (Bullseye Blues, 2000).

## Chapter Eight: Retro Jivesters
**Duke Heitger and His Swing Band**
Porter, Bob. *Rhythm Is Our Business* (Fantasy, 2000).
**Joe Jackson**
Jackson, Joe. *Jumpin' Jive* (A&M, 1981).

# WEB SITES

## Artist and Band Sites
**The Andrews Sisters**
www.cmgww.com/music/andrews/andrews.html

**Louis Armstrong**
http://tinpan.fortunecity.com/riff/11
www.geocities.com/BourbonStreet/7541
www.satchography.com
www.satchmo.net
**Asleep at the Wheel**
www.asleepatthewheel.com
**Big Bad Voodoo Daddy**
www.bbvd.com
**The Boswell Sisters**
www.singers.com/jazz/vintage/boswell.
  html
**Cab Calloway**
www.isp.nwu.edu/~ethan/calloway.htm
**Cherry Poppin' Daddies**
www.daddies.com
**Nat "King" Cole**
www.alamhof.org/colenat.htm
www.homestead.com/natkingcole
**Bing Crosby**
www.geocities.com/BourbonStreet/3754/
  bing.html
www.kcmetro.cc.mo.us/~Crosby/
**Ella Fitzgerald**
www.cnn.com/SHOWBIZ/9606/15/ella/
  index.html
**The Flying Neutrinos**
www.flyingneutrinos.com
**Slim Gaillard**
www.pocreations.com/slim.html
**Ray Gelato & His Giants of Jive**
www.raygelato.com
**Dizzy Gillespie**
www.bowdoin.edu/~aboisver/jazz/diz.
  html
**Babs Gonzales**
www.geocities.co.jp/Hollywood-Kouen/
  5953/babsgonzales.html
**Lionel Hampton**
www.musicsearcher.com/h/Hampton,Lionel
  .php3
**Eddie Jefferson**
www.gallery41.com/artists/eddie_j1.htm
**Louis Jordan**
www.primenet.com/~swlbrjjp/ljordan.htm
www.worldmall.com/wmcc/kcblues/
  yesterday.htm
**Lambert, Hendricks & Ross**
www.singers.com/jazz/vintage/lh&r.html

**Louisiana Music Directory**
www.satchmo.com/nolavl/noladir.html
**Steve Lucky & The Rhumba Bums**
www.luckylounge.com
**The Rhythm Boys**
http://mypage.direct.ca/r/rsavill/Rhythm.
  html
**Royal Crown Revue**
www.rcr.com
**Brian Setzer Orchestra**
www.briansetzer.com
**Lavay Smith & Her Red Hot Skillet Lickers**
www.lavaysmith.com
**Squirrel Nut Zippers**
www.snzippers.com
**T-Bone Walker**
www.island.net/~blues/tbone.html
**Fats Waller**
www.geocities.com/BourbonStreet/Delta/
  6704

*General Sites*
http://abjazz.com
http://home.earthlink.net/~spaceagepop/
  index.htm
http://jazz.edionysus.com
www.52ndstreet.com
www.africana.com
www.allaboutjazz.com
www.allmusic.com
www.amazon.com
www.anyswinggoes.com
www.billboard.com
www.blueflamecafe.com
www.borders.com
www.cdnow.com
www.jass.com
www.jazze.com
www.jazzhistory.f2s.com
www.jdscomm.com
www.jivejunction.com
www.jiveon.com
www.neoswing.com
www.notz.com/jazz_pages.htm
www.redhotjazz.com
www.specialeffects.com/a1/jazzworld.html
www.totalswing.com
www.visionx.com/jazz
www.yehoodi.com

# INDEX